istory Series

1984.
J. Schaffner. 1985.
ch. 1986.
d David Shepard.

kins, 1987.
utch. 1989.
ine Parker. 1990.
*hite,* interviewed by

Atkins. 1991.
ntonio. 1991.
ins. 1993.
y Norman Corwin

dited by Ira

*seen by 21*
by Ira Skutch.

# The Days of Live

*Television's Golden Age
as seen by 21
Directors Guild of America Members*

Edited by Ira Skutch

*Directors Guild of America
Oral History Series, No. 16*

The Scarecrow Press, Inc.
Lanham, Md., & London
and
Directors Guild of America
Los Angeles, California
1998

# SCARECROW PRESS, INC.

Published in the United States of America
by Scarecrow Press, Inc.
4720 Boston Way
Lanham, Maryland 20706

4 Pleydell Gardens
Kent CT20 2DN, England

British Library Cataloguing in Publication Information Available

**Library of Congress Cataloging-in-Publication Data**

The days of live : television's golden age as seen by 21 Directors
Guild of America members / edited by Ira Skutch.
      p. cm. -- (Directors Guild of America oral history series ; no. 16)
  Includes index.
    ISBN 0-8108-3491-X (cloth : alk. paper). -- ISBN 0-8108-3492-8 (paper : alk. paper)
    1. Television broadcasting--United States--History.  2. Television
producers and directors--United States--Interviews.  I. Skutch, Ira.
II. Series: Directors Guild of America oral history series ; 16.
PN1992.3.U5D38   1998
791.45'0973--dc21                                            98-17630
                                                        CIP

# Contents

# Participants

| | |
|---|---|
| Paul Bogart | 7, 37, 43, 44, 88, 137, 143, 146, 159, 171, 179, 181, 185 |
| Allan Buckhantz | 26, 38, 40, 45, 62, 97, 185 |
| Fielder Cook | 7, 37, 43, 50, 51, 67, 68, 128, 136, 137, 139, 158, 169, 181, 186 |
| Marc Daniels | 3, 36, 48, 61, 168, 169, 183, 186 |
| John Frankenheimer | 10, 38, 62, 130, 132, 137, 160, 180, 187 |
| Livia Granito | 8, 41, 42, 102, 113, 135, 148, 162, 187 |
| Walter Grauman | 27, 95, 136, 172, 188 |
| Franklin Heller | 5, 35, 52, 57, 154, 181, 194 |
| George Roy Hill | 8, 50, 70, 129, 138, 143, 157, 158, 161, 170, 188 |
| Arthur Hiller | 13, 38, 41, 105, 149, 162, 173, 189 |
| Lamont Johnson | 14, 44, 108, 173, 181, 189 |
| Buzz Kulik | 8, 36, 65, 68, 70, 127, 138, 157, 159, 174, 180, 190 |
| Adrienne Luraschi | 17, 42, 73, 92, 123, 194 |
| Delbert Mann | 20, 39, 77, 134, 139, 164, 170, 178, 184, 193 |
| Ralph Nelson | 21, 40, 44, 59, 131, 133, 142, 152, 163, 175, 184, 190 |
| Arthur Penn | 23, 39, 43, 81, 131, 163, 164, 170, 191 |
| Daniel Petrie | 23, 38, 83, 172, 173 |
| John Peyser | 1, 34, 47, 56, 138, 143, 164, 191 |
| Martin Ritt | 4, 35, 59, 138, 158, 172, 176, 192 |
| George Schaefer | 25, 42, 46, 114, 141, 145, 165, 176, 180, 182, 192 |
| Franklin Schaffner | 4, 38, 44, 47, 50, 61, 129, 158, 159, 175, 193 |

# Preface

Although few were aware of it, experimental television was being actively pursued during the thirties. It first burst upon the public on April 30, 1939, at the inauguration of the RCA exhibit at the New York World's Fair. The dedication ceremony featured President Franklin D. Roosevelt, who was seen arriving and delivering the opening address.

By the time of Pearl Harbor, approximately three thousand receiving sets had been sold in the New York area. The only programming they could receive came from CBS and NBC, which had experimental stations on the air prior to the war, but when hostilities began television activity was suspended, except for once-a-week broadcasts to maintain the licenses. For example, in 3H, its only TV studio, NBC produced a live, half-hour Air Raid Warden training program on Friday evening around seven-thirty. In 1945, the two networks were joined by DuMont, a manufacturer and broadcaster founded by the inventor, Dr. Allen B. DuMont. All three began to expand their programming, although great stretches of the day and evening hours were devoted to broadcasting test patterns. These were charts with circles and radiating lines that aided technicians in aligning cameras and receivers. They also served to maintain a picture for appliance dealers to show potential customers.

The CBS studios were at 15 Vanderbilt Avenue, adjacent to Grand Central Station; NBC operated out of the RCA Building at 30 Rockefeller Plaza; and DuMont, which originally broadcast from their offices at 515 Madison Avenue, built a studio in the John Wanamaker Department Store.

In the late forties, the one factor slowing the expansion of television was the dispute between CBS and RCA over color. CBS developed a mechanical method involving a spinning disk. The color it produced was beautiful and true, but the adoption of this system would have made all the black-and-white sets in existence obsolete. RCA was developing a compatible electronic system, so that extant receivers could continue to receive the color broadcasts, albeit in black-and-white. RCA, as a manufacturer and patent holder, was eager for the industry to grow as quickly as possible. CBS, riding a flood tide of profits from radio broadcasting, would have been content to let things go more slowly. Hence, they each

ix

campaigned heavily to have the Federal Communications Commission accept their color system. In the early fifties, that body finally came down on the side of RCA, following which the sales of television sets exploded.

By 1952, when CBS and NBC announced their intention to broadcast the political conventions from Chicago, the Philco and Westinghouse corporations decided there were enough sets coast to coast to justify sponsorship. Like RCA, both companies manufactured and marketed receivers. They paid about a million dollars each for the coverage, which also included the broadcast of election night returns. The coaxial cable did not yet reach the West Coast, so the telecasts in those regions were of kinescope recordings, which were poor quality, 16mm films photographed directly from the face of the kinescope tube.

The conventions were intensely interesting, not only because of their novelty, but because the Republican meeting featured the dramatic battle between the right wing's candidate, Senator Robert Taft, and the moderate group's preference, General Dwight Eisenhower. The session was marked by spirited floor fights, sidebar caucuses, and glimpses of backstage maneuvering. The Democratic gathering saw the passing of the leadership of the party from President Harry Truman to Governor Adlai Stevenson.

All this excitement propelled television viewing to new intensity, causing the sale of receivers to increase geometrically. The networks grew in power and wealth. The industry continued to reach new heights in the ensuing few years, but with the advent of tape in the late fifties, the years of live television became, inevitably, only a nostalgic memory.

Ira Skutch
Sherman Oaks, California
August 16, 1997

# Acknowledgments

The twenty-one DGA members in this book were interviewed separately about their experiences in live television — Paul Bogart, Allan Buckhantz, Fielder Cook, Marc Daniels, John Frankenheimer, Livia Granito, Walter Grauman, George Roy Hill, Arthur Hiller, Lamont Johnson, Buzz Kulik, Delbert Mann, Ralph Nelson, Arthur Penn, Daniel Petrie, John Peyser, Martin Ritt, George Schaefer, and Franklin Schaffner by Steve Cohen; Adrienne Luraschi and Franklin Heller by Ira Skutch. The interviews have been broken up and integrated to illuminate various perspectives of related subjects. The result is a firsthand picture of the onset of what was, perhaps, the last revolutionary technological development — with an impact comparable to motion pictures and radio — in the long history of entertainment.

We thank the interviewers, as well as the following individuals who contributed their time, talents and resources: Adele Field of the DGA Communications Department, who oversaw the project; David Shepard, who commissioned the original interviews as part of the Guild's Oral History program; Ira Skutch, who compiled and edited the book; Daniel McGowan who assisted with fact-checking and proofreading; and Selise E. Eiseman.

**John Peyser**: I graduated from Colgate in 1938 and went to NBC in New York, as a page. It was a very tough job to get — you had to have a college degree and you had to be socially acceptable — for which they paid you fifteen dollars a week and gave you clean white shirts. I'd been there about six weeks when they opened something called the Television Department, and I volunteered, along with a bunch of young guys. We didn't broadcast, we were just learning the business.

Television was pretty much an American phenomena. All the development in Europe, where practically every television operation is government owned, really came after the war. They went to much higher resolution because they had a limited number of channels. Over here they knew it was going to be commercial, and RCA wanted the greatest amount of competition so as to sell receivers.

At the opening of the World's Fair in the spring of 1939, I was transferred to RCA and there I became a demonstrator of television. The picture resolution was pretty good, with the same number of scan lines they use now. I interviewed people outside the building, saying, "Aren't you glad you're on television? Where are you from? My, that's a long way from home." We did this kind of mindless interview so people's relatives, inside, could see them on television.

Bill Patterson and I came up with an idea that we took to the RCA people, saying, "Hey, this is pretty dull stuff. People aren't all that thrilled with seeing themselves on television. They'd like to see what kind of entertainment it can perform." RCA let us go ahead. We set up shows, and did them ten times a day. One of the first acts that we booked was Burr Tillstrom. Bill Patterson was from Chicago and had seen Burr working in a Chicago department store at Christmas, doing hand puppets. Ollie was born at a party one night where we were all pretty drunk. Burr sat on the floor cross-legged, sewed Ollie and tried out his voice. So *Kukla, Fran and Ollie* — without Fran — was born at the World's Fair at the RCA Exhibit. We had Burr under contract until we went to war and I had to release him. He went on to be a star on television.

In 1940, the second and last year of the World's Fair, I directed the first remote ever done on television, to see if the bloody thing worked at all. It originated in the RCA building and was transmitted over NBC's facilities on top the Empire State Building, using two cameras and a bunch of acts. It was broadcast over Channel 4 — the only one operating — although G.E. had done some test broadcasting up in Schenectady.

Also in 1940, I did the first baseball game that NBC tried with their new portable truck. It was the opening game of the season between the New York Giants and the Brooklyn Dodgers, at Ebbett's Field. We went out at seven in the morning to get ready for the ball game that was going to take place at one in the afternoon. Because we had a very small crew, I helped them set up. I remember almost killing myself, because we had coax [coaxial] cable that, with all the other crap in it, was about two-and-a-half inches in diameter and about five or six inches in circumference. The goddam stuff was unbelievably heavy, and I think it cost an incredible ten dollars a foot. One of the first things we did was to get up on the roof and start to pull this bloody cable up by hand on a rope. As I started to pull, the weight got heavier, I started to slide toward the edge and I knew if I ever let the cable go, I might well go over the roof. Somebody grabbed me just in time.

That day was really wild, because it drizzled and we did the ball game in a light mist. We had no way of doing all the fancy things you do now. We had three cameras and no dissolve equipment — we'd cut everything. Communications broke down, and in the middle of a shot a hand would come in and wipe the lens off!

There were about twenty-five hundred sets, owned by executives, stockholders, friends. The sets were all turned on, and people just sat and stared at test patterns. Then they used a Miss Television, who, when the test pattern came on, would sit and wave at the audience. We got tremendous response. Unfortunately, we never got any reviews because no newspaper people ever saw the thing. And on top of that, there was no way of recording it, so what we did is somewhere out in space, on its way to wherever it's going.

Early in 1940, the Army decided to make a test of television, using it as a spotting weapon. I went along to handle the equipment. They put us in a B-25, we took off from Mitchell Field and flew west. I had a lock-mounted camera pointing down, and my little Jeep equipment and transmitter. They were controlling us from Washington. They could see the ground, which they thought was wonderful. This was in the middle of

December, and when it started snowing, we said, "Hey, that's enough of this"

They said, "Oh, keep going, we want to see what it looks like in the snow." We flew west, almost to Illinois, where we ran out of gas and crashed in a field! Luckily, nobody got killed. I got transverse fractures in both my knees.

Then came the war. I went overseas with everybody else, and when we came back I decided that I wanted to get into a more stable line of work, so I went into the record business. I opened the first all-vinyl pressing plant, in Allentown, New Jersey, which I ran for a year or two. I didn't like that very much, and Worthington Miner was setting up at CBS, so I went to work for him in 1948.

**Marc Daniels:**   After the war, about 1946 or 1947, I was on the faculty, as well as taking courses, at the American Theatre School, which had been set up under the G.I. Bill to rehabilitate the skills of members of the profession who had been in the Armed Forces. I was teaching acting and stage management.

Television Production was one of the courses offered at an experimental station in Jamaica, Long Island. There was a control room, earphones, a headset, and so on. I took the course because I knew nothing about it and thought I'd like to learn something. It was taught by Harvey Marlowe, who had been directing television at DuMont. He gave the class some general guidelines and taught us what he knew, which was not very much. We were basically making it up as we went along.

The only professional person there was the guy who ran the studio. He did the maintenance, but we were the camera crew and we did everything else ourselves, so I got some familiarity with the system. I think you learn camera composition fairly quickly, and if you have good cameramen they give you pretty good composition by themselves. When you were doing a three-camera show, the custom was to keep one reserve camera just in case one of the other cameras conked out. I figured what the hell, if it conked out, so what.

Marlowe divided the company into two groups. One week one group would do a show, and the next week the other group would. Ours was the first group, and since he knew that I had some experience directing summer stock, as well as teaching acting at the American Academy [of

Dramatic Art], Marlowe made me the director on the first show. I took off from there.

**Martin Ritt:**   I came out of the war and began looking for work in the theatre. However, the Broadway theatre was terribly difficult to crack, so around 1948 I got a job at CBS. I entered as a director. It was the beginning of a new medium, so, from a work point of view, it was very interesting, it was exciting, and it was live.

Obviously, the technology was different, but live television wasn't all that different from theatre, except that television was definitely small. It was done on studio sets rather than on outside locations. We had continuity of performance, with a beginning, middle, and end. In addition, all of the actors were from the theatre.

Working with images was new, but, as with anything else, if there is no substance, the images are meaningless. We all had the opportunity to work with the caliber of material that you don't have the chance to work with today — except on PBS [Public Broadcasting System].

I had a good time. I enjoyed working and those were good days. I could do virtually anything I wanted, and I did. As a matter of fact, television was a help when I started to direct films.

**Franklin Schaffner:**   Originally, I did not plan to be in this business, nor in the theatre. I had intended to be a lawyer. However, after four and a half years in the United States Navy in the Second World War, I came to the conclusion that four more years of education and a couple of years clerking in a law office was just too much. So, like everybody else, I went to New York to look for a job.

In New York, a bizarre series of circumstances led me to the business. I was working for an organization called Americans United For World Government. Along with the public affairs department of ABC radio, they sponsored a weekly broadcast called *American World Security Workshop*. I was handed the opportunity to produce this show, and after twenty-six weeks, I thought seriously about starting a career in radio. But job-wise, there wasn't anything happening.

Luckily, around 1947 I was able to get a job through a friend of mine who knew the man who was producing *The March of Time*, Richard DeRochemont. After I interviewed with him, he told me to speak with the production manager and I was hired. *The March of Time* was a series that wasn't really a documentary but rather a combination of newsreels and staged creations that were put out under the aegis of Time-Life and distributed by Twentieth Century-Fox.

While I was working on *March of Time*, Robert Bendick, who was head of the department at CBS television in charge of sports, public affairs, news, religious programs, and so on, asked one of our directors if he wanted to work in television. This director didn't want to go into television, so he told Bob Bendick that he would send someone else whom he thought had some promise. He sent me.

I talked with Bob for about a half hour, and he hired me as a director. This was in 1948. I had never seen a television camera, nor had I ever been a director. Normally, all the new television directors went through a kind of "basic-training" period, which meant you observed for a while, then you would start directing the little musical that CBS began its broadcast day with. It had two cameras and a pianist who entertained for whatever number of minutes were required. You were supposed to learn the technique, if any, of using two cameras.

After "basic training" you directed a fifteen-minute news show shot on a set with a desk but no video monitor. The news consisted mostly of the "talking" anchor. I can remember Douglas Edwards, Quincy Howe, and Elmer Davis all being anchors. Occasionally, you included feature stories, that consisted of film that was very fresh if it was only a week old. Often it was as much as a month old.

**Franklin Heller:** I had been an actor in stock and in Shakespearean repertory, then a Broadway stage manager for ten years. During World War II, I was producer of dramas and comedies for USO Camp Shows that played all over the world. After the war I spent two abortive years trying to keep from slipping between the cracks at Paramount in Hollywood as a producer-director. I slipped, but that's another story.

In 1949, I had been mostly unemployed for two years. Although stage manager jobs were available, I aspired to be a director and got some directing in summer stock. The rest of the time I just hung in there with the ever-present majority of New York's inactive show-biznicks.

A friend introduced me to NBC-TV where the program director kept me waiting three hours, then told me that since neither he nor anybody there knew anything about show business, I could not be hired because I was over-qualified. "I'd have a severe personnel problem if someone like you came to work here."

Another friend suggested CBS. I was not enthusiastic, expecting all broadcasting people to be like NBC's man. My friend said that Jerry Danzig, second in command of programming at the CBS TV Network, (which then got as far as Pittsburgh) had been his Dartmouth classmate and he could call him. I did not have anything else to do anyway, and besides, figured anybody who had gone to Dartmouth could not be all bad. An appointment was arranged.

Much to my surprise, Danzig told me that my background in Shakespeare, Broadway plays, musicals, ballet, the worldwide USO, and Hollywood was exactly what television needed. He asked me if I would consider coming to work there. But — he could not hire me. His boss, Charles Underhill, had that authority, and he was not in. Could I come back tomorrow morning? Could I!

At home, my atypical mother-in-law was visiting. A very smart lady, she didn't think TV was a fad, as some people did then. She also thought I should have a job. She pointed to my already-graying hair and said I must not go see the chief of CBS-TV programs looking like his father. She got an eyebrow pencil and a hairbrush and darkened my hair very effectively.

The next day I went to see Underhill, and met a handsome man — maybe two years younger than I — whose hair was completely white!

He made me an offer I couldn't refuse and I was "working" that very day observing Frances Buss, a very fine and experienced TV director, who generously shared her knowledge and experience. From that starting day, I knew CBS had to be a first class workplace, and, in the many years I did shows there, I never had any reason to think differently.

I was thirty-seven years old when I was hired on as a staff director — pretty old for TV even in those days. I didn't like my crayoned hair. My hands and pillow were stained by it. After about three days of trying to keep up the sham, I got a shampoo and knocked it off. Nobody at CBS cared about that at all.

Several years later I was lunching one day with an actor, Paul Tripp, who had a nice kid's show on CBS called *Mister I Magination*. We had worked together in the theatre.

"You know, Frank," he told me, "you are a legend in television." Since I hadn't done anything I thought would deserve such an appellation,

I asked what he meant by that. "Oh," he said, "everybody talks about you. You came to work at CBS and within a week you were gray!"

**Paul Bogart:** I got out of the Air Force in the late forties, and, in 1950, I had given up trying to get into television. I didn't know anybody and I didn't know how to do it! I didn't even know what kind of job I wanted because, at that point, I had no experience other than driving trucks, working in gas stations, and being a puppeteer.

My luck changed when a man I knew, Hal Friedman, and his friend, David Young, got together to become play investors. As a sort of trial flight, they hired the puppet theatre that my wife and I operated called the *Berkeley Marionettes*. Just to go through the motions of putting on a show, Friedman and Young hired us for a week's worth of performances at the Pythian Temple in New York, while they handled advertising and getting audiences.

After that, Hal Friedman called and asked if I wanted to work for him on television. He had a new hour variety show at NBC called *Broadway Open House*, which aired at eleven o'clock every night. He thought I would be good for it.

They were just establishing the jobs in television and there was very little form to those positions because nobody really knew what to do. They did have a rough idea there were cameras, and they had a director somewhere. They put me on staff at NBC before I'd even filled out an application, which was lucky because I had no qualifications for the job. When NBC sent me the application forms to fill out, I lied terribly about my schooling and my experience and then lived in terror that they would find out, but it didn't seem to matter, because by then I was firmly entrenched, earning eighty-five dollars a week.

I was lucky to get into television when I did. It was just before the door slammed shut, though a little too late for plum jobs, because all the directors who subsequently went on to make big movies were already directing live television, while I was still a floor manager.

**Fielder Cook:** I graduated from Washington University in 1948, and came up to New York to go to Columbia School of Radio because I had nothing else to do. I needed to get a job to support myself. I learned about advertising agencies, which I'd never heard of before, because in Virginia we didn't talk about those things. I interviewed them all, and they all offered me the same thing, which was twenty-five dollars a week as a messenger. Since J. Walter Thompson was the largest agency and had a great deal of commercial radio, I went to work there as a messenger.

**Buzz Kulik:**   Before being drafted into the army during World War II, I was in college for a couple of years, where I developed a theatrical background. After the war, I got married and was living in New York when I decided to try to find a job acting. It was impossible, because there were so many men and women who wanted to take a crack at it, it was just overloaded.

I had to get a job, but the only entertainment work I could find was as a messenger for J. Walter Thompson. At the time, Fielder Cook, who is an old, dear friend of mine, was also a messenger boy. Thompson had a very large radio department and was just beginning to move into television. I was hoping that through radio I would get an "in" to theatre.

**George Roy Hill:**   After the Second World War, I went to New York and then to Ireland, where I became interested in the theatre. I left Ireland in 1949, came back here, and started acting in Margaret Webster's Shakespeare company. Then I was called back into the Korean War as a Marine pilot.

During my stint in the Korean War, I found that I had a lot of extra time on my hands, so I started writing scripts. I sent the scripts to *Kraft Television Theatre* in New York, where I had done one small part as an actor. When the Korean War ended, there was a job waiting for me at *Kraft* because they'd bought three or four of my scripts, and they wanted me to continue on their staff as a writer, adapting plays and novels. Among others, we adapted *A Connecticut Yankee in King Arthur's Court* for Edgar Bergen.

**Livia Granito:**   I had been on the road with an operetta, and I got into television while I was making the rounds as a singer. I applied for a job with an independent television producer, who hired me as a gofer — a production assistant. Since the director was from NBC, I got to know quite a few people there.

The show was a night court type of thing. The only professional [actor] on the show was the judge, otherwise we used all real people. We looked for "characters," so you can imagine the kind of people we got!

We got drunks off the Bowery — well, at least the guys did. We went on the subway, gave out little cards to people and asked them to come to the storefront that housed our office and rehearsal hall, down the block from the 21 Club, on 52d Street. A lot of professional actors tried to pass as amateurs, but we would see right through them. One day, Marlon Brando was passing by the store, came in, and applied — incognito. We went along with the prank and told him not to call us, we'd call him.

The whole thing was improvised. The judge would have a rundown of the script and how we wanted the story to go. By certain questions, the judge would elicit certain responses. The others would know what they were going to be booked on, and whether or not they were going to be guilty. They could embroider or do whatever they wanted. We had some hair-raising escapades with that show, but it was a lot of fun. It was all live, and there was no editing or anything, but most of the people knew not to say certain things because they didn't want to embarrass themselves.

The show was a critical success and did pretty well, but not enough to renew it. It went off the air at the end of the year. The producer kept me and the three men on staff a while, and we had an absolutely marvelous time being young in New York.

When the producer got called to do something else for NBC, he called me again to work for him, and that's how I officially got connected with NBC. We were hired to coordinate the hour-and-a-half *Your Show of Shows* and the one-hour *The Jack Carter Show* as well as the commercials.

*Your Show of Shows* was done at the International Theatre on 59th Street at Columbus Circle. *The Jack Carter Show* came from the Hudson Theatre, which was near 48th and Broadway. As our base of operations, NBC gave us a third studio, at NBC in Rockefeller Center. We did most of the commercials there, they were all live. We spent the day going from place to place, catching up on what was happening. We would study the rehearsals and know what the rundown was, so the producer could write lead-ins that would tie in the last skit with the upcoming commercial. As the liaison and representative for NBC, it was a very interesting job and a marvelous way to learn television since I was working with top people. The guests were always fabulous people.

Mel Brooks walked around as an extra. Neil Simon, Carl Reiner, and Howard Morris were up-and-coming. *Your Show of Shows* was not only the top show on any of the networks at that time, but it's still a classic. It was a fascinating world, and before I knew it, I had forgotten about singing.

At the end of that season, I got a chance to be a script girl at the local station. They liked my work, so I began scripting on many of the local shows. I also got to script for the network, as what they called a floater. Whenever they needed an extra person, or when somebody was on vacation or out with an illness, I filled in. A lot of us were all learning at the same time; we were all in training to become directors.

**John Frankenheimer:** I was in the Air Force in 1952, '53. I was stationed with a film unit in the photographic squadron at Lockheed Air Force Terminal in Burbank, California. I wanted to get into movies, so I'd go to see anybody who would see me, but Hollywood was very similar to now, in that the movie business was really in the toilet. They were firing a lot of people. Television had made tremendous inroads into movie attendance and into movie revenues.

I met an agent, Al Rockett, who said, "If I were you, what I would do is go into television."

I applied at NBC out here, and they offered me a job as a parking lot attendant. At CBS they said, "You could start in the mailroom." I was offered a job at ABC as a scenery construction supervisor. I didn't like any of those jobs.

I got out of the Air Force in 1953. In July, I went back to New York, where most of television originated, and tried my luck at getting in to see people. I knew someone who was a stage manager at NBC — I'd acted with him, and we'd gone to college together. He was very pleased until he knew what I wanted, which was a job.

I had my interviews at NBC, and I knew somebody that knew somebody at DuMont. ABC was not really a network to contend with. Just on a dare, I went to the CBS employment office, where they hire secretaries. The guy who was head of the whole thing heard me, and said, "I'd just like to meet some guy who's damn fool enough to come in here and ask for a job as an assistant director."

His name was Dick Stanley, I'll never forget him. We talked for a long time in this hot office — 485 Madison Avenue wasn't air-conditioned. He said, "Jesus, I just don't understand the nerve of some people. How you can just come in here and expect — you're in the wrong building, everything else. Let me call the guy and get you an interview with the right person. When could you get your résumé there? It's at 15 Vanderbilt Avenue."

I said, "Oh, I could probably get it there tonight."

He said, "Well, it closes in fifteen minutes."

I said, "I can handle that."

I ran down Madison Avenue from 53rd Street to Grand Central Station at 44th Street and got to the office just as it was closing. I was to see a guy named Hal Meyer, but the secretary said, "Mr. Meyer can't see you for a week and a half." And — I don't know what made me say this — I said, "I can't do that. I'm going back to California, and I have to see him much sooner than that."

She looked at me, and said, "All right. Can you be here at ten tomorrow morning?"

I said, "Yes."

Now, in point of fact, I had about two hundred dollars left out of my mustering-out pay, and that was it. I was living at this hotel in New York, and I didn't know what the hell I was going to do. I went in to see Hal Meyer, and the woman said, "Now, look ..." I'll never forget this "... don't be upset if he doesn't spend much time with you. He's very busy."

I said, "Okay," and went in. I sat down at his desk, and sure enough, he was very busy on the phone. He looked like Lloyd Nolan. We started to talk, and it turned out that he had been in the same photographic squadron that I was, only in World War II, and this was Korea. We talked a lot about that, and then he walked over to the side of his office, where there was a stack of papers — now, mind you, I was twenty-three — and he said, "You know what those are?"

I said, "No."

He said, "Those are all applications, for the job that you want. These people have years of experience. Stage managers from the theatre, directors from the theatre — all kinds of people. What makes you think that you could do this job better than them?"

I said, "Well, it's really very simple. Number one: all these people have obviously got terrific experience, but they've never been in television, so you don't have to unlearn any bad habits with me."

Some days when you're hot, you're hot, and I was quite good at that interview. We talked and talked. Finally, he said, "Somehow, I don't think you'd be lost in a crowd. If anything happens, I will call you, one way or another, in about a week."

I believed this man. I went back to that terrible hotel. It didn't have any message service, so I never wanted to leave the room, for fear he was going to call. I'd go out early in the morning before he got into his office, get myself a sandwich for lunch and sit there all day long and wait.

Sure enough, on the fifth day, he called and said, "John, I'm promoting one of my assistant directors to director. There's going to be a job for an assistant director for four weeks this summer. Are you interested? I've no guarantees that it will go on. It could be five weeks."

I said, "Absolutely."

I didn't know what the hell I was doing, but I went the next day, and there was another guy who came in the same way I did. They promoted two assistant directors temporarily, and we were sent through training as assistant directors. It turned out that this was a tremendous job to get, and that a lot of people in the company really resented it — floor managers and people like that who wanted to be promoted. Because of my name, they all thought that I was related to a man named Van Volkenburg, who was running the company — somebody I'd never met.

To make a long story short, I did very well, and at the end of six weeks, I was much in demand as an assistant director. Hal Meyer called me into his office and said, "Look, you've done a very good job. I want to give you a permanent job, but I'm going to put you up in Control," which was a demotion. "Would you do that?"

I said, "No. I won't do it"

He said, "What do you mean, you won't do it?"

I said, "I will not do it. You should have put me up in Control in the first place, and taken somebody from Control and put them in the job that you've given me. Because if I go into Control, it's going to look like I screwed up, it's going to be a total demotion, and I don't think I deserve that."

That, coupled with the fact that two directors asked for me to stay on their programs, convinced him that perhaps I should be a permanent assistant director. I got the job at a hundred dollars a week plus overtime, going to a hundred twenty dollars a week in six months.

Within about five months, I was making a tremendous amount of money, because I was very much in demand — I was Sidney Lumet's assistant director on *You Are There*, which was two days a week; I was on a show called *Danger*, which was two days; and then Edward R. Murrow's *Person to Person* on Friday nights. I was making about three hundred dollars a week because I was getting a lot of money under the table from people to do their shows, and on _Danger_, I was directing the Ipana Toothpaste commercials, which were done right there in the studio. It was terrific. I was not married, I had two days off, on Wednesday and Thursday and I didn't have to be at work until well in the afternoon on Friday for _Person to Person_. I had an ideal existence, and by this time I was twenty-four.

**Arthur Hiller:** I have always been interested in the theatre. My parents formed a Yiddish theatre company up in Edmonton, Alberta, in western Canada, and when I was eight or nine years old I was helping to build and paint sets. That turned me on to theatre, and later my parents decided that I should try acting.

We put on plays, which I always liked. When I finished high school, I was offered a scholarship to study drama at the University of Ohio. Since I thought theatre was something that you did on the weekends, and not something you did as a career, I turned down the scholarship.

Later, after World War II, I entered a graduate school at the University of Toronto, where I studied psychology, and was completing a master's degree. It was very interesting. One day, succumbing to my interest in communications and theatre, I went over to the Canadian Broadcasting Corporation headquarters, where I went up to the front desk and said, "Who do you see about a job?"

The woman at the desk said, "What kind of job?"

I said, "I want to be a director." She told me to speak to a Mr. Doyle, who was manager of the network.

I went home and phoned Mr. Doyle's office. His secretary said, "The name is Boyle, not Doyle. What did you want to talk to him about?" I told her and she said, "You can't speak to him but you can speak to his associate, Mr. Palmer."

I met with Mr. Palmer and told him that I wanted to be a director. I didn't know that you started at a transmitter on the prairies and worked your way up. Palmer said, "Just a minute." He left for a minute, then came back and took me to meet the supervisor of public affairs broadcasting. We had a very pleasant hour-and-a-half conversation. However, I later realized that he was pumping me as to how I felt about certain social issues and civic problems, what books I read and which periodicals I preferred, as well as engaging in various philosophical discussions. As a result, Palmer suggested I apply for a job that he had available.

I joined sixty-four other people in applying. Three weeks later, in the late nineteen-forties, I was working as a director in radio, on public affairs programs. I started doing talk shows, pro and con citizen's forums — things like that. Because of my particular interest in drama, I started to do what you'd call social documentaries and social dramas dealing with specific issues.

The following year I transferred over into what we called general production. I was a director on music shows and dramas, as well as the dramatic segments of the public affairs programs.

Then, along came television. When I first shifted over to television, I worked in public affairs, and eventually moved into drama.

I remember the first live show that I directed. It was set on the bridge of a ship in fog. The art director had designed the bridge with the front part out, so that you could see the backdrop past the steering wheel. I said, "We're looking at the back wall. That's not visually interesting. Let's take out one of the sides so we're at least looking through a window, so you can see the fog."

The art director said, "Fine. If you want to try that."

I realized later what I was letting myself in for. Although I was prepared and organized, when we got down to the floor and were moving the cameras around, because of the number of windows on the bridge of the ship, the cameras were forever looking at each other. I was in total panic throughout that show. It seemed that there was a problem everywhere, but the cameramen helped me, so that somehow it all sort of worked out.

I fell into some things. On one show, looking through a chain link fence towards a boat, I was supposed to cue dry ice so that when we made the cut to the boat, there would be the feeling of water. In my panic, I was a little late on that cue, and by the time we cut to it, the dry ice was just starting to form. Well, it gave the feeling that the boat was in motion. It all worked so well. That was the beginning of live television for me.

**Lamont Johnson:**   The beginning was the bit of direction that I did in school, when I was simply out to show myself off as an actor. I staged the epilogue to *St. Joan* by Bernard Shaw, because I had a wonderful notion in mind to turn on Pasadena City College by doing a cheap Hollywood stunt. I rented a limousine and dressed myself up as Bernard Shaw, in a white linen suit and a full beard and floppy hat, which concealed a great deal of youth — I think I was seventeen.

I pulled up to the reflecting pool in front of the college, where there were some two thousand kids sitting around eating lunch. I had my beautiful, red-headed girlfriend, Gloria, meet me, open the door and guide me, as I feebly felt my way with a cane. I was loudly denouncing the entire establishment for cramping my play into that little theatre. I got the whole crowd to follow me in, which caused the entire theatre department to just go into a state of shock.

That was the kind of nonsense I did, taking directing not at all seriously. It was delightful and fun, but it was only so I could play parts I wanted to play. I was a very greedy actor and an ambitious one.

I played in a production of Ferenc Molnar's *Liliom* at Pasadena City College. I had a whole different notion of how I'd like to see it done, because I had disagreed with my director, so when I got to UCLA as a student, I did, I think, a pretty damn stunning version of it as a director. I was eighteen at the time. When I was nineteen, I did a few Equity Library Theatre things in New York. Because I had a limp, I always had to do two things: first of all, disguise it very carefully in auditions and readings so that they wouldn't think I limped, and, second, give myself parts where I could show off how dazzlingly I could cover it all.

My wife and I were married in Paris in 1945, and when we finished a seven-month tour of the USO European Theatre Operation we spent some time with Gertrude Stein. She had just come out of her enforced idleness in the South of France, being perhaps the only American Jewess to stay through the entire German occupation. She was wildly lionized and I sought her out in Paris, because I'd heard that she liked to talk to G.I.'s. We had a wonderful time with her.

She wrote a play for us, *Yes Is for a Very Young Man*, which she dedicated to me and to my wife. We took an option on it, and produced it as a world premiere at the Pasadena Playhouse, with my wife and me playing the two leading roles.

I controlled the rights to the play, and I was fascinated with what could be done with it that hadn't been done at Pasadena, so, in 1947 or '48, we took the Cherry Lane Theatre in New York. I directed, with a rather astonishing group of people: Anthony Franciosa, who was nineteen, was the young man; Michael Gazzo, who wrote *Hatful of Rain* and was in *The Godfather*, played Anouilh; Gene Saks, the director, played the German; Bea Arthur was Constance, the part my wife had played. It was

Kim Stanley's first performance in New York, and Brooks Atkinson did the usual kind of classic line, saying, "We will hear more of Miss Stanley." All of us were totally, totally, totally brand new.

I had such terrible fights with the actors, because we were all in different schools — there were devout Strasbergians, there were Stella Adlerians, I had left Strasberg and gone to Sandy Meisner — so we didn't really talk, we used vocabulary on each other, argot of the various teachers. I was fired at one point and then Gene Saks called me a week later and said, "Now we fired Mike Gazzo. He was trying to take over. You've got to come back."

I said, "I'll do it on one condition only. That everybody shuts up, I tell you exactly what to do."

He said, "Okay. That's what we really want."

The whole thing was a very unpleasant experience. We had gone through seven weeks of this kind of masturbatory group therapy, and we opened and it ran for eight weeks, which was a big success. Now, an Off-Broadway production has to run two years before it's considered a hit. I wanted Miss Stein to see it, but she died before we opened.

I went home to my wife and said, "That is it. I never want to direct again. I can't stand actors. I can't stand all the crap. It's not worth it. I'm really an actor myself. I want to be an actor only. That's all I'm going to do for the rest of my life." And this was my first serious job of direction.

From 1947 to 1955, I doodled around a little tiny bit with some directorial things, but mainly I was very happy just being an actor. I was doing the last of radio. I started in radio when I was fourteen years old, and did all the radio shows there were to do. I made a very good living always as a radio actor — they had bought my first house — but radio was now going down the tubes.

I was finishing off my last year of *Tarzan* for Dr. Ross dog food and things like that, but I was getting very discontented with parts I was getting in television. I was doing some rotten filmed television jobs, and I loathed that early television stuff.

I was still working back and forth between New York and L.A., but we'd moved to California in 1951. I was a terrible snob about being a New York actor, and showing them how New York actors don't respond to this kind of crap and garbage. I'm sure, at that point, I was a very arrogant and unpleasant young man to direct.

Ethel Winant occasionally sent for me, I worked for Daniel Petrie, and with Martin Balsam. I made occasional forays back to New York, where I began to ask people like Jack Smight, for whom I acted on *Philco/Goodyear Playhouse*, and Arthur Penn and Dan Petrie if I could sit in the booths and watch what they did. What happened in that marvelous booth, where everything took place, was a total mystery. As far as I was concerned it was a space satellite, it had that much mystery and glamour. They would say, "Yes, as long as you don't give me any suggestions."

Jack was very sweet. He said, "You're not on in the second act of this. Take the script, break it down, do your own moves, block it, figure out what you want to do with it, just don't tell me. Come and watch what I do, and see what you would do. It'd be a good exercise for you."

It was a brilliant suggestion, and it totally turned me on. I so loved it, not only the mystery, but the real magic of what the director could do in that booth. One had as close an approximation to being a total tyrannical emperor as one could get in the arts. You did everything. You picked out the music, you brought it in, you swelled it, and sometimes you even reached over and handled it physically, raising and lowering the sound levels. You ordered the cameramen to change lenses and what lens to flip, telling them where to move, over whose shoulder to shoot, while you gave notes to your secretary to pass on to the actors on the floor about changing their performances. Even as you were on the air, you were still shaping it. I had the opportunity to prove this just two years later when I fell into *Matinee Theatre*.

**Adrienne Luraschi:**  I was born and brought up in New Rochelle, New York. My first job was with the New Rochelle Water Company. Most of the young men were off to war, and I was assigned to work with a wiry little old person — well, he may not have been that old — who went around to the various townships in Westchester County, checking all the little water meters, where they were and that they were working. He had big charts and maps and tape measures and so on. I had my little dress on and my stockings with the seam up the back, being very proper, and he said, "None of that. Wear your slacks because we're going to be in a pickup truck."

In the middle of winter with snow around, we'd go to Dobb's Ferry and Ardsley and who knows where. He'd say, "Now there should be a water meter about two feet from here." We'd scrape until we could find it, then we'd mark it down.

It was the dumbest job, but it was sort of fun because it wasn't a regular 9-to-5, sit-down-at-the-table job. From there, instead of going to college, I went to work at the FBI in Washington, D.C. I heard they were in town looking for people and I thought, Well, I'd like to do something like that, go away from this town. So I filled out all of their forms and talked to the agent in charge. I went home and I told my mother. I was very excited because I felt I had a good chance of being accepted.

My mother didn't think it was a good idea, as I had never been away from home. After I had gone to bed, she said to my father, "We can't let her go. She doesn't know anything about anything. She can't even boil water! Can you imagine what it must be like in Washington now?"

My father said, "What are you going to do? She's grown up and she can do what she wants. Now is as good a time as any for her to go out on her own."

Years later, my mother told me she went to the office of the agent and introduced herself. She said, "My daughter told me she came here, and filled out all of your forms. I have a feeling she probably filled out something falsely because she did not know the truth. My husband is not a citizen of the United States. He was born in Switzerland, and he never became a citizen." I always thought Daddy was a citizen. They were floored by the fact that my mother would come and tell this. She said, "I'd rather she didn't know. I'll tell her someday. Or my husband will."

Anyway, I got the job, and I went to Washington. In 1945, shortly before the end of the war, I left the FBI and came home. I was running toward a nervous breakdown from all that activity in Washington, D.C.

Then, I was working for the Community Chest in New Rochelle as a secretary, making contacts on the phone, putting flyers in envelopes and so forth. I had seen something about NBC in New York hiring people for this new television department. One of the people I was working with who knew I was interested in theatre and motion pictures, said, "Adee, why don't you go down and see about that?"

I think it was February of '46. I was interviewed by the NBC personnel department, and they said, "All we have at the moment are secretarial jobs in the pool."

I said, "Well, okay. But how long before you could move me out of the pool?"

The interviewer said, "I can't really be sure. But I would say maybe a month."

I said, "If it's all right with you, I'll work here for two weeks. If nothing comes along that I can at least apply for, I'll leave."

So they put me in the pool. Before two weeks were up, they sent me up for two jobs. One was as secretary for Nick Kersta, a nice-looking man who was in charge of the TV department. He had his own office and a small office for his secretary.

The other job was being the receptionist for the TV production department, and as secretary for the casting director, Owen Davis Jr. I remember thinking, The activity's here. There were people moving back and forth, phones ringing, lots of chatter. In the other job, I was going to be sitting in that little secretarial office, and I didn't want to do that. Both of them had said they would take me, which was nice, but I said, "I want Mr. Davis."

They said, "Well, Mr. Kersta pays more."

I said, "I know." So that's how I started, as a secretary-receptionist.

A number of funny things happened my first year there. Sometimes, it was like a circus atmosphere with the many weird specialty acts for the variety shows we were putting on. Once, I remember going to the elevator and when the door opened there was a grizzly bear standing all alone in the elevator. (His trainer was probably behind him.) I almost fainted. I went back to tell everybody, and they said, "Oh, Adee, come to your senses." A little later the bear came into Room 688 with his trainer to see Ernest Colling [one of the NBC producer-directors]. I let everybody know that indeed there was a bear in the building! There was a bunch of us in 688. I can always see Warren Wade [executive producer for NBC Television] way at the back, and Bill Garden [a director] over on the side. All the directors had their own cubicles, and the secretaries sat outside them.

Another funny episode was when I had been away from the desk for a while, and when I came back, I heard a flute, or something, coming from Owen Davis's office. I went in the room, and Owen was sitting there with his head in his hands, as if he was saying, "Please, let it all go away."

There was a man with a little animal. The man was playing "The Star Spangled Banner," and this *thing* was walking on its hind legs, carrying an American flag. I thought, Poor Owen, he probably thinks he's got the DTs, and it isn't happening. I got the man and his animal to leave, and I told Owen, "That was indeed a squirrel or a *thing*, crawling along your desk."

He said, "Oh, my God! How did he get in? Where were you?"

For weeks, when we talked about it, we'd get hysterical. Owen was a nice man and a very funny man. It was terrible when he drowned in Long Island Sound on the 4th of July weekend.

Whenever I could, I would sneak downstairs to studio 3-H. That was the tiny place where we did most of those early shows. I'd hide behind the sets, watching the goings-on. One day I heard a voice, "Adee, will you get off the balcony please! We're about ready to come up, and you're in the shot!" Oh, it was so embarrassing. I thought I was being so careful to keep out of the way. After that I became more aware of what was happening and what was done. About two years after I started working with Owen, I became a script girl.

**Delbert Mann:**   I knew Fred Coe from the days when we grew up together and acted together at the community playhouse in Nashville, Tennessee. I graduated from college in political science, but during the war I decided I wanted to go into theatre. Right after I got out of the service, on Fred's advice, I got into Yale Drama School. Then, on his recommendation, I went to Columbia, South Carolina, where he had directed the local community theatre for four years during the war. I had my first professional directing job there from 1947 to 1949.

In the spring of '49, I called Fred once again. A few years before, he had gone into that thing called "Live Television" in New York. I asked him what's doing, and he said, "Come on up, I think I can get you a job at NBC."

I went to New York and, once again, through Fred's recommendation got a job. At that point they were hiring people like crazy, mostly people with a theatre and stage background, because they saw the network was primarily going to a lot of dramatic things. Robert Sarnoff hired me at NBC as a floor manager and assistant director. I had never even seen a television show or a television studio or a television set — I didn't know what television was, so I didn't really know what I was getting into.

I spent twenty-four hours a day observing, watching, learning, questioning, and being on the floor throwing cues. One of my very first directing jobs in that summer of '49, was on the first film series that I can recall the network running. It was *The Life of Riley*, which was done on film here in California and shipped east. The beer commercials were done live. One week Kingman Moore would direct the commercials, while I would get my nails properly done and my hand would come in and pour the glass of beer with just the proper head on it. The next week he would pour the glass of beer and I'd direct the commercial.

In the summer of '49, the old *Lights Out* show was sustaining — no sponsor — so I, as a new director, was allowed to direct the first time. The opening was on film, superimposed over a candle, with the sepulchral voice saying, "Lights out, everybody." You always had a seven- or eight-second delay after you rolled the film, hoping to time it out properly so that as the film came up on the chain, you could cut to it and put it on the air.

On my first time in the chair: "Roll the film," and just as we went on the air, the candle flickered and dwindled and died to black. The projector upstairs had blown a fuse, so no film came up and the voice said, "Lights out," over a bit of nothing — a little unnerving.

Fred Coe, from being without any question the best director in television, had moved up to producing the *Philco Television Playhouse*, which was NBC's premiere, prestige one-hour dramatic show. By Thanksgiving time of 1949, he was seeking directors he wanted to work with. He promoted me, so that, about six months after I had joined the network, I found myself directing and learning from Fred. It was, I think, more than anything else, simply a matter of incredibly good timing and luck and friendship and help from Fred Coe.

**Ralph Nelson:** I had been in the Air Corps as a pilot in World War II, stationed down in Georgia. I had married there, it did not turn out too well, and I returned to New York in 1948. New York was not only my home town, but I had been an actor and a writer in the theatre on Broadway.

In December of 1948, as I recall, the head of production at NBC, Warren Wade, called me in and, just to get some income, I appeared on what was then one of the two dramatic shows on the air, the *Kraft Television Theatre*. The other one was *Philco Television Playhouse*.

To my surprise, NBC called and asked me if I'd like to join their staff as a director. I thought at the time it was a sneaky way to keep me off the screen, but it turned out that Fred Coe, who was the producer and director of the *Philco Playhouse*, and whom I had never met, had seen a play of mine on Broadway, and had seen me perform in the *Kraft Theatre*. I learned later that he convinced the brass at NBC that television was about to burgeon, they would need directors, and here was somebody from the theatre who acted and wrote and would possibly be useful.

My friends in the theatre thought I was crazy, but I said, "Well, I think television has a future." And there was nothing available for me on Broadway. I didn't have a new play written, nor were there any parts available.

I joined the staff at NBC and was given every kind of odd job in directing — we did cooking shows with Dione Lucas, a show with Wendy Barrie, and an early Sunday morning show called *Powwow* with a bunch of New York Indians. I don't know where they got them.

At the same time, NBC had hired a number of motion picture directors, but they were used to working with one camera at a time, and they just didn't seem to be able to adapt to doing three or four cameras. They were let go after awhile.

I remember the terror when I was given my first show to direct, after the Wednesday night fights. We were just a standby, but suddenly there was a knockout and I was on the air with one camera and this three-piece orchestra. I was glued to the monitor, glued to the clock to make sure I got off on time. I was in total confusion, but an old-timer of a technical director pulled me through on that one.

In the spring of 1949, NBC's head of personnel was Robert Sarnoff, who had somebody up there who liked him. [His father was General David Sarnoff, chairman of the board of RCA, NBC's parent company.] He offered all of the NBC directors a new five-year contract with no escalation, and no commercial fees at all. Everybody signed up except me. I thought it was outrageous. They were going to dismiss me, but about that time, out of the blue, I had a call from Charles Underhill, the head of programming at CBS, whom I didn't know at all. He invited me to lunch, said he had been watching my work and liked what I had done — I had directed a *Philco Playhouse* and a couple of other dramatic shows by then — and would I care to join CBS. They had on the air *The Goldbergs*, which was a very popular ethnic series about a Jewish family in the Bronx, and they were planning three new pilots. One, as I recall the name, was *The O'Flahertys*, about an Irish family; one I've forgotten; and one was based on *I Remember Mama*. Well, both my parents were Swedish, and I had a feeling for the property, so I said, "I'll come if I can do *I Remember Mama*."

I moved over to CBS, we did a pilot titled *Mama*, and it sold in record time to Maxwell House Coffee. I did it for the next six years because it became a mink-lined rut.

**Arthur Penn:**  Sometime in 1951, I was off the streets looking for a job, and I got one working as a floor manager trainee at NBC. If you survived the first couple of days of that, you stayed on. I floor managed news shows and some dramatic shows. After a couple of months, I got assigned fairly regularly to *The Colgate Comedy Hour*, which was a Sunday night show out of New York featuring rotating comics. I was one of the floor managers, Bud Yorkin was the other. We stayed with the show for quite a while.

Around late 1952, the coaxial cable, which linked the network from the West Coast to the East Coast, was being opened. This made it possible to have direct transmission, so they shipped out the whole show and moved to the West Coast. Bud and I were sent along to do the floor managing and also to train some additional network level floor managers out there.

We were at the El Capitan Theatre on Vine Street, which had been converted into a television theatre. We would do the show at five o'clock in the afternoon, West Coast time. The show was live at seven o'clock in the central states, eight o'clock on the East Coast, and they would show a kinescope at eight o'clock on the West Coast.

I had some aspirations to becoming a director, but everything was quite chaotic, and everything was moving very swiftly. Before very long, it was clear that those who could survive in television were going to do well. Those who couldn't were going to fall by the wayside rather quickly, and that happened. It was a very high-risk, high-tension job. There's no question about that.

**Daniel Petrie:**  I was an actor, in New York. After two productions, I went out to Chicago with the road company of *I Remember Mama*. While I was there, I decided to go back to school, because I figured I didn't really know anything about acting — I'd just been lucky to get into Broadway shows. I went back to Northwestern to become a drama major and work toward my Ph.D. in drama. I took courses in directing and producing television shows. Northwestern University had a summer institute which was taught at NBC's WBKB in Chicago. About 1948, WBKB was, I think, the only television station on the air in Chicago, and was where *Kukla, Fran and Ollie*, the little puppet show, started.

I went to Omaha, Nebraska, to teach at Creighton University. I thought the academic world was what I wanted. I'd finished all the class work toward the Ph.D., and I would finish my dissertation while I taught.

One of the attractions of going to Creighton University was that there was equipment on the campus for a full-scale television operation. WOW TV, the NBC affiliate in Omaha, had not gone on the air yet. Their building was still being constructed, but they had all their equipment. The only place they could store it was on the Creighton campus, so that equipment was my plaything for a year, and it was a good teacher, too. Nobody knew anything about television. I was the resident expert, because I had taken one summer course. We did little dramas on closed circuit.

When the station opened, that equipment went over there and I was brought in as a sort of director. I was there for about a year. As a matter of fact, I directed Johnny Carson, because he came with his magic show to do a noontime program.

I decided that, although there was a very nice atmosphere on the campus, teaching at Creighton University was not the life for me. I wanted to be in what I then considered "the real world," where it was happening. So I went to NBC in Chicago at Christmas in 1949, and pleaded with the guy who was the head of the programming or the production department to give me a job. He said he didn't think that there would be anything until early 1950. I said that wouldn't do me any good, because I couldn't leave in the middle of a semester, but if he would give me a job right then, I could give a month, or a month-and-a-half, notice so that they could get somebody to replace me for the second semester. He said, "No. No chance."

The next day I got back to Omaha, very despondent. By this time I had really decided that I didn't belong in teaching, and wanted to be in production. The whole idea of teaching another semester was very onerous.

He called me and said, "Something has come up very suddenly."

I said, "When would you need me?"

He said, "As it turns out, from about two hours after you left yesterday."

I said, "Oh, great. I'll hurry on in."

**George Schaefer:**   After I graduated from college, I spent just one year at Yale Drama School, intending to go into the theatre. I'd written a lot of the producers saying I hoped they'd have room for a "hopeful, maybe reasonably bright, young, aspiring director." I admit I was going to be going into New York to get a job as an assistant stage manager, if I was lucky, or, more likely, a gofer sweeping out the corners. Instead, Pearl Harbor came in the middle of my year at Yale, so I went directly into the Army, where I stayed for three years. Due to the success of the many shows I directed there, Maurice Evans got to know me and to respect my talents, I guess.

When we came back to New York in '45, Mike Todd had heard about the production of *Hamlet* we had done in the Pacific during the war — all Shakespeare, but slightly streamlined and done with a lot of gusto and kind of Ruritania clothes so that it would connect very definitely with the soldiers. So my first job in New York was directing Maurice Evans in *The G.I. Hamlet*, for which George Jean Nathan awarded me the Best Director of the Year award. It was very successful and ran a year in New York and a year on the road. I started out in just the right way, and the years in the Army turned out to be a shortcut, instead of the other way around.

I stayed with Maurice and directed *Man and Superman* for him. We brought over from London a J. B. Priestley play, *The Linden Tree*, which I directed and which did not succeed, but Maurice knew my work very well and put complete confidence in me.

At the time that *The G.I. Hamlet* production was on tour, I began to get kind of fascinated by television. I had some friends on the Milton Berle show, the number one, big-rated variety show. I used to watch from the control room, and I really thought I should get in it. I recall writing letters to seven or eight stations around the country saying, "Hey, I'd like to just come and do everything at your studio for a while, work for next to nothing." I never got a job offer, although one of them said, "Look, we've seen your record of what you've done and you're obviously not going to stick with us. To have you come out to Cincinnati for three or four months just to learn and leave us is not what we really want."

I used to watch *Studio One* and *Kraft* and *Goodyear* — a lot of original, hour shows, none of which I ever did. I did get a chance to do one live show. In the summers I would go down to Dallas, Texas and direct the musicals, which I loved doing. We'd put on five, sometimes six, very huge productions at the State Fair Auditorium, with all-star casts. Just before I started with the *Hallmark Hall of Fame*, one of the NBC people tied in with it felt it would be a very good idea for me to direct in the control room, so we brought the production of *One Touch of Venus*, the Kurt Weill musical, from Dallas. Janet Blair and George Gaines, Iggie Wolfington and Herbert Marshall were in it. In a week's time, we blocked it, we staged it, and did it live — in black and white — out of the old Brooklyn studio. There was a lot wrong with it, but there was a lot that was quite exciting about it too.

**Allan Buckhantz:**  I was referred to as a "comer" while employed as a messenger at Fox [in Los Angeles] and was able to circumvent the union requirements and get experience in all of their departments. I was paid thirty-seven dollars and fifty cents a week in the mail department, so that they could place me for a couple of weeks in the editing room, for a couple of weeks in the art department, for a couple of weeks all over the place. I had come from theatre, so I used to do a substantial amount of work with the Fox contract players. One of our big claims to fame was that we found Marilyn Monroe.

At Fox I met Cecil Barker's wife. She mentioned me to Cecil, who was at one time Selznick's right-hand man, and he asked me to come down and talk to him. Cecil was in charge of programming for KNXT, which was a local CBS station not connected to the network because this was about 1949 and there still was no cable. He asked me whether I would consider leaving my very important post as a messenger at Fox to come work in television.

I didn't know anything about television except that it was pictures coming through a tube. I wanted to know how it worked, so he asked me to come and see a show that they were doing that night. It was called *NTG*, and the reference was "Not Too Good." Seriously, *NTG* stood for *Nils T. Granlund* — a daily talent-scout show which was a popular event.

I was absolutely fascinated by the medium, by the booms and the cameras, but more important than that, by a guy running around the stage with headphones. He was the stage manager, and he did all kinds of stuff. Everybody talked into the headphones, and I couldn't figure out how anybody could understand who was doing what.

Cecil said they'd pay me seventy-five dollars a week, but I would have to work three days on the network side and two days on the local side because local couldn't afford seventy-five dollars. So I quit Fox and went to work at KNXT.

At first there was no job. Cecil was doing *The Alan Young Show* — which was national by means of kinescope — at the CBS studios on Sunset, with Ralph Levy directing. So I was at CBS for three days, and over at KNXT for two or three days, just hanging around.

One day Cecil called me in and said, "All right. We're ready for you to make a move to be a director."

I said, "No." He looked at me. I said, "No, if anything, I want to be a stage manager because this is all too confusing. I'd like to know what makes it tick."

He said I was crazy because a year from now everybody and his grandfather was going to be a director. In other words he meant relatives would be coming into the industry. So I got the job as a stage manager and did everything — *Hopalong Cassidy*, the movie intermissions, *NTG*, news, everything.

We had a show on the air called *Peter Potter*. It aired three times a week. Twice a week it was *Peter Potter's* something, and once a week it was *Peter Potter's Jukebox Jury*, which became very popular. I was stage managing that show when Peter got very unhappy with his director, and Cecil called me up and said, "As of tomorrow night, you're directing *Peter Potter's Jukebox Jury*." He would not take "No" for an answer.

I was worried about directing for the first time, so I called my good friend Bob Adams, who was a director, and said, "Bob, I will only take the job if you sit with me in the control room because I'm going to panic." I didn't, but only because I knew that he was sitting there. Immediately, I started a love affair with live television. There was something about live that doesn't exist today. It's an entirely different medium.

**Walter Grauman:** I was a pilot in the Air Force in World War II and then I got a job as an apprentice publicist at Universal Studios [in Los Angeles], through the head of the studio. He'd been a friend of my father's. That lasted for less than a year. I got canned in one of their cutbacks, so I went to real estate broker's school, got a broker's license. I hated the real estate business, because I hate dealing with the public. I'm very short, people are arrogant when they have money to spend, and I used to get very hostile.

I quit that, went into the candied popcorn business and then I got married. I didn't have any money, but my wife's parents gave us a television set as a wedding present. In 1949, there were a lot of local stations — KTLA, KTTV, KHJ, and ABC had a local outlet, KCOP. There was a variety of really primitive local programming, all of it live.

One night, when I was looking at a local program, I turned to my wife and said, "If that's entertainment, I can do better than that."

She looked at me, and said, "Well, why don't you?"

I dreamed up an idea for a talent showcase for young actors and actresses, *Lights, Camera, Action*. I went to my wife's cousin, Alan Armour, who had also become a friend of mine. He was an unemployed announcer. Later, he was a very successful producer in television for quite a long time, and now he teaches writing at Northridge.

I said, "Listen. You don't have a job and I don't have a job, and I've got this idea. Do you want to go partners?"

He said, "Sure."

So we wrote a format of the idea, and I tried like a sonuvabitch to sell this idea, because I was always sort of the hustler, the salesman. I went to the local NBC station — I think it was called KNBH at the time — and the local program manager was a marvelous, short, tough man, Ed Sobel. He's been dead many years now. He had been in radio and he packaged shows, and I don't know what all, and this callow kid walks in off the street, and says, "I have this idea. It's a talent showcase for young, professional actors and actresses, and we'll hold open auditions."

Ed Sobel said, "Look, what are you going to use for material?"

I said, "I have a very good friend from universal casting who said I could use the material that they use for screen tests for actors."

Ed said he didn't think that would work.

He was right, because they were just excerpts from plays or pictures, and they have no beginning or end.

I said, "I tell you what. We'll write the material."

He said, "Well, give me a sample of your writing."

I wasn't a writer, so for maybe three or four days Alan and I broke our butts writing these things, took them in to Ed Sobel, and he said, "Oh, they're not bad."

We wrote, eventually, a hundred fifty playlets that were five to seven minutes long, and which, several years later, we compiled into book form called *Vestpocket Theatre*, and sold it to Samuel French. They sell to schools and to little theatre groups. Within the last three months I think I got forty dollars in royalties.

The format of the show was actors competing. Every thirteen weeks there was a grand prize winner, who got a guaranteed Screen Actors Guild [SAG] contract to appear in a picture. On Monday afternoon I had to have this prize set, and I was beating my brains out. I was desperate. I never forgave my partners, because they were at the racetrack having a good time, and I was sweating bullets trying to get that deal made.

Saturday afternoon I went into Sammy Kramer's office, to talk to his publicist. I said, "We will talk about your Harry Popkin Cardinal Pictures if you just give a SAG minimum contract to the winner every thirteen weeks and you get all this publicity in return."

Kramer said "Well, they'd like to, but they don't make enough pictures."

I walked into Harry Popkin's office at Cardinal Pictures, and I talked to Joe Eadel. He said, "Hey, that's a pretty good idea, kid. Just go in and tell Harry."

So I went in and told Harry. I was quaking in my shoes, because he was a big shot sitting at his desk and everything.

And he said, "Yes, that's pretty good. I'll write you up a letter."

He gave us a letter, and we did promote Harry Popkin's pictures. I don't remember what they were any more. He didn't have many, but he held up his end of the bargain.

I needed a partner, somebody who could get us actors, actresses, writers, producers, directors to act as judges on this little stinking show that we did. I went to an old friend of mine, a much older man, who'd been a Shubert musical operetta star on Broadway. He had given that up, come out here, and been under contract in the old days of Fox Studios. His name was Walter Woolf. The owner of Fox Studios said, "Walter Woolf's too Jewish. We want you to change your name."

And Walter Woolf said no, he wouldn't change his name, but he'd add another name to it, so he became known as Walter Woolf King. He worked in pictures, never too successfully, then he became an agent, and because he was an agent, he knew everybody in this town. He became our partner as well as the emcee.

We got a hundred dollars a week for the three of us to put on the show. There were no unions involved, the actors got no pay, and we got whatever we could get out of it. I think we each cleared about twenty-two dollars a week.

Alan and I wrote and staged the scenes and produced the entire show. It was a half-hour, once a week, played to an audience on a proscenium stage. As I remember, there were three cameras, and Bud Cole, a staff director, called the shots in the control room.

We produced the show at the local NBC radio station, on the corner of Sunset and Vine. It was sort of an art deco, modern, green building, and in the back end of it they had added a couple of television stages, with live cameras and live control rooms. Then there was the parking lot, the offices of KNBH, and scene docks of flats. That's where we held our open auditions. I think we put an ad in the trades, but word gets around very quickly when you've got openings for actors.

Alan and I and Walter Woolf King picked who we wanted to be on the show. People like Richard Anderson, Leonard Nimoy, Nita Talbot, Beverly Garland, Jacqueline Scott got their first exposure on with us.

When Nita Talbot came in — her name then was Ginger Gray — Oh God, she was so sexy! She was very tall, built like a ton of bricks, striking looking. She read a scene and she had on a knit sweater with a huge — like a mock turtle — collar.

I said, making a joke, "This character's more sexy."

She said, "You want it more sexy?" and she took the neck of the sweater and pulled it wide and pulled it down so it was just half covering her boobs.

I said, "That's sexy enough!" And she got the role. She had a marvelous, sardonic, Eve Ardenish kind of quality. Quite a good actress, actually, and I've directed her since.

First, it was a sustaining show, then Republic Van and Storage bought it for local sponsorship, and it did very well for them. There was no network in the sense we have it today, but NBC had a cable from New York as far as St. Louis, and we sold it on the network. We got a thousand dollars a week to do the show here, to kinescope it, and send it by air mail to New York, where it was played back on the cable. They may have bicycled the prints around to other network stations.

We were in the chips, the three of us, getting a thousand dollars instead of a hundred dollars, and I was celebrating our big sale in a nightclub. An actor, Robert Quarry, said, "Oh, do you know you're being sued?"

I said, "What are you talking about?"

Lester White, whose daughter I've since directed on a filmed television show, sued us, because he had a show called *Hollywood Screen*

*Test,* which I didn't know existed. It originated in New York, and it was similar in concept.

NBC said, "Well, you have to defend the suit, you indemnified it." I took whatever money we were getting, flew back to New York and hired a lawyer. It cost us everything we'd made, but the show was on for at least a couple of years.

# Technical Matters

A salient fact of live television was the intense need for cooperation and teamwork. Like the theatre, everything happened in real time, but, unlike the theatre, the technical complications were multiplied twenty-fold. In the very early days, a camaraderie developed between engineers, stagehands, stage managers, and directors that was closer to a college atmosphere than a commercial enterprise. Nobody made much money, but everyone felt a part of something new and exciting, something that seemed to have unlimited horizons.

NBC engineers belonged to NABET [National Alliance of Broadcast Engineers and Technicians], CBS technicians to the IBEW [International Brotherhood of Electrical Workers]. All operating personnel at DuMont were members of IATSE [International Alliance of Stage Employees]. The DuMont technicians had their own local, while stagehands belonged to Local 1, which also had jurisdiction over the stagehands at CBS and NBC, and in the Broadway theatre.

Union contracts for actors, directors, or musicians did not yet exist. Production budgets were minuscule — actors were routinely paid twenty-five to fifty dollars for a performance, with up to a week of rehearsal. When music was desired, television was restricted to playing commercial recordings, until a deal was made with James Petrillo, the head of the New York local of the American Federation of Musicians.

Both CBS and NBC studios were equipped with three cameras, one mounted on a Fearless motion picture dolly, the other two on custom-built pedestals that could be raised and lowered by air pressure. CBS used florescent lamps for base lighting; NBC used incandescent floodlight bulbs arranged in banks of six to twelve. Since eight hundred foot-candles was the minimum needed for a quality picture, an operating studio became very hot — NBC unbearably so. It was not uncommon for those working the studio floor in the RCA Building to lose eight or more pounds of fluid during a long day. That afforded an added inducement to repair to a neighborhood watering hole after work.

**John Peyser:** When I went to CBS in 1948, there had been a few technical improvements. They had found a way to mount the cameras and put them on pedestals. The cameras themselves had become much more sophisticated. Field equipment had never existed before World War II.

Sports were a big thing. Boxing — not because it was the kind of entertainment they wanted to do, but because it was easy, it was something we could handle. Then baseball. I did the Brooklyn Dodger games for two seasons and the one thing we loved about Branch Rickey was the Labor Day and Memorial Day twin games. They were not doubleheaders. He did a game at ten in the morning, emptied out the stadium, filled it up again, and did the afternoon game. There was nothing happening back in the studio, so we'd line up some interviews with ball players, and for two and a half hours we vamped.

Commercials were done live on the spot. We stuck one camera in the back room at Ebbett's Field, where Ballantine's beer and Coca-Cola had their displays set up. Between innings we'd cut back to the room, where we had an announcer who had nothing to do with the ball game, because Red Barber [the Dodgers' play-by-play announcer] wouldn't do commercials.

There was a Radio and Television Directors Guild — it wasn't the DGA yet. [The merger with the Screen Directors Guild took place in 1960.] The only directors were people who worked for the network — there were no outside people. Nobody had ever heard of paying a director to do commercials. You worked for the network, so you just did them along with the show for your salary. I said, "Hey, wait a minute, this is ridiculous. They're getting a free meal here." So, when we started doing *Suspense* at CBS in Grand Central Station — where we had all our studios — I went to the agency and said, "I want a hundred dollars a week extra for doing your commercials."

They said, "We won't pay you."

"Well," I said, "I ain't going to do the commercials."

They said, "We'll get somebody else."

I said, "I'm not going to let anybody in my booth. Either pay me or that's it."

We instituted the commercial payment. From then on, everybody got paid for doing the commercials. It was a tremendous source of income.

**Franklin Heller:** In the early days, CBS grew a lot — and fast. The main thing about television in those days was that nobody knew anything about how to do it. As a result, nobody criticized anybody else, because they knew they could be criticized right back. The more ignorance you confessed to, the better you were able to get along with the other ignorant people. As a result, we didn't earn a lot, but we learned a lot because nobody knew that whatever was wanted was impossible. We just did it, and sometimes there were some pretty dicey experiments. It was exciting and great fun.

The management at CBS was very receptive to creative ideas. Every Thursday morning, there was a meeting in the rehearsal hall, above Grand Central Terminal and anybody who wasn't rehearsing or was not otherwise occupied was required to attend. That went for stage hands, scenic artists, directors, producers, anybody who was working there — maybe a hundred people. Charles Underhill, Jerry Danzig, and occasionally Jack Van Volkenburg, who was president of CBS at the time, and other executives from uptown would be there. They would stand at the head of the table and say, "Now tell us what we're doing wrong, and how we can correct it. Maybe we'll have a good reason why we can't do it, but at least we can talk about it." They listened to everybody; everybody was welcome to talk. This was so different from the way things were done at NBC, I learned. It was most helpful, and I think Charlie Underhill was responsible. He was really a very good man, and was misunderstood and underappreciated at CBS.

**Martin Ritt:** I rehearsed and photographed the shows as I would in the theatre. Every week we rehearsed the new show, learned lines, staged everything, picked all the camera shots and lenses. A day or so before we aired, the technical director [TD] came in to watch the last rehearsal, and I'd go over the show with him.

Directing a live television show was really like conducting, because everything was happening at once and you could talk directly to the crew. Everyone could hear you except the actors. You could say to the camera operator, "That's it. Now just his ear and mouth. That's it. Hold it. That's nice." After working with different crews week after week, you discovered who was the best and who could do what the best, and you utilized those people.

There was only one studio; we only had one camera. We'd finish a scene, go to black, and take fifteen or twenty seconds to scurry over to the other side of the stage so we could open up on the next scene. Because there weren't any emergency cameras, if something went wrong, that was it. We made all kinds of technical mistakes which the audience forgave because they understood the nature of the piece.

The essence of directing a live television show was that you could really affect the live performance and end up with something special. Not every director could do that. Being a good live television director was not necessarily a reflection on how well you could direct, but on how well you managed to keep control of the show.

**Buzz Kulik:**   When I first started, the network had only three stages. We accepted a lot of things. The sets were small and made of canvas, because the unloading ramp at the 39th Street entrance of the CBS studio in New York at Grand Central Station was a window, and the only way we could get the scenery into the building and into the studio was to lift it through. A guy would be there to fold the canvas so it would fit.

Of course, nothing was secure. If you slammed a door, it would shake for hours. Now, drama is not about a solid door, but as time went on, we become more sophisticated and said, "No, that's no good. We have to have the real thing." Well not only does the "real thing" cost more to build, but you've got to find a way of not having to go through that window.

**Marc Daniels:**   We started with very rudimentary conditions. We did the *Ford Theatre* shows out of Studio 41 in Grand Central Station, where they later produced *Studio One*. When we did the first show, the studio wasn't even completed. There were only two walls, and the builders were pounding all through rehearsals, which drove us mad. The control room was a plywood box. We had field cameras, which means that the monitor screens were only about five by seven inches. The switcher was also what you might call rudimentary.

As technicians, there was only IBEW personnel at CBS. During that first show at CBS I had a technical director, but it was still a rather horrendous thing trying to set up all the shots and call takes, even though I had every cut pre-planned. About twenty or thirty minutes into that show, the TD said, "Let me have the script." He took my script and punched the takes as I had pre-marked them. I thought, This is the way to go. So, from then on I prepared him a script.

The CBS system had an associate director [AD] set up the shots, so the director could talk to the cameramen. NBC, however, had the other system, where the technical director set up the shots, and the director had to talk to him. But when I first went to NBC to do a show, which was the pilot for *Mr. and Mrs. North*, I said to the TD, "I have to tell you what the shot is, and you tell the cameraman?"

He said, "That's right."

So I said, "Well, in the first shot, I want camera 1 to bring the man in the door and carry him to the bed where the girl is sitting, hold the two-shot, then carry the girl when she goes to the closet."

He said into his microphone, "Camera 1, did you hear that?"

The cameraman said, "Yes."

He said, "Well, do it —"

From then on, I just talked loudly. Actually, I never found that they were too strict about their system. You could talk to cameramen if you wanted to.

**Fielder Cook:** CBS had much more freedom. It's a much more flexible network. NBC was an engineer dominated network and NABET said there had to be a technical director, because the director was not qualified to speak to the cameraman.

**Paul Bogart:** At NBC and ABC, if a cameraman thought he wanted to do something better, he was enjoined by his technical director to keep his mouth shut. They only allowed you to speak to the cameramen up through the dress rehearsal. It was strict because there was a mad scramble to protect jobs. I haven't worked at NBC for many years and refused to do so on the account of that system.

The only time in my whole life that I ever walked past a picket line was when NABET went on strike. I liked the people individually, but their system was so counter-productive that everything took twice as long. It eventually broke down when the Directors Guild threatened to strike, which forced the issue into arbitration. When the issue was explained to George Meany [President of the AFL-CIO], who handled the arbitration, he said, "Of course a director has to talk to his cameramen. It's insane that he cannot," so they readjusted the system.

**Allan Buckhantz:** Since I had learned to direct at CBS, I had to adjust to the NBC system. The TD at NBC was always salvaging everybody's life because he was pushing the buttons and repeating what you said.

**Dan Petrie:** I worked at all three of the networks at various times. I felt most of the time that the camera guys would stand on their head in order to get an interesting shot for you. They made suggestions. Even at NBC, where you had problems while you were in the booth, when you went out on the floor, the three camera guys would come up to you with their shot lists, and they'd say, "Did you notice on the monitor that when he was saying this — I can then move over very quickly between my shot six and my shot seven, and get you a great closeup of the kid listening in on all of this."

I would say, "Oh, great!" I never felt a sense of enmity between myself and the technical guys at all.

**Arthur Hiller:** The union requirements in Canada had been very different from those at NBC, but I found that there was a lot of leeway in that area. While it's true that only the technical and associate directors could converse with the crew, all instructions still came from the director. I kind of liked that approach. I was amazed at how many good people there were on the floor and in the booth. I felt suddenly that life seemed easier, but when we sometimes began two days a week at four in the morning — it wasn't all that easy!

**John Frankenheimer:** I did most of my stuff for CBS. I did only about four shows for NBC. Because of my reputation, which was really large when I went to NBC, they waived the whole TD system, and I was able to talk to the cameras and so forth.

**Franklin Schaffner:** I preferred the CBS control room method over the one used by NBC. That's how I was trained. I think that everybody will tell you that those of us who had trained in the CBS system found working at NBC not as free as an experience as we might have liked. However, Arthur Penn — who trained at NBC — probably couldn't move with ease and comfort to the CBS system of directing *Playhouse 90*. Please note that I'm talking on a *technical* level rather than on a *creative* level. I don't think that anybody changed strokes from show to show on a creative level.

**Arthur Penn:**  The chain of command continued to exist at NBC, but on a show like *Philco*, you were dealing with the same technical director and the same camera crew. The cameramen would come to the rehearsal, see what was being done and often suggest stuff from the floor. Although the "letter of the law" said that you spoke to the camera crew through the TD, it was not rigidly enforced by a long shot. In point of fact it was a very loose and open situation, but it was adhered to on the air.

Everything was growing very quickly. The techniques were emerging. Those were the days of a lot of camera flaws and of missed shots. A lot of the live aspects of television were dangerous and terribly exciting.

**Delbert Mann:**  The TD system was a thing that NBC became stuck with back in union negotiations fifty years ago or more. I have a hunch it was a routine they would like to get rid of, because I know that every director is much more comfortable working with the so-called CBS system, where an AD is on the line, readying the shots for you, and you have direct communication with the cameraman. I grew up on the NABET TD system, so it never bothered me to operate that way.

All shows in those earliest days were done with three cameras and no more — two pedestals and one crane camera, which was a very, very small crane at that. NBC's restrictions on equipment and so forth were much more rigid than a lot of others. You could not dolly a pedestal camera, because it was too big, too awkward, too difficult for the cameraman to do it smoothly, keep in focus, and follow the action. You simply had to plan for static shots from your pedestal cameras and mobile shots from your crane camera. So there was a kind of rigidity of shooting that became almost mandatory.

As a film director, I had to learn to break away from that and to gain more freedom of expression through the camera, but it also helped me a great deal. With Fred Coe, you had to justify whenever you made a camera cut. You couldn't just cut from a medium shot to another medium shot, without a real reason for doing so. It led to a kind of economy of camera work that I have found useful over the years.

**Ralph Nelson:**  At NBC we were all complaining because we could not move a pedestal camera on air. Fred Coe was particularly incensed by it, because we would watch the shows on CBS, see the fluidity of the camera moves and want to achieve the same thing.
It was an entirely new industry, with no rules. We would all watch each other's shows to see what somebody had developed. We followed motion picture patterns mostly. I did not like a lot of camera cutting. I was more interested in the characters and their performance than in trying to show any razzle-dazzle in my direction.
On *Mama*, I did the first split screen, and the following morning just about every director at CBS called me up to find out how I had done it, because there was nothing on the console board to allow us to be able to do that. It was a very simple trick. There was a telephone conversation between Mama and her sister, Aunt Jenny. I had one flat with them both in front of it facing toward each other, holding telephones, and I just split the flat with two different kinds of wallpaper. It was a one-camera shot, but it looked like a split screen. Later, I tried to do that in the motion pictures in a film called *Soldier in the Rain* with Jackie Gleason and Steve McQueen, but it did not work as successfully.

**Allan Buckhantz:**  Albert McCleery arranged it so that I could go to New York to do a *Kraft Theatre*. My friend, an actor-director, also went to New York for a *G. E. Theatre*, and we stayed in the same hotel. He was a maniac workaholic. I'm a workaholic, too, but I don't bother other people. I bother myself. This guy was on the phone every five minutes, "Allan, what do you think about this?"
This was during the time when we were fighting with NABET to let the director talk to the cameramen. Finally, NABET said, "All right. We'll agree to a trial period. But you have to say everything, so we get a decent test of it."
On the air he says to camera two, "Pan left." So the camera panned left — three hundred sixty degrees! He never told the cameraman to stop.
It was a question about who had the last word in the control room. For example, when I was still at CBS, doing *Peter Potter's Jukebox Jury*, I used to enjoy challenging the equipment, so I decided to use a black piece of velvet as part of the set design.
Just before going on the air, the TD, whose name was Fred Muller, said, "I'm not going to put it on the air."

I said, "What do you mean?"

"Well, Allan, this is black."

"That's not what I asked you. What did you say?"

"I won't put it on the air."

"All right, let's hold everything." I left the booth and went upstairs. The CBS vice-president, Merle Jones, was in the office when I walked in. I said, "Who is responsible for what goes on the air? The TD or the director?"

He said, "The director."

I said, "You better tell the TD because he's just refused to put my show on the air."

They called the chief engineer, and before you knew it there was a big squabble, and we had to wait two hours before CBS in New York determined that the director is responsible. Later, the TD came over and said he never thought it would work. But it was a principle question. Call it the first creative rights challenge.

**Livia Granito:** I had my orientation from NBC, where talking over the intercom was not allowed by principle. It was extremely inefficient, because I'd have to tell the stage manager and then the stage manager would have to tell the actor. However, when I was in a dress rehearsal and something was happening so fast I couldn't wait, or when the stage manager was at the opposite side of the stage, I'd just flip the switch and talk. But I tried not to do this, because they didn't like it.

As a union those guys were absolutely impossible. They were extremely territorial about the crew's division of labor and were always jealously hoarding their prerogatives. I'm not saying that the crews at NBC weren't any good. I had no quarrels with their performances or their abilities. It was just the way that they tried so hard to keep people out and maintain so much regimentation. The experience was like being in the army, and I hated that.

I think that the CBS setup was much better creatively. I worked there for a time directing a soap opera, and I just loved it.

**Arthur Hiller:** In Canada, there was less money in television than in the States. Also, you had to do everything yourself. There was no such thing as an associate director. As the director, I had to prepare and call the shots, the sound effects, and the music bridges. I can remember saying to myself a dozen times and meaning it, "This is it. Okay. I'll go through this one because I took it on, but never again." But, somehow, because it did come off, worked well, and some of the mistakes even helped me, I stuck with it.

At NBC there were people to help you. It was a nice change. I remember preparing to direct and the script girl saying, "Can I get you a cigarette?"

"Well, thanks but I don't smoke."

"Do you want a drink?"

"No, I don't drink."

Finally, she said, "Well, what can I do for you?"

"Just keep an eye on my script." In rehearsal I had a habit of putting my script down and forgetting were I'd placed it. So, she did that.

I made some comment once about how I felt like I was at a party, and someone brought in a cake, explaining, "Well, you said it was like a party."

**Livia Granito:**   At NBC, the people who did scripts were always women and the stage managers were men. There were no associate directors. The script girls essentially did all the work.

**Adrienne Luraschi:**   The transition to people becoming ADs was when the Radio and Television Directors Guild came. Before that, we were called "script girls," or we were called "program assistants," but we did the same thing. We ordered equipment, sound effects, props — everything! Then they brought in a production manager, and he was in charge of some of that.

After we became ADs, we could get a script girl to handle the time sheets; to schedule actors for publicity, wardrobe, and wig appointments; and so on, freeing us so we could work closely with the director, doing the actual production. I always claimed I was the oldest living AD, not in the point of age but in the point of service.

**George Schaefer:**   In those original days you had to be on staff at the network in order to do the show. Adrienne Luraschi was one of the few associate directors at NBC. She worked with Fred Coe for years and with Paul Bogart and with all of us early directors. She was so wonderful and so much the best of the lot that shortly after the Directors Guild had arranged for there to be freelance associate directors, I persuaded her to leave NBC.

**Arthur Penn:** After the first season of *The Colgate Comedy Hour*, Bud Yorkin moved up to being associate director on some of the shows, and I became the head floor manager. Later on in that season, I also moved up to being an associate director. It was just too much for one man to do it every week, since it involved participating in the camera blocking with the director.

There were two directors on the series at that point, and then it expanded to three or four directors because the shows were growing increasingly complicated. The comics became more demanding of techniques and coverage and that sort of thing.

We kind of ran the rehearsals and participated in the camera blocking and did everything that the director did, except that we were responsible to various departments for getting the stuff done. It would then flow down from us to the floor manager who was backstage working with props, costumes, and the scenery. All of that went through us.

It was a very small team, and so the lines of communication were very short. We'd all get together at the beginning of the week, figure out what the show was going to be like, then figure the costumes, set, and prop requirements. We'd put all that stuff in the works and then start rehearsing. The idea essentially was to keep abreast of all the changes because with comics there was so much improvisatory work.

**Paul Bogart:** I also worked as a floor manager on *The Colgate Comedy Hour* for a few short years before becoming an associate director. The job of associate director at NBC was minimal, and an associate director was assigned only if someone requested an extra person to take some of the production burdens off the director.

**Fielder Cook:** Herbert Brodkin was a producer on *Studio One* and after that started his first series, *The Defenders*, where he made his fortune. Then he did *Fast Lightning* out here because CBS had built nothing in New York, but had built a great television center in Hollywood, with the most modern and brilliant stages that you could get, marvelous facilites, suited for dramas, big shows, spectaculars.

**Franklin Schaffner:**  In 1955, I did one of the first hour-and-a-half dramatic shows out of the West Coast, *The Caine Mutiny Court Martial*, which was on *Ford Star Time*. The only reason we did this show on the West Coast was that CBS had just opened their facility at Fairfax and Beverly. I came out from New York to direct, and it was the one time that I was not only rehearsing and staging a television drama, but also running a classroom, because their technicians were not as experienced as those who had been in New York.

**Ralph Nelson:**  In L.A. there was more of a hungry desire with the crews. They were determined to prove that they were as good or better than New York crews. Indeed, on the *Playhouse 90* crew, the technical director was Brooks Graham, and he didn't mind chewing out anybody on his staff who he thought was doing a sloppy job. The reverse of that came when he was given an Emmy for his work on *Playhouse 90*. He insisted that every member of the crew get an Emmy as well! And the Academy had to bow to that.

**Lamont Johnson:**  It took a little while for the live crews out here to take on the efficiency of the east, because at the beginning, most of the live originated in the east.
     There has always been a marked contrast in the two coasts. You can get a very excellent crew in New York, among the best in the world, but they're not ideal crews. There's an anarchic quality about them somehow, they don't have the same cohesion or efficiency or professionalism that a Hollywood crew has.
     By the time I started, there had certainly been forty years of constant work in California, and it had built a tradition that carried over into television, as many of the same people re-worked, re-trained, transitioned from film into doing live work. There was a tremendous revolution, as there was when sound came to film.

**Paul Bogart:**  There were some bad boys around who would move equipment noisily. I remember looking into the studio and seeing a cable puller slap his cable on the floor just to make noise. I went through all sorts of subterfuge. If I had a quiet love scene going on while the crew moved equipment to another set, I tried to make sure that I had sound effects, music, or something that would mask the noise.

For the most part, I thought the cameramen were remarkable. Those black-and-white cameras were like little toys anyway. They were wonderful, very flexible, and all on pedestals, which weren't even pneumatic. You couldn't afford a crab dolly or anything like that, but the shots came out better than I had dreamed because the cameramen wanted them too! Sometimes the technical directors would balk at something complicated. The safe way was to shoot it straight on, the interesting way was to pan from monitor to monitor so that it would be a little more daring. I always tried to experiment.

At the beginning, I used to set the shots. Some high pedestal, some low pedestal, depending on which angle was the best. I found that by the time I got on the air, the cameramen would usually ignore my precept and operate at their own height. The tall men were operating high and the short men were operating low. To counteract this problem, I used to block the low shots on the short men in order to insure my getting the low shots.

I worked with wide lenses because I had to. The sets were so small and limited that you tried to make the action work toward the lens instead of horizontally. You literally didn't have the room to put the people in. That became standard television shooting, the grandfather of which was Orson Welles. He shot his early films that way.

Usually the shows that I did were broadcast on the coast two weeks later on kinescope. L.A. got everything on those lousy kinescopes.

**Allan Buckhantz:**   When I left CBS it was all black-and-white, when I went to work at NBC, it was all color. Everything was brand new. NBC had the latest technology. For example, they had a twenty-four-hour maintenance service. It was fantastic. I'd come in early and find three or four maintenance men realigning their cameras and monitors. Everything was ready by the time our crew or the shift crew arrived. When we were rehearsing, they were working on the other side of the stage. We'd finish, and they'd have a night crew come in to do all the measuring and everything. It was like NASA. I don't recall CBS at Vine Street having that kind of thing.

The first show that came out of Burbank in color was *Our Town* directed by Delbert Mann and starring Frank Sinatra. Our show was the next show, so we went to observe Delbert Mann and to get a look at the size of the cameras. They were huge, like tanks.

The pictures looked great. It's difficult to say if they were better than everybody else, but the fact is, NBC had a great stake in color. That's why they and RCA financed *Matinee Theatre*, five days a week, which was not a cheap exercise.

You never got a chance to really check yourself out. NBC used to make color kinescopes, but the quality was very bad, and it was hard to lay your hands on them. However, the shows were reviewed, and *The New York Times* told you that you were full of shit a lot.

**George Schaefer:** There were two big studios in Brooklyn, and we did all but maybe three shows from there. My favorite was Brooklyn One. We did the first two-hour dramatic color show, *Alice in Wonderland*, when the studio was just being built — they didn't even have a control room. It was very accomplished, but when I think of how few sets there were to watch it, I wonder why we made all the fuss about it.

Almost all dramatic shows continued to originate at the Grand Central Station studios, but by 1948, when Ed Sullivans's *The Toast of the Town* debuted, CBS had begun to expand their facilities by converting legitimate theatres. Conversion generally entailed widening the stage apron, building a camera ramp back through the center of the audience, and installing a control room. These booths were usually very small, the cramped quarters accommodating an absolute minimum of personnel.

Theatres were used mainly for the production of variety and game shows. CBS took over a number of houses, including the Biltmore and the Mansfield on west 47th Street, and what was later named The Ed Sullivan Theatre on Broadway. As production moved more and more to the West Coast, these facilities closed down.

\* \* \*

**John Peyser:** After the war, sets were being sold so there was a whole new approach to programming, as we were now going out to get an audience. The public was tremendously interested in television, but the country was still not hooked up with a network.

The emphasis was on music, because it was cheap — Fats Waller at the piano, some little songbird doing a fifteen-minute program. The seven o'clock news show with Douglas Edwards didn't come on until much later.

**Franklin Schaffner:** CBS began its program day around six-thirty at night. I believe the network consisted only of New York and Philadelphia. Later, it incorporated Boston. The programs were very loosely scheduled and nothing was by the clock. For example, if the news was ready at a quarter of seven, it went on, but if not, it didn't go on for three, four, five minutes, and it was often fifteen minutes late.

Using remotes was not terribly unusual. There were Dodger baseball games and basketball games out of Madison Square Garden, where John Henry Faulk did the color.

In addition to directing the news, occasionally I'd direct sports, parades, public affairs, and programs like *People's Platform*. On the opening day at the United Nations, I did the first *United Nations Broadcast*. I worked in news for almost a year, at which point Worthington Miner noticed me. He had seen something I did on the parade celebrating the Golden Jubilee of New York. Moving into the so-called drama area was an absolutely different education.

Miner ran the CBS drama department, where he started such projects as *Studio One* and *The Toast of the Town*, which eventually became *The Ed Sullivan Show*. He also produced *The Goldbergs* and *Mister I Magination*.

**Marc Daniels:**  Our first season on the *Ford Theatre* was 1948 to '49, the second was '49 to '50, with each beginning in September. We did eight shows the first year, sixteen the second. It was an eight-month season, with no reruns. We shot it live in New York, using CBS personnel and crews, and sent the kinescope to the West Coast for broadcast a week later. Ford, represented by Kenyon and Eckhart, was the sole sponsor of the program; I was the sole director. Ford wanted quality programming, so we had pretty good budgets, mostly pretty good stage actors, and nice long rehearsal periods.

Scripts were developed a couple of months ahead; generally, there wasn't a problem with them. We had a group of three writers who adapted all the programs: Max Wilk, Norman Lessing, and Ellis Marcus, who was my brother. We were limited by space for scenery, and limited by time for set and costume changes, because when you came back from the commercial, you had to be ready to go.

It was particularly difficult to find material, because we never did any original scripts. They were mostly Broadway plays, which had either not been sold to the movies, or the movie rights allowed us to do it on television. Some of them were current. For instance, our first program was only about two years old, a play called *Years Ago*, written by Ruth Gordon. We also did *Joy to the World*, a play about Hollywood; and the old English classic, *Night Must Fall*.

We were going to do *Edward, My Son*, a British play, but it was about to be done as a movie by MGM and Mr. Mayer called Mr. Ford and said, "Would you please not do that, because we have our movie coming out and it might affect the box office." Mr. Ford agreed, so we had to find something to get ready in about three or four days. We took *Light Up the Sky* by Moss Hart, which had just closed on Broadway, because we knew those actors would know the parts. The main problem was to get them to learn the cuts, because it was only an hour show, about half of what they had done on stage.

*Subway Express*, adapted from a Broadway play, was the first remote drama shot on location. It was a murder mystery that took place in a subway car and at a subway barn. There wasn't any way to do that in a studio, so we took the cameras to a subway barn in the Bronx, where we were able to have the use of an actual subway car. We did the whole thing live from the location, including putting a camera in the maintenance pit underneath the subway car, to get a decent angle. Incidentally, the camera had to be moved down there and moved back during commercials.

Many times we had fast wardrobe changes. I can remember one particularly with Judy Holliday, who played in a production of *She Loves Me Not*, along with Marsha Hunt, Paul Stewart, and a wonderful actor named Richard Hart. I knew we had a very difficult wardrobe change and if she didn't make it, I had to be able to improvise something. The only way I could tell if she was going to make it or not was to put a camera on her. We watched her making the change with great interest.

The designer was Samuel Levitt, who was a New York theatre designer. When I wanted to be able to get certain angles and there was a wall in the way, we used to make a camera port that would open and close. To give us more flexibility, we designed a system of no walls at all. We had a neutral cyc [abbreviation of cyclorama — a stretched cloth or backing that surrounds the rear of the stage] which looked like a grey wall. If we wanted to hang a picture, we'd hang it on wires that you couldn't see. For a door, we had just a door frame, and, since the show was black-and-white, you couldn't tell that it wasn't a solid set. It enabled me to get a camera all the way around the back of a set and shoot. We did shows of more and more complication, resulting in more and more accidents. The good old live television accidents.

I took Sam with me to *Nash Airflyte Theatre*, and sometimes we used the no-walls technique, but once we got into color, it didn't work any more.

**Fielder Cook:**  Every show was created by a different person, and bore his basic imprint. *Studio One* was Tony Miner. *Philco* was Fred Coe and was writer oriented. *Kraft* started out very old-fashioned and then went into the modern.

**George Roy Hill:**  *Studio One* was a CBS product and was a brilliant creation of new forms in television — an imaginative, highly creative, technical breakthrough. Worthington [Tony] Miner jammed *Julius Caesar* into forty-eight minutes. He blew the horizon out on the technical side. He did the last cruise of a submarine and had submarines going underwater and coming up. He created deep-depth focus, by using large foreground objects with actors and action in focus in the background. He really pushed the imaginative limits of the live camera as far as it could go.

He hired Franklin Schaffner and Paul Nickell — very bright and challenging, highly intelligent guys who pushed it to the wall for him.

**Franklin Schaffner:**  Worthington Miner initiated me into drama by having me direct a situation comedy written by Sam Taylor, which ran for fourteen or sixteen weeks. It was essentially a *Henry Aldrich* setup. There was a young kid who was always getting into trouble, his mother, his father, his sister, and the kid next door. Unfortunately, we never got a sponsor.

When that was finished, I asked Tony if he'd take me on *Studio One* as a director. Tony agreed, with the understanding that I could do one *Studio One*, and if I proved facile, I could go on. Tony must have liked my work because I continued on *Studio One* up until the time that I left CBS in 1952.

What I think distinguished *Studio One* from the others was Miner's unique sense of programming. His routine involved alternating between a kudos show, melodrama, drama, comedy, and sometimes he would slip in an unexpected piece. He also had the advantage of airing every week.

But what made *Studio One* an attraction was the sense of adventure that Tony Miner brought to that show in terms of challenging the limitations of doing television programs live inside a studio. His insistence on exploiting the possibilities for staging in terms of depth made *Studio One* markedly different from *Philco*, *The U.S. Steel Hour*, and *Kraft*. Everything that I know visually came out of that experience with Tony Miner.

Under a single producer on *Studio One,* it is not surprising that there wasn't the kind of difference that there might have been from week to week. All of us started with public domain properties, but *Philco* began earlier to produce original material. There were also a great many half-hour spots. These shows were enormous consumers of material, and eventually everybody had to take that step of unearthing original scripts.

I was with *Studio One* for two years before I left to do the *Ford Theatre*, another live, one-hour anthology that alternated weekly with *Motorola TV Theatre. Ford Theatre* originated out of the advertising house of Kenyon and Eckhart.

*Ford Theatre* and *Motorola* were totally different — staff, everything. Airing during alternate weeks was always a terrible worry because we never knew whether the other show would produce the same high-quality programs in terms of provocativeness, excitement, and technically well-done shows.

I worked a year on *Ford Theatre* before returning to *Studio One* in 1953. Parenthetically, while I did the *Ford Theatre*, I also directed a show at NBC called *The Victor Borge Show.*

When Tony Miner left CBS and went to NBC, *Studio One* changed its producership many times. After Tony came Donald Davis, Fletcher Markle, and then Felix Jackson. What I got from him was a sense of storytelling and an understanding of writers and the writing process.

**Fielder Cook:**  There were marvelous network productions. On Monday night you'd have *Lux* at eight o'clock, which was high glamour. Then at ten o'clock Monday night, was *Studio One.*

Tuesday nights on CBS you had *Suspense*, which was a half-hour, high-technology show. Robert Stevens directed and produced it. Robert Mulligan was his associate director, before he got his first shot at directing.

CBS Wednesday night brought *Danger*, a weird, spooky half-hour. It was very off-beat stuff that started out with Martin Ritt producing and Yul Brynner directing. Sidney Lumet was Yul's assistant director, so, when Marty and Yul left, Yul got him the job to direct it. That was Sidney's first directing job. *Kraft Television Theatre* was also on Wednesday night, on NBC.

Thursday night was *The Theatre Guild on the Air* on ABC, with Alex Segal directing. Friday night was *Mama* on CBS with Ralph Nelson directing. And, sometimes, Saturday night was the one-hour *Actors Studio* on ABC.

**Franklin Heller:**  In 1949 I shared an office with Gil Fates in that three-story building behind Grand Central, where the Pan Am building is now. He was staff at CBS where he produced a number of shows, including *Winner Take All*, which was owned by Mark Goodson and Bill Todman. It was a radio show they had brought into television in the earliest days.

I had known Gil since 1939, when we were both in a Broadway play. He told me about a show he was working on for Goodson and Todman called *What's My Line?* We didn't have pilots then. There were test kinescopes made, but they weren't very good, and weren't really worth showing. The network would put a program on sustaining and encourage agencies and sponsors to look at the shows on the air and maybe buy them. *What's My Line?* was going to go on the air, with Gil as the producer. He explained the show to me, and I said, "Sounds pretty good. It's very simple. It's nothing but 'Twenty Questions,' and if you get good people, it might work out."

By the way, the game was invented by a kind of a Broadway-radio hanger on, Bob Bach. He made a deal with Mark Goodson that, if the show went, Goodson would give him a job, and I must say for Goodson that he did. After *Line* went off the air, until the day he died, Bob was employed by Goodson, and Bob studiously swore that he didn't create the show. Goodson, of course, changed it a lot, but the fundamental idea was Bob Bach's, just as the ideas of *To Tell the Truth* and *The Price is Right* and *Password* were Bob Stewart's, and the idea for *I've Got a Secret* was Allen Sherman and Howard Merrill's. Mark Goodson became a multi-millionaire on the basis of other people's ideas.

At first, *What's My Line?* was a half-hour, every two weeks. Then it went to once a week — I think in the fall of 1950 — on Sunday night at ten-thirty. They did it at the Maxine Elliot Theatre on 39th Street, which was where *The Ed Sullivan Show*, originally called *The Toast of the Town,* was done.

I saw the first *Line* on the air and it was awful. It consisted of a panel of four people who were a strange aggregation. Louis Untermeyer, a revered poet; Dorothy Kilgallen, a journalist/gossip columnist; and would you believe *two* men named Hoffman? The Hoffman's were Dr. Richard

Hoffman, a slick society psychiatrist, and Harold Hoffman, a blustery former governor of New Jersey. Newsman John Daly was the emcee. There was actually a cheap easel with a blackboard, where people would come in and sign their names.

A staff director, Paul Monroe, was assigned to direct it. Paul was Familiar with the standard 50 and 90 millimeter lenses, but he was not so sure with a 71/2-inch lens, which tended to wobble. As a result, he was moving the cameras in and out, and back and forth to get closeups, and the way he had laid it out on the stagemade it absolutely impossible not to get the cameras in each others shots. I watched it and told Gil I thought the game was pretty good, but I also told him what I thought was wrong with the show, from a purely mechanical point of view.

The second show was two weeks later, and although Paul Monroe tried to correct the mechanical things, he was unable to do so. There were no laughs — people said funny things, but there were no laughs. Gil said to me, "What can we do about it?"

I said, "Well, in the first place, it's very badly set up."

I remembered a Hollywood story about Samuel Goldwyn, when he was producing a film called *The Goldwyn Follies*. Somebody hired George Balanchine, who had recently come to this country, and didn't speak English very well, to do the choreography. The budget was submitted to Mr. Goldwyn, and on it was, "choreography — X dollars." Goldwyn said, "What is that, choreography, what is that?"

The production person said, "Well, it's this George Balanchine. He came from Russia. He's very well known. He's very capable."

"Well, I don't know what that is. Send him in here."

So Balanchine came in, and Goldwyn said, "Hello Mr. Balanchine." And Balanchine responded in Russian. Goldwyn said, "Tell me, what is it that you do? What is this here choreography?"

Goldwyn had a big desk, with an ink well and a pad and pencils and pens and a clock and various things.

Balanchine said, "You see this clock? That's six girls." And he said, "You see this ink well? That's two fellows." And then he took all these pieces and he put them around on the desk, and he said, "Now the music starts and these six fellows go over there, and these two go over there," and he hummed something musical while he moved all the desk fittings around on the desk top. Goldwyn is looking around and he says, "You know — I like it." And he hired him.

I was a model maker, so the first thing I did was to go home and make little models of a four-panel desk, and the two-panel seat for Daly and a guest, and a different kind of sign-in board, which was not just an easel. I went to the theatre, measured the stage and made a scale ground plan. Nobody had ever before had a ground plan for any CBS-TV theatre stage.

We brought it up to Goodson and Todman. I laid out the plan of the stage, and I said, "Now this is what you have now. This is where the panel is, and this is where Daly is, and this is the guest. Don't do that. Take the panel and put it over here, take Daly and put him over here, and put the guests here, and the guests are coming from the center," and so on. They both looked at it, and, much to my surprise, they both said, "You know, we like it."

And I said, "Samuel Goldwyn rides again."

They said, "Well, try it once. Do it your way."

I had two weeks to prepare. All I had were a curtain and those desks, which I didn't rebuild. I got a new sign-in board, and I got 7 1/2-inch lenses, so that we didn't have to move the cameras, they could stay back and take the close-ups, without having to show each other. We had lens turrets with a 50, a 90, a 135, and a 7 1/2. They had to flip from one to the other, and I had to be careful not to catch them in a flip.

I also discovered that the cameramen were reveling in their notoriety. This was in February of 1950, when the simplest television set cost four hundred dollars and that was a lot of money, so very few people had sets. They could see television in bars, rich people had television, but common, garden variety people didn't have any. So most of the people who came to the theatre were fascinated with the cameramen and the cameras and what was going on, more so than what was being said or done on the stage. The cameramen knew this, so they always wore fancy Hawaiian shirts — like Harry Truman, who was president at the time — and when they flipped the lens turret, they would do it with a flourish, and then they'd take a bow. They would do all these extravagant things and make themselves very prominent. So, I bought three black Alpaca coats, and told the cameramen they had to wear them, and they couldn't make any gestures, and they weren't to get in each other's shots, and they were to act like they were not there, like Chinese property men. They didn't know about that, but I explained it to them.

As a result, the audience was sort of forced to watch the stage, and when funny things were said, the audience laughed. There were no cameras in the shots, there were no booms in the shots, we filled the requisite number of minutes and seconds, and I was a genius. And that was the only thing I ever did. I did that once in 1950, and, although eventually we got color and zoom lenses, I never changed it for seventeen years.

One of the main things I insisted upon at CBS for *What's My Line?* was continuity of technicians. In seventeen years, because we only had three crews, we worked up an entente among us, and thought as one. As a result, I didn't have to call any shots. The men knew what to do.

I wouldn't say it was noted for it, because I don't think the public knew what they were liking, but one of the things that *What's My Line?* was appreciated for was the fact that it was so crisp. At a moment somebody was asking a question, when you wanted to see the questioner, you saw the questioner; and when you wanted to see the person being questioned, you saw the person being questioned.

There was hardly any rehearsal. The cast, of course, didn't rehearse, but we would check the equipment with the crew. Another thing I did was against the rules. I had a silk stocking on the 71/2-inch lenses that took the pictures of Dorothy Kilgallen, Arlene Francis, and the guests. We tried to make them look as good as we could. The cameramen had it made up out of a filter frame, and they would very quickly slip it on to the 71/2 when nobody was looking. If a supervisor was in the theatre who might have objected to it, we'd just take it off.

The usual black-and-white TV technique was hard, bright, cruel pictures, and I wasn't interested in that. I was interested in a picture that was neither hard, nor bright, nor cruel, but was real, and made this show about real people. I knew most of the sets at home were out of whack, so it was foolish to try to do any better than that. And we did pretty well. As a matter of fact, we had practically every big star as the Mystery Guest, and I know that a lot of Hollywood people and show business people, particularly women, said they were told they looked better on *What's My Line?* than they looked on any other show.

Although later it became par for the course, I dare say at the beginning there was nobody who did it as slickly as I did. And I did it mostly because I had a quick mind, but also because I had marvelous help from the cameramen and the switchers, who were extremely skillful and wonderful people. Vernon Gamble, Carl Schutzman, and George Gould — those men had nimble minds and fingers. With rudimentary early equipment they did very well.

We never shot the audience. Towards the end we had a big screen in the theatre, but not in the beginning, not for fifteen of those seventeen years. There were little ones, but out of the way. I wanted the audience to look at the stage, so that their reactions were reactions to what they saw on the stage, and what they heard from the audio.

That was another thing: Goodson was from radio and a bear about audio. He wanted it to be very clear and very loud, and he was right. We had an extraordinary audio man, Billy Taylor — Buell Taylor — he was a genius at this kind of thing. He knew how to pick up errant phrases that wander around, ad lib. He never got caught with a closed pot, he was wonderful. Something else very important about audio is the balance between the cast and the audience. You had to hear the audience, and the cast had to hear the laughs. Billy knew all about that, too.

Because *What's My Line?* was topical, we very often would have as the Mystery Guest the fellow that hit the home run that won the game for the Yankees that day. Bob Bach did that. I couldn't believe it, but we once had a rating of 49. [That meant forty-nine percent of all homes with television were tuned to the program. Anything over twenty was a success.]

**John Peyser:** From '48 to the end of '54, when I left, I did so many programs I can't tell you. The second year of *Studio One*, I directed eight shows for Tony Miner. Bob Stevens and I did *Suspense* together. That was probably one of the most innovative productions of the beginning of television. Both of us were camera nuts, both of us were big fans of John Huston, and both of us had gone to see *Asphalt Jungle* many, many times. That was the kind of camera work we brought to *Suspense*.

At first, it was all studio. I did film inserts on a pilot called *Pentagon, U.S.A.,* a series about the counter intelligence corps, that was supposed to take place in New York. We shot all the exteriors on film and incorporated it into the live studio stuff. That was the first show that really did it, intensively. We shot on 16mm, black-and-white, and it was a big thing — it sold the series right away. They loved it.

In 1952, I directed *The Frank Sinatra Show*, for Bulova. It was an hour show with Ben Blue, on Saturday nights on CBS. And we did that for thirty-nine weeks.

Here's a cute story. We used to fire the producer every other week, so I could never get fired. I'd get new producers every other new week, and on the weeks when I didn't have a new producer, I produced the show. Frank came to me one week and said, "Hey, listen. I want to do 'Soliloquy' next Saturday."

I said, "We have to get permission from The Theatre Guild. You know, we can't just do that."

"Oh, don't worry about it. Armina Marshall's a good friend of mine. I'll handle it."

"Well, Frank, please get the release, because it would cost a fortune."

"Oh, don't worry about it."

And off he went to California. I staged the whole thing and, just to be sure that we didn't get caught, I changed the staging quite a bit from the original Broadway staging. Frank came in and we rehearsed. He loved the whole thing and we shot it that night.

On Sunday afternoon, I got a call from William Paley, who said, "Be in my office Monday morning, you've got a big problem."

"What happened?"

"The Theatre Guild is going to sue us for a million dollars."

"What for?"

"You did a show and you didn't get a release."

"Frank got the release. He told me he went to see Marshall and got it all released."

"He didn't do it."

I went to see Paley that Monday, and said, "Did they see it?"

"No, they didn't see it. They just heard about it."

"Frank did a beautiful job, it's a lovely thing."

"I know, I saw it."

"Let me show them what we did, We'll pay whatever fee they want to charge us for it and get off the hook."

I called Miss Marshall up and said, "Hey, can I bring this down?"

She said, "Okay."

I went down with a projector and the film. The whole Theatre Guild outfit was sitting there. At the end they all applauded, and said, "You can come work for us any time. We'll just charge you a minor amount." I think we paid a hundred fifty dollars and we got away with it.

**Franklin Heller:**  In May 1950, I experienced one of those impossible assignments. I was already directing *What's My Line?* and I also had a fifteen-minute musical with Earl Wrightson singing Broadway show tunes, that came on right after *Studio One* on Monday nights. I was told that they wanted me to produce and direct a half-hour mystery drama every week as well. Of course. Wasn't that why I came there?

The producer-director of *Suspense*, the mercurial Robert Stevens, had suddenly decided not to work during the summer. Since *Suspense*, with its radio repute, was his baby, I was to do a similar chiller show to be called *The Web* — inspired by "Oh, what a tangled web we weave ..." It had no radio background and no backlog of scripts with which to get a start.

I was given a script editor who only had some radio experience. He was my entire staff. In five weeks, from behind scratch, with help from the CBS story and casting departments, we were to select stories, find writers, get scripts written, assemble casts, have a backlog of scripts, and be ready to go on the air on July 4 for eight weeks, as the summer replacement for *Suspense*. I don't remember the budget, but it wasn't very much. Maybe $2,500 above the line and $5,000 below.

I would have five days of rehearsal in a hall, plus one day in the studio with five hours of camera "fax" [facilities], some of which I had to give up to the live cigarette commercials — which I also directed.

Tuesday started, for me, at six a.m. The scenery had been lugged up three flights of stairs in Grand Central Station the night before. With the designer, I had to make sure it was properly deployed and lit for my planned camera moves. The three cameramen and the rest of the crew were there for the first time that day. The actors came in at nine a.m. They had never seen the cameras or the scenery before. We blocked on camera, rehearsed all day, had no dinner, dress rehearsed, and went on at nine p.m. We were expected to be at our peak in the last half-hour of that day and week.

I had chosen a well known short story, *The Twelfth Juror*, and recklessly elected to do it with a subjective camera playing the title role! Anyone who has ever tried the subjective camera technique will know that it is not easy. And we were on the air live. Hopefully, no mistakes. Certainly, no stops. And no retakes.

Who knew from easy? We didn't even know it was impossible. And we did it! Came out exactly on time, too. Time is always a factor in television. Show number two started rehearsals the next day at ten a.m.!

I was living in Old Greenwich, Connecticut, by that time. After we got off the air at nine-thirty and I had taken the call from Underhill saying he always knew I could do it, I went down to the New Haven train to go home. I had not been home since Sunday, as I did *Line* on Sunday night at ten-thirty, stayed at a hotel in the city so as to make *Web* rehearsals, and then did my Monday night musical show at eleven. It was beastly hot. The train was not air-conditioned. I walked home from the station. My wife had retired but was awake and ready to comment on the show (she liked it). Then I took a shower to cool off.

It was well after midnight when I came back to the bedroom. I went to my bureau and took out underwear and socks — put them on. Then a shirt. My wife watched in amazement as I started to pull on my trousers.

"What do you think you're doing?" she asked. Of course, I had lost contact with reality. I was dressing to go back to work!

With some medicinal help, I got some sleep that night. The next day I found time to face Underhill, told him what I had done, and demanded that I be assigned an alternating director. I said I would produce the show and direct every other week, but that was that. As I recall, it was Ralph Nelson who came on first to help out. He was followed by a succession of excellent colleagues. *The Web* stayed on for four years but I only did two of them.

Whenever Charlie Underhill and I crossed paths he always asked, "Are you putting on your pajamas to go to bed these nights, Frank?"

**Martin Ritt:** I was with several series. I directed *Starlight Theatre*, and *Danger*, which was very successful. Sidney Lumet was an AD on *Danger*. Robert Mulligan worked next door to me as did a lot of other good directors. It was in many ways a very good creative time. I worked at CBS as a staff director until the problems escalated in 1951, when the Cold War just enveloped everything.

**Ralph Nelson:** *Mama* scripts were mostly written by Frank Gabrielson, and very high quality scripts they were. But the pressure was always on him. The first day of rehearsal on a Tuesday morning, we might only have three pages of script out of thirty that we needed. It would sometimes be Friday, the day we were on the air, before we would get the final pages. The cast was accustomed to their characters, it was the same crew all the time, and we grew more and more easy with it. We eventually got to where it was so simple that we rehearsed about nine hours a week, went on camera, and were on the air that night at eight.

We were fortunate in that there was only an opening and a closing commercial so there was no interruption in the body of the program. We had a very good relationship with Benton & Bowles, the advertising agency.

I was the sole director. I did thirty-nine shows a year — two hundred sixty-two of them in six years. We had the summer off. When I took time off to go on a honeymoon with a new bride, John Peyser, John Frankenheimer, and Franklin Schaffner filled in for me.

I did not have an exclusive contract with CBS to do *Mama*. The schedule was so simple that I was able to do all of the other big dramatic shows in town — *Omnibus, Philco Playhouse, Ford Theatre*. I did a lot of work for Herbert Brodkin at ABC: the *ABC Album* [*Plymouth Playhouse*], which was a half-hour, and then later *The Alcoa Hour*.

Franklin Schaffner and I had a deal. Occasionally I would make an appearance on *Studio One,* and he would make one on the *Mama* show, until the head of Business Affairs issued an edict that no CBS directors were allowed to appear on shows on the network.

Long before I had a beard, I was in one show, *Mama and the Carpenter,* playing the young carpenter. The part had been written with a lot of Norwegian dialogue in it, and we couldn't find a Norwegian actor who we thought was a good enough actor, nor could we find any actor who could learn that much Norwegian in time. While I didn't speak Norwegian, I could speak Swedish. As a matter of fact, the grace that they used to say at the table before a meal was one that I had been raised on. It was Swedish, and only the Norwegian Consul in Brooklyn picked up on it.

I took a credit, as Alph Elson. I just dropped my initials. The head of Business Affairs called up, irate. I said, "Well, speak to the producer," who was Carol Erwin, because it was she who cast me. I hadn't wanted to play it, because I had to run from the control room out to the floor, and turn the directing over to the associate director.

One episode, "Along Came a Spider" with E. G. Marshall, almost got us thrown off the air, because *Mama* was a warm, largely sentimental show, and families made it an eight-o'clock-Friday-evening habit. It was an ideal time spot because there was no school the next day. The families trusted the show, there was always a kind of basic moral lesson in it, and suddenly Dagmar, the youngest child, alone in the house, was put into jeopardy by this man threatening her. In retrospect, it was so out of character for *Mama* that there were a lot of phone calls and letters afterwards denouncing us for having done it.

I had a three-year contract, and after the three years, I didn't want to do it anymore, but they kept adding more and more money to the pot, and so, eventually, I stayed with it for six years before I finally broke loose. It was very successful, we were always up there among the top ten.

**Marc Daniels:** Early TV consisted mostly of dramas, because drama was simpler. The *Nash Airflyte Theatre*, a half-hour drama on CBS, came after my second season on *Ford Theatre*. It had to go together pretty quickly — I think we had two weeks to prepare. I was freelance, and I worked with the same writers that I had used on the *Ford Theatre*, although we did have some others beginning to come in. We did originals or original adaptations, including a couple of book musicals — an original, *The Box Supper*, and a production of Gilbert and Sullivan's *Trial by Jury*. We prepared a very nice production *The Importance of Being Earnest*, but the CBS engineers struck and it never got on.

I was the only director of *Campbell Soundstage,* a half-hour show, broadcast every week. We did a mixture of comedies and dramas, a lot of which were originals.

I went from *Campbell Soundstage* to *The U.S. Steel Hour*. After that, I did a lot of David Susskind specials during the end of the nineteen-fifties. Then I came out to Los Angeles for good.

By that time I wasn't producing much. I was just directing, so I didn't have the problem of getting the actors. Sure, whenever you decide to do a special, you immediately want Henry Fonda, but then you work your way down from there.

**Franklin Schaffner:** Around 1954, I got the assignment of in-studio director for *Person to Person* with Edward R. Murrow. I must have done that for about three years. Sometime before that Friday night broadcast, we went out, along with the technical director, to survey how adaptable the location might be. They took the equipment out there the day of the show. The show went on the air at nine or ten, so we would get our first check-in from the crew at around seven-thirty. Then we'd do a rough rehearsal with the crew and Ed, just so everybody knew what the continuity of the program would be.

Nobody knew what to expect. There wasn't any of the sophisticated hardware that is available in television these days. We used the old, heavy, turret-lensed, RCA cameras on their weighty pedestals. As for audio, radio mikes really hadn't been perfected yet. We would go on the air and never know whether the radio mikes we used were going to stand up or even if we were going to get an audio signal from them. Very often we would go on the air without previously having had an audio check from the location. We would cross our fingers and hope.

**John Frankenheimer:** *You Are There* went to film, and Sidney Lumet left to direct it. It had to continue live for another ten weeks while they caught up with the films, and I was asked to direct an episode, with the idea that there was nothing after that if it didn't work. Well, it did.

It was a show called *The Plot Against King Solomon*, written by Walter Bernstein under a pseudonym, because the blacklist was in effect then. I have the kinescope of it still, the first show I ever did. Shepard Strudwick was in it, Martin Brooks, Kathyrn Barker, some good actors. And the show was a success, people loved it. From there, I did three *Danger* shows.

The area I concentrated on mostly was in rehearsal with the actors. In the beginning, I was so nervous that I remember staying up with no sleep the first couple of shows, blocking everything out, and then I just started to trust my instincts. I would block it with the actors and figure out how to shoot it afterwards. Lining up shots and all that came naturally to me, and I was very good at it.

**Allan Buckhantz:** At CBS on the coast, we didn't do a show a day. We didn't do a show a week. We did five, six, seven shows a day. Rehearsal was a luxury. I was doing news, *Peter Potter's Jukebox Jury*, commercials, and whatever else needed to be done. I probably did the first band show ever to hit television — a local show, out of the Palladium. The orchestra would sit on the stage while I made notes on when the trumpets came up. Then I'd add whatever I could do to make it look more staged. As a matter of fact, the reviews of it were sensational.

After we finished *Peter Potter's Jukebox Jury* at midnight on Saturday night, we'd stay an hour, setting the lights for a live religious show Sunday mornings on KNXT. There were four or five staff directors who alternated. Everybody hated directing it, because the various religious groups were always changing things.

One Sunday the Jewish group was scheduled, and sure enough everything was different. There was a choir of forty instead of the twelve we expected. They were supposed to have six children, but they had twenty-five. Every child had a line to say, to show the world that they spoke Hebrew. I lined them up, so that each child would say the line, then walk out as the next child stepped forward. There was nothing ingenious about it. It was simply a quick means of not having to relight.

The first child did her line of the prayer in Hebrew, and the second little girl moved up. Because she was nervous, someone on the floor tapped her hand to remind her that she was holding a card with her line written on it. It fell down! She looked into the camera and said, "Jesus Christ, what do I do now?"

But this was only a minor mishap. There's a famous story that happened on one of the game shows that's much funnier. They used to kinescope a show with members of a soldier's family, then send it to him. On one show a little girl and her mother were talking to the host, and he said, "Make a wish for whatever you'd like."

This little girl said, "I would like to have a bed."

"Don't you have a bed?"

"Oh," she says. "Yes, I have a bed. I sleep with Mommy. But you see, on Fridays, Uncle George comes."

That went on the air!

Now that is live!

# J. Walter Thompson: 1947 to 1955

For a few years, NBC operated only out of the RCA Building. Kraft Television Theatre began its long run in tiny 3H, Philco Television Playhouse and Robert Montgomery Presents were produced in 8G and 8H, respectively. Expansion forced the network to take over former motion picture studios in Brooklyn and on 106th Street, as well as theatres like the Colonial at 59th Street and Columbus Circle. Like CBS, NBC abandoned almost all these facilities as Hollywood drew television westward.

At NBC, only staff directors were allowed to function in the control rooms. In 1946, when the first one-hour, commercial variety show, *Hour Glass*, sponsored by Standard Brands, was produced by the J. Walter Thompson advertising agency, NBC's Edward Sobel was assigned as director. In spite of the goodwill and common purpose of all involved, there was constant friction between Eddie and the agency producers. When Thompson brought *Kraft Television Theatre* to NBC in 1947, they broke the NBC taboo by insisting that their man, Stanley Quinn, be allowed to direct as well as produce.

\* \* \*

**Buzz Kulik:**  At J. Walter Thompson, John Reber [vice president of J. Walter Thompson in charge of radio and television] was one of the two or three originators of commercial radio, the entrepreneur of the great radio shows of the twenties, thirties, and forties. Some of the radio shows in which he became involved included *Bing Crosby*, *Kraft Music Hall*, and *Lux Radio Theatre*. He hired Rudy Vallee, Eddie Cantor, and Edgar Bergen to do radio — the list is limitless.

When television started, Reber decided that J. Walter Thompson should produce shows the way they produced radio, because the agency received a fifteen percent commission on whatever was billed. He was also determined to get his clients involved early, and he didn't feel that an advertising agency should just get a free ride.

After spending eight months as a messenger and in the mailroom and as a gofer on a couple of the bigger radio productions, I was assigned as an assistant on a couple of radio shows. Then, J. Walter Thompson decided that I would go to NBC and be given a course in television directing. Ralph Nelson was in that gang with me, as well as Joe Cavalier, who is now a production manager.

In 1948, the recognized directors of radio, stage, or motion pictures wanted nothing to do with this little nonsensical beast. Nobody knew anything about it — or cared to. Also, cities were just developing their first local stations, and nobody dreamed it would turn out to be the colossus that it is.

After a two-week crash course, J. Walter Thompson assigned me as the camera director to a show on WNBC-TV called *Say It with Acting*. [This show's first title was *Look Ma, I'm Acting*. It then became *Act It Out*, and, finally, *Say It With Acting*.] It pitted the cast of one Broadway show against another one in a game of charades, and it was there that I first met Eli Wallach and Jack Warden, who were doing little walk-on bits in *Mr. Roberts*.

It was basically on-the-job training. I swear to God that I didn't know what the hell I was doing, but I had a technical director who really did the work, and made sure that I didn't get into trouble. I did it for about eight months.

J. Walter Thompson had a beer account, Ballantine Beer, that sponsored the Yankee baseball games on radio. They decided to televise the games, using a very primitive setup. I was hired to direct the cameras up at Yankee Stadium, which was a dream come true for me — one summer, as a kid, I was a ball player in Class D, in Pennsylvania. In 1949. I even got the opportunity to attend spring training with the Yankees. It was a terrific job, but J. Walter Thompson told me that they had another assignment for me and it broke my heart. I was to be an assistant director to a man named Earle Levy who was going to direct *Kay Kyser's Kollege of Musical Knowledge*.

Kay Kyser was a hit in radio. He had a quiz show format with a big band. It was the most expensive show on television at the time, with a budget of twenty-one thousand dollars. Kay Kyser got four thousand dollars, which was an enormous amount of money. Perry Lafferty, who became head of NBC on the West Coast, was the producer; Bob Quigley, the game mogul, was the head writer; Mike Douglas was the tenor. I was on that for half a season.

Earle Levy's wife, who hated New York, just couldn't take it anymore. She wanted to go back home, so Levy quit and went with her. John Reber said to me, "Well, you're the director now." I directed that show for a year, and while I became known as the musical guy, Fielder Cook went on to direct dramas. You always get typecast in our business.

When the Kay Kyser show went off the air, J. Walter Thompson put on a show with Patti Page, who was a very big star. I produced and directed that show for about a year. It aired in a half-hour slot on Mondays, Wednesdays, and Fridays. Jack Lemmon and his ex-wife did a situation comedy in that time-slot on Tuesdays and Thursdays.

**Fielder Cook:** About a year after I joined Thompson, I got a job as the assistant to the first producer-director of any live commercial dramatic show on television, Stanley Quinn. He was a marvelous producer. The first year of *Kraft Television Theatre*, which was '47 to '48, he did a show every week, and then he did one every other week. I remember, with great excitement and pleasure and joy, that *Kraft* set the production side of it. Every week, they were able to produce a regularly scheduled hour. The shows were mostly adapted from old plays, such as *The Dover Road* or *Wuthering Heights*. They would buy them from Samuel French and cut them down.

Because it was making no money, television was paid for by radio's profits. The first *Kraft Television Theatre* budget was about thirty-six hundred dollars for the entire hour, everything. We were given rehearsal space at NBC, free.

I worked for Stanley Quinn for a year and a half as an apprentice-learner. I carried the coffee, helped put the floor plans down. I helped select and cue the music on the air. We had records that played background music.

I earned a good friend in John Reber and got promoted from within. He assigned me to direct my first play in April of 1950. It was a half-hour series called *Believe It or Not,* where they dramatized King Tut's tomb's curse, and the sinking of the *Titanic*, and all sorts of weird things. It was a perfect show for somebody who was born with an exceptional gift and was very young and totally ignorant. I had a chance to learn my craft. I'd never talked to actors — I'd watched them. I was so busy running around and creating effects and cameras and pizzazz, that I didn't have a lot to talk to the actors about.

I did that for about four months, quite well, so that I was given the first live glamour show with Hollywood stars on television, *Lux Video Theatre.* It was the television equivalent of what was, at the time, the number one queen of radio shows, *Lux Radio Theatre*, with Cecil B. De Mille. *Lux Video Theatre* was done Monday nights in New York on CBS from 1950 to 1952. It was the biggest production in New York, only half an hour, but it should've been an hour.

I got married three days before I directed my first show, but those things you can do when you're a baby, with a vast amount of ignorance, and the fact that there was not a lot of money involved. I did it every other week. I had one show cast and designed, and one show in rehearsal. None of this belonged to the network, they just rented us space and equipment.

For every Veronica Lake and Joan Caulfield, I would get a Fredric March, a Claude Rains, when they came to New York. I did one or two of Eugene O'Neill's one acters, like *Iowa*, that I'd shake down to twenty-three minutes, but mostly we did originals. There was some very beautiful sentiment and a lot of fodder, too. We found the best writer to this day of any half-hour, Rod Serling. He was writing a lot of our shows at the same time he was working as a commercial director in Cincinnati. The J. Walter Thompson Company brought Rod to New York and helped fund his house because he was costing so much money flying back and forth.

**Buzz Kulik:** When *The Patti Page Show* went off the air, I was asked to direct *Lux Video Theatre*. By 1951, the network had been connected all the way to Chicago but went no farther west, so this show was being broadcast live from New York. In 1953, the Lux people decided that the show should come from Hollywood. It remained on CBS until 1954, when it moved over to NBC. I came out here with *Lux* and stayed with it and J. Walter Thompson until '55 when I got an offer from CBS.

**Fielder Cook:** While I worked at the J. Walter Thompson Company, I was an executive. For the first three or four years, they didn't even give us credit. I did *Lux* for three years, and then I went abroad, did some work and some study for myself. When I came back, I was given a producer-directorship of a session of the *Kraft Television Theatre*.

In 1953, John Reber had *Kraft Television Theatre* on NBC, nine o'clock, Wednesday night. It was so successful that he talked Kraft into doing a second one on ABC on Thursday night, so we had two *Kraft Television Theatre*s on the air, live, every week. No repeats. No summer reruns.

Stanley Quinn and two other director-producers were doing the NBC show, I was going to take over the ABC. I hired George Roy Hill as an assistant on my production staff; later he and William Graham alternated with me. It was like I was training assistants. One of my great friends, Dwayne McKinney, did the sets. Gorgeous. He also did the movie of *Patterns*. And died of a heart attack a couple of years later. Brilliant art director.

The crew and everything else was the same each week — a package that lasted until 1956. The only things that changed were the writers and the actors. At the end of *Kraft*, we would introduce every actor and give a biography and a long credits. But that was before the network grabbed the time.

We had a very fine vice president in Ed Rice, who was in charge of scripts. I guess they paid three or four thousand dollars for an hour script. Ed would send them to me, or I would find scripts or plays that I liked. I had to approve the screenplay, or I wouldn't do it, which is true of any director. One way or another, we would get together and program their year for different producers. There was no backbiting or grabbing.

A lot of writers came into our building. I had my first really big breakthrough with Rod Serling's *Patterns*. I put a lot of work in myself, and that was a great lift. *Patterns*, on *Kraft*, cost twenty-five thousand dollars, complete. It was two days in the studio — 8-H at NBC — the cast, everything. It was done twice, and then I made a film out of it for United Artists.

*Kraft* began to make a very large push to get original material. One year, they gave a fifty-thousand-dollar award to the playwright of the best script. They wanted the publicity, and it was obviously a good thing to do for the writers, but it was kind of a gimmick to get submissions of the better material before it went to *Philco* or to *Studio One*. *Snap Finger Creek* by William Noble was submitted to *Kraft* in the hope that they might nominate it for the award, and it was voted the best script of the year.

*Snap Finger Creek* was a marvelous show. It was the first thing Hope Lange ever did, and she was absolutely incredible. Joshua Logan saw it, called me the next day and said, "Can I see the kinescope?"

I said, "Well, I'm not sure it's ready yet. Why didn't you see it live?"

He said, "I did see it live."

I said, "Then what do you want to see it for?"

He said, "Because I don't believe that girl. And if she's as good as I think she is, I'm going to put her in *Picnic.*"

So, two days later she was in a plane going to Hollywood with Don Murray. They were going together at the time, and they later married.

**Buzz Kulik:** I did *Kraft Television Theatre* one summer in New York. I wasn't given a choice because there weren't that many scripts available. Fifty-two scripts a year was a great amount of material. Therefore, even though most of our plays were original, the story editor, Ed Rice, and I went to places like the Drama Bookshop on 52nd Street to get ideas. We'd look for a play that had few strings attached to it and that you could buy cheap. I remember one called *At Mrs. Beams*, which had been produced in 1904, and ran for twenty performances. We bought it for fifty dollars and adapted it ourselves.

We used to get an actor for three weeks of rehearsal and shooting, with the top pay being four hundred dollars. I did my blocking out on the stage, and I had an assistant in the control room. I like both working with actors and the technical end, but basically I was never concerned about the technical aspects until I had fairly well set the drama for itself. I put the camera to the performance, rather than the performance to the camera. Even in film, I try not to straitjacket myself with the camera.

**George Roy Hill:** I did *Kraft* for about two years. I worked as Fielder Cook's assistant, and did nearly all of his adaptations. When they decided to extend *Kraft* to Wednesday and Thursday night, an opening as a director appeared and Fielder got it for me, although I wasn't highly motivated to make my career as a director. I considered myself as possibly an actor, a teacher, or a writer.

I did one *Kraft Theatre* every three weeks. I had to show which outlets the cameras were plugged into, and I had to move cameras around so that they couldn't cross each other. It was like those puzzles that you get, of how you draw a line and you only go through this part of the line once. After rehearsal, I'd work straight through until three or four o'clock in the morning figuring all that out.

The crew came around on the last day of rehearsal in the rehearsal hall before we got on the set. By that time, I had my whole script marked, with all of the cameras, all of the shots, and where I was going to take them. My assistant would make a script for the technical director, and I would go through the whole thing pointing out where the cameras would be. That was a very specific kind of exercise that made you very disciplined. The day before air I would go into the studio.

Live shows incorporated techniques of stage direction because they were performed straight through; you couldn't go back and retape a section. When it went on the air, all our mistakes showed and we made many of them. I've caught more than one camera by calling for a shot too early and not letting a camera get out of the way.

*A Night to Remember* on *Kraft* was a show that I would never attempt to do again in a million years. We sank the *Titanic* in a studio! It was a live show with two hundred and fifty cues in an hour. There were one hundred and six actors, or something like that, and about thirty sets in a very small space. The sets were built with different angles of the ship as it was going down, and some of the sets had tanks with water in them. There were so many cuts that we had to have the cameras fairly static and build the sets around them, so that whenever we had to make slight adjustments the camera would just pan instead of running all over the studio, which was what happened in other shows. We had a desperate dress rehearsal, but I had confidence that it would come out right on the air, and it did. It was the largest production I ever did, and I think it was the largest production ever done on live television. It was youthful energies and my ignorance that made it work, and the fact that it didn't work except once on the air didn't bother me.

I used to love the kind of excitement you don't get in anything except live performances. I would get happier and happier as the air time approached because so many things could go wrong, everybody was very geared up, and the release was wonderful when we got it on the air and it was going well.

*Kraft* was just a wonderful place to work. We were all very young, we were just starting out, it gave us the training in directing actors and camera, and in editing, since we were editing it all on the air. We were using good material. The film business was going through a kind of depression, so I got to work with Claude Rains, Paul Muni, and a lot of wonderful actors. It was great experience for a young director.

I did television all through the fifties. After *Kraft*, I directed *Ponds Theatre*, which was produced by J. Walter Thompson at ABC, and then some shows in California, including *Playhouse 90*.

*Philco Television Playhouse* went on the air in October of 1948. Anxious to promote their line of television sets, Philco Corporation sponsored the program both as an advertising medium and as a demonstration for their dealers and the public that there was something worthwhile to see.

Since the Hutchins Advertising Agency had a deal with Actors Equity Association to help procure talent and properties, the former president of Equity, Bert Lytell, acted as host. Fred Coe, who was on staff at NBC, functioned as the sole producer/director on the weekly series. The first season consisted mostly of adaptations of Broadway plays, but the start of the second year brought the end of the Equity participation, and the beginning of an arrangement with The Book of the Month Club, which was supposed to smooth the way for acquiring novels for adaptation. This proved less than felicitous, so, in the third season, Fred Coe began emphasizing original material. That became the touchstone of the program.

\* \* \*

**Adrienne Luraschi:** *Philco* was the first show that I worked on as script girl/program assistant. I believe I started on it the year after Fred Coe knocked himself out. That was the first year, '48 to '49, when Fred produced and directed all the shows — a one-hour drama every week!

I worked for Gordon Duff, while Nelle Rahm worked for Delbert Mann. Del came in at the beginning of the second *Philco* year. Gordon and Gary Simpson were the first two directors. Gary was replaced by Albert McCleery, who thought the TV cameras were film cameras. And I thought, Oh, does he have a lot to learn.

Dear Gordon Duff. It was hard for him to show his feelings. I mean, he didn't want to get very sentimental. And me — I could get very emotional and sentimental.

The first show I worked on with him, we had rear-screen projection, film inserts, everything you could think of. I was running around like crazy at the last minute — "Oh, did we get the routine down to the film chain?"

Running, running, running.

At the end of the show, he got up, and walked out. He didn't say doodley-squat to me. When I came in Tuesday — at that time we were in a couple of large rooms with a lot of desks — Craig Allen [a director] was already in. He said, "Well, Adee. How did it go?"

I started to cry.

He said, "What's the matter?"

I said, "You know, I was awful."

"What do you mean you were awful?"

"He didn't say anything. He must have thought I was just terrible. He was hateful."

Craig said, "Oh, that son-of-a-bitch. I'm going to really give it to him. Adee, we both came in early on the train. All he was doing was saying how lucky he was to have you. You were just wonderful. You never let up. You were determined to get everything. You would fight with him at every point."

And I cried all over the place — this time out of anger. I said, "Why couldn't he give me one little bit? I mean, I don't want people just slobbering over me. I just need one little thing, that's all."

Eventually I think he said something. But even then, it wasn't in his nature to do that. I learned a lot from watching and listening to Fred and some from Gordon, but Gordon wasn't open about what he knew.

I'll always remember Gordon. I was invited up to his house in Connecticut a couple of times, met his wife and children. But he was a very private man. He kept his family out of it.

We did the show on Sunday night, nine to ten p.m. Monday was off. Tuesday I came in to hand in all my time sheets, make out the report for central files, turn the script in, and get hold of the next script. On Wednesday, we'd have a production meeting. I had to have a breakdown of the show for props and all that jazz, which I did at home by myself. Then I'd run off copies, so that all those at the production meeting had whatever they needed. Then they would talk about casting the next show. Friday was the first reading.

I'd do a preliminary timing on the reading. Stop and go, because they'd discuss it like crazy. I can't remember if we gave Saturday and

Sunday off for the actors to learn the lines, but Monday through Friday we rehearsed.

The rehearsals were at the Palladium Ballroom. It looked so glamorous at night, when it was dark, with the lights on and people dancing, but it was so ratty in the daytime. We used to think there was nothing but wall-to-wall dust, with rats and garbage under all the pleated cloth that lined the ceiling, and that it was all going to fall down.

I remember that big baseball season when I was in the manager's office with the actors, watching the ball game. Gordon said, "Would you get those people out here!" He was so mad at me, he just carried on. He didn't give a hoot about that baseball game. After Bobby Thomson's home run [that won the National League pennant for the NY Giants against the Brooklyn Dodgers, on the last day of the season], we came marching out and behaved ourselves.

I kept my own script, and during rehearsals I cued the actors. I marked the floor, where the scenery and the furniture was supposed to be. Sometimes I'd stand around and be a camera, and the director would be a camera. Most directors had the camera shots in their head until the last minute. I had to keep pursuing them to get it in the script.

By Thursday night I had to have all the shots made out for the TD's script and the cues in the stage manager's script because they and the cameramen came in on Friday to watch run-throughs of the whole show.

That was a terrible day, because Fred would come in. If he liked the show, everything was fine, but sometimes at the end of the run-through, he'd say, "Oh, Pappy. My God. We're in a lot of trouble here, Pappy. We're going to have to make a lot of changes."

And I'd think, Oh, God. How? When? Why? There's no time! So we'd sit down, and he'd say, "This should come first, and that should come second. Cut that out." He could be terrible when he'd suddenly say, "No, it all has to be changed," but the interesting thing is that he was mostly right. He had a wonderful instinct for knowing what was wrong and how to correct it. He was a genius in that respect. But he could be so hard on his directors, and poor Gordon didn't know how to battle and fight.

One thing that worked well between Fred and me — Gordon had no interest in picking the music, had no feeling for it, so he would accept practically anything I selected. Fred had very definite ideas as to what the music should be. Most of the time, we were on the same wavelength. Sometimes he would come and change everything, and sometimes he didn't change a thing. He'd pat me on the back, and say, "Hey, that's really great." And I'd think, Thank heavens.

Saturday we were on camera, blocking all day. Sunday, we started in the afternoon with a run-through, then notes. Dress rehearsal. Notes. An hour later we were on the air.

Once we were doing a story about the war in the Pacific. Supposedly the Marines were on an island, and the fighting was almost over. There was a fire in the studio. We had a couple of Japanese actors who were not really actors. They were lying in a cave, and the only sign you could see from one of those actors was a flicker of an eye as he noticed that there was a fire over there. The scene continued while everybody was running around to get the fire out. Gordon said, "My God, we can hear them. Do something."

I said to the sound man, "Cue the bombardment." Great. Suddenly, out of nowhere, came bombing. We got the fire out, everything was back to normal. "Okay, that's enough," said I. Quick thinking it may have been, but the wrong sound effect. At least I didn't say, "Start the rain" when there was no rain. And we were all so proud of that actor who wasn't an actor.

To do even two or three shows in six months that were really good would be fantastic. They had such little money. When you look at some of those old shows in black-and-white kinescopes, you can tell it's a set and not a real exterior. You can tell it's rear screen. But if you shut your eyes to that and watch the performances and listen to the dialogue and get involved in the story, you can say, "Yes, that's good." You can sit at home as I did many, many times and watch that television set, with a story like *Marty*, and cry. Nowadays, it's just the production values.

A lot of snobby film-lighting men would talk about how motion picture lighting was so wonderful and the lighting in live TV was so tacky. I'd say, "Most people in this country don't know from lighting. They want to know if they're laughing, if they're crying, if they're involved with the story. *That's* what they care about. You and your group can care about the lighting and win awards. I care about the script and the acting."

We did *The Great Escape*, before it became a movie. It was a marvelous production, and to think we did it all in studio 8G. I can't conceive how we did that, but we did. A show like that made me want to get up and sing, "There's no business like show business." Nothing else I know can get the adrenaline going the same way. It is very exciting when it's all working together.

**Delbert Mann:** Fred Coe was my mentor, my guardian angel, my teacher and the man to whom I owe my whole career. Fred was a wonderful, sensitive person with a very volatile temper, a very low boiling point. A great Southern accent that would explode all over the place when things did not go to please him. But Fred was marvelous and really quite phenomenal in a couple of specific ways.

One side of Fred, and the one that is the most remembered today, was his work with his writers. The other side was his work with his directors. Fred, being a marvelous, wonderful, sensitive director, had great difficulty in turning the show over to those of us who were his staff — Vincent Donehue, Gordon Duff, myself, and shortly after that, Arthur Penn — without intruding his own personality and his own way of doing things on us. His counsel and his distress made us very aware that we were doing wrong things, but we wanted to do better for Fred.

His famous method of criticizing, I remember so vividly, was to sit in the chair behind me while we were blocking a show on camera. Quite often, he'd watch, then there would be a kind of a pause, and then Fred would say, "Pappy, do you really like that shot?" to which I would say, "God, no, Fred, I hate that shot. What's the matter with it?" And we'd talk it out.

He was wonderful in teaching us the craft of not only directing for television, but directing in general, of inspiring everybody to do the best that they could do under the harassed and pressured circumstances of live television. So he was, in many ways, a kind of genius. A lot of people feel as I do. They also owe their careers to him.

Deep down, I think he always wanted to go back to directing. In later years, he did direct some television shows, and when he returned to the Broadway theatre, he turned to both producing and directing, and then directing for other producers. It was always in his blood.

I was under a contract to NBC for the years 1949 through '55, always on the staff of *Philco*, never freelance. NBC was completely staffed in-house. We had our own resident scenic designer, Otis Riggs; our own resident costumer, Rose Bogdanoff; our staff of technicians; our staff of assistant directors, and so forth.

In the beginning, I did a show every other Sunday night. It was a fifty-two-week-a-year job that everyone worked twelve-hour, fourteen-hour, fifteen-hour days on. It was horrendously pressured. You didn't have a chance to erase your mistakes and go back and redo. You simply had to live with them, cover them up as best you could, and go on and try to get the show off the air on time. A job for young people, I think. I'm not sure that those of us today who are as old as I am could take that kind of pressure.

We were always fighting the battle of space, the battle of time, the battle of money. Studio 8G, from which we did the *Playhouse*, was a tiny little studio. All the sets of the show and all of the commercials, which were also done live, were encompassed in the same studio, so it was kind of a scramble.

Fifty-three minutes of playing time, that was the hour. Six minutes of commercial time and opening and closing. That was standard for all of those dramatic shows. I didn't have to direct the commercials, thank God. The commercial director would get into the chair as I'd get out at the end of an act. While I'd stretch, he'd do his two or three minutes of commercial, then he'd slip out of the chair and I'd drop back into it to start the next act.

On any of the shows, the battle for the producers was to fill up the appetite of television. We ground out so much material — fifty-two hours a year on *Philco*, fifty-two hours a year on *Studio One*, fifty-two hours a year on *Robert Montgomery*, the same on *Kraft*. The search and the rush for material was quite horrendous, and that was always one of Fred's primary concerns. It was never really one of ours, except when we'd get a script that was not quite ready or needed a lot of work. I was simply there to direct. I was given a script that was my assignment for the next show.

I would finish a show on Sunday night, come in Monday afternoon to pick up the next script, read it, and start casting that evening. Tuesday morning was production meeting, and I'd be ready to go into rehearsal on Friday of that week.

We participated in the casting, along with Fred and the casting directors, and we had marvelous casts, particularly in the early years in New York. There was a whole group of young actors just coming out of the Actors Studio and so forth, trying their wings and learning their craft, both in theatre and television. It became a tremendous source of income and training for them.

Each show had its own nucleus of actors. They'd work back and forth from one show to another and across the network line. *Studio One* had its little sort of stock company — Charlton Heston and Maria Riva and Mary Sinclair worked week after week after week for them. John

Newland, Rod Steiger, Eva Marie Saint, Grace Kelly, Julie Harris, and Paul Newman — the list goes on and on — worked for us many, many times. It became a situation where, if you didn't watch it, you would tend to fall back on the old reliables and use them over and over and over again, because you knew they were professional, and that under the pressured circumstances of live television, they could produce.

Rather than thinking in terms of trying to make it different or unique, you were trying to cope with that week's show — how to solve those problems of transitions, of actors making costume changes, of getting from one set to another. The writers had to be made aware of it. For instance, in rehearsal you would have to cut half a scene, and now it had a different ending. The writer had to rewrite in such a manner that there was time enough for you to hold actor A on a closeup, while actor B leaves the set, changes his coat, gets into the set across the studio; and so that the camera and the boom had time to get around to pick up actor B in this other set.

We were trying to expand and explore. A few times we experimented with live pickups in those early *Philco* days. I remember one romantic comedy in particular that we did with Julie Harris and Leslie Nielsen. The show was in Studio 8G, but we opened it with Julie being interviewed by Ben Grauer at the skating rink downstairs in Rockefeller Plaza. Then she came into the studio to play the rest of the show. They were to play the last act on the observation deck of the RCA Building at night. We built the show so that while we played a scene with other actors in the studio, they raced out of the door of the studio, were taken by the studio guard to a waiting elevator, down the eight stories and across the lobby to the express elevator going to the top of the building, where we had a camera live and hot. It was timed so that as they arrived at the top they played the last scene. And it worked. It was very exciting.

On another show, we sent Valerie Bettis — she was a dancer [as well as an actress] — down the elevator and across the street, through the waiting traffic, into the old Center Theatre across the street from the RCA Building, where we had a couple of cameras patched up.

One show had a last act that took place up at Grant's Tomb, on Riverside Drive. After the dress rehearsal, Frank Sutton, who was playing General Grant, left the Sixth Avenue entrance of the RCA Building, hailed a cab, jumped in and shouted, "Grant's Tomb." The driver looked in the rear view mirror, saw General Grant sitting there and practically wrecked the cab. Probably an apocryphal story, but we got a lot of laughs out of it.

We also had film available. It was almost always stock, but once in a while, we would go out and shoot something in advance on 16mm film, and then integrate that into the show. A show that we did with the Seeing Eye Training School in Morristown, New Jersey, had a whole act on film. We took Phyllis Kirk and Philip Abbott out there and shot for three or four days with the dogs, and up and down the streets of Morristown, and in the Seeing Eye School. On the air, they played the first act live, then the film rolled, then they played the third act live. So we were trying as best we could to sort of expand a bit, but we were still focusing on personal, intimate stories rather than on car chases.

Audience reaction was amazing and immediate. A show like *Marty* just had an overwhelming response the very next day. The actors particularly were aware of this, because any time one of our shows made any kind of an impact on a Sunday night, on Monday morning the cab drivers, the elevator operators, the people on the commuter trains, the people on the subway, would be talking about the show, and they'd recognize the actors.

Television was intriguing; it was new. Not everybody had sets. I think that the entire audience in those early days, the early fifties, would be the equivalent of the audience that today watches PBS, a much more selective kind of an audience. The cable didn't even go across the country at that point.

It was more of a special event to see television, and people made an effort to watch it. When Milton Berle came along on Tuesday night, it is really quite true that things would shut down and people would stay home to watch Uncle Miltie.

We young directors, like Arthur Penn and Bob Mulligan and Frank Schaffner and Sidney Lumet and Johnny Frankenheimer, were learning our trade by doing these shows week in and week out. All of us young, and all of us learning by doing and working together. We would watch what everybody was doing, and it was kind of a whole way of life, but it didn't exist long. It was from about '48 or '49 until the mid to late fifties, and by that time, it was really gone.

**Arthur Penn:** I was asked by Eddie Cantor and Jerry Lewis to direct their shows for the upcoming year of 1953. Cantor, Martin and Lewis, Danny Thomas, and Bob Hope alternated shows.

Fortune intervened. I got a call from Fred Coe in New York. He had heard about me from another director, Vincent Donehue, who I had worked with as a floor manager. He was one of the directors of *Philco*.

Fred was then the producer of the *Philco Playhouse*, which was the most prestigious live dramatic show on the air. He was beginning a new series called [*Gulf Playhouse:*] *First Person*, a summer series that was replacing *The Life of Riley*. It was a half-hour, kind of special-techniques show with the camera as the first person. We had scripts by Horton Foote, Paddy Chayefsky, and Robert Alan Aurthur. Fred called me in to direct five or six of them, and that was my first shot at directing live with dramatic actors.

It was all very experimental, very interesting, and very exciting. It was a terrific test of whether or not I could handle directing, particularly in light of the fact that I didn't have a lot of security yet in working with the distinguished actors that we used.

The marvelous thing about working in New York was that one was working with the major actors of the day: Kim Stanley, Kim Hunter, Joseph Anthony, Mildred Dunnock — all stars on Broadway. That was the sort of cast that I had in my first and second show. People of that astonishing caliber.

At the end of about five weeks, Fred offered me the chance to be the third director on *Philco*. They decided to increase their directors from two to three in order to relieve some of the pressure on the other directors, because up to that point they had been alternating every week. That's when I, with great pleasure, said, "Absolutely, yes."

I stayed with *Philco* for the next three years, and I did almost all the shows that Tad Mosel wrote.

# Other Shows: 1950 to 1955

Until 1940, when a federal government consent decree forced their separation, NBC had operated two radio networks, the Red and the Blue. Edward J. Noble, the president of the Life Saver Corporation, bought The Blue Network and eventually sold it to a new management, headed by Leonard Goldenson. Its name was changed to the American Broadcasting Company. Mainly because of limited finances, ABC was somewhat slower than the other networks to leap into television and lagged behind for a number of years.

Although New York was the principal center of origination, Chicago television produced some of the brightest, most innovative of the early programming. NBC's Chicago studios were in the Merchandise Mart, in total area perhaps the nation's largest office building. *Kukla, Fran and Ollie* originated there from November 1948 until August 1957. *Garroway at Large* debuted in April of 1949, bringing with it refreshing informality and off-beat humor. It ran until 1951, after which Dave Garroway moved to New York to become the host of the *Today* show.

* * *

**Dan Petrie:** On January 6th of 1950, I went to work at NBC in Chicago. I was hired as an assistant director, and also functioned as a floor manager. I joined the Radio and Television Directors Guild when I went into New York, but wasn't a member when I was in Chicago. The union setup there was very loose; we talked directly to the cameramen.

Everything was live, so everybody had to do everything, and we were on the air quite a bit of the day. We were all young at the time, so I worked eighty hours a week, getting a larger overtime check than I did for my regular hours.

There were the usual talk shows, interview shows, commercials, very, very simple in their format, and frequently only a two-camera operation. Oftentimes we ran movies and we would set up the [commercial] cutaways at used car lots. I would be the floor manager on something like that. At the same time, I also got a shot at directing, so in any given week, I would direct two shows, floor manage three or four others, and be the assistant director in the booth on two or three others.

There was *Walt's Workshop*, which was an afternoon show, where we went into this guy's workshop and he showed how to build a coffee table, or repair a windowsill, or a drawer that was sticking — simple home repairs, cabinet work, working with wood for the most part.

Herbie Mintz did a show in which he banged away on the piano for fifteen minutes. Herbie and an announcer would reminisce about the good old days at the various clubs around Chicago, recalling a certain performer or a certain song, and Herbie would play that number. Then, there was the news. The news was usually read live — there was no teleprompter. Sometimes, there were cue cards, but very seldom.

The Dave Garroway show was in operation, a variety show, which was very popular. Bob Banner directed it, along with Bill Hoben.

In the drama area, they did a show on Saturday night called *Saturday Square*, in which there were four or five segments that would all take place on the same little square in Chicago. One of those was the show that I was assigned to, *Studs' Place*, a sort of a rib joint, that starred Studs Terkel. Studs was a writer, a commentator, a personality. He had done a lot of emceeing of various shows, and he was a stand-up comic in a kind of way, but he was not really an actor. Then there was a piano player, a waitress, and the handyman. Those were the four principals.

Chet Roble was the pianist, and we made jokes about how bad an actor he was. But he was himself, and whenever he spoke it was right out of him. He never had to say somebody's lines, which made him wonderful. Win Strockey, who was a guitarist and a folk singer, played the handyman who pushed the broom, did a little cooking, and cleaned up in the kitchen. Each week there was a story involving an outside influence coming into that atmosphere.

Physically, they worked in a very small area, I guess about twenty feet wide and about ten or so deep. You saw the entire set, and we didn't have any scenes that took place outside. The idea of the series, right from the very beginning, was that it would be an ad-lib situation, that the dialogue would be created by the cast.

We had about ten hours of rehearsal. The stories were three- or four- or five-page outlines. I knew the whole story, but on the very first day of rehearsal, I'd read them only the first paragraph. Then I'd say, "Okay. Let's go ahead."

We would then devise what action would be going on. In the material it might say, "A delivery boy comes in and he's got a great big box and it's for Studs and it comes from some place in Iowa, and he's really surprised by this."

It was easy to just pretend in the rehearsal that the big box came in, and all four of them would get around the thing and make jokes, like, "I hear something ticking." Then I would read the next paragraph. "Ohhhh!" they'd say. "I see where it's going now," and they would start ad-libbing again.

We'd go all the way through it, and when the story finally came out, they would realize that they had gone astray in many areas. We would go through it again, just paragraph by paragraph. Now they knew where they were going, and it would start getting distilled and cut down to the half-hour time format that we had to fill. Sometimes I would say to somebody, "Instead of saying, 'Yes,' at a certain point, say 'No'," which threw them a challenge. They knew that they had to get a "Yes," or they wouldn't have the end of our story. I would do that just before the air show, but even with that, you could put it on a stopwatch to the second. When it got on the air, you could time it, even though it was ad-lib, and even though they often made changes. The show was sustaining. One would wonder, if it had a sponsor would they want to see the content of the show they were doing.

I did it for the full time that it was on NBC. It was very highly thought of by the critics in New York. John Crosby was the chief television critic for *The Herald Tribune.* He loved the show, and he reviewed us almost every week. After about twenty-six weeks, it went off the air, at which point I moved to New York and started to direct there. After a summer off, the show went on ABC for the whole season in Chicago.

Billy Rose, the impresario, was a great fan of *Stud's Place.* One day in Chicago I got a call from him, asking if I would come to New York to direct his show. He was going on the air with an anthology-type, half-hour series for the Hudson Motor Car Company — they're out of business now.

I started *The Billy Rose Show* in October of '50. I did one a week. I rehearsed four days, the fifth day we went onto the stage, and that night it would go on the air. The next day I worked on the casting and the script of the following week's show, took one day off, and started rehearsing again, the very next day. This was ABC, in Manhattan, on 66th Street, just off Central Park. Their equipment was indistinguishable from NBC's and CBS's.

Billy Rose wrote a column made up of little anecdotes, *Pitching Horseshoes*, which I think was in the *Daily News*. Now, Billy didn't really write them, they were ghost-written by a lot of writers he knew in New York. The writer would submit the story to Billy, who had an aunt over in Brooklyn. Billy would narrate the story, "I have an aunt over in Brooklyn who —" Some of the stories came from that, some were classic stories.

We did *The Juggler of Notre Dame*, for example, changing it to an old actor in the St. Patrick's Cathedral in New York. Walter Hampden played the old broken-down actor. Then there were a couple where we featured Billy himself, and Burgess Meredith played Billy in both of those.

To produce *The Billy Rose Show*, Billy reached out for one of the great theatrical producer/directors, Jed Harris. Jed was a man of the theatre, and was not into television producing at all. All he was interested in was story. He dealt with the writers from time to time in deciding what story was to be done, although Billy took part in that activity as well. Jed never got involved in the casting except for something like "get Mervyn Vye for that part, the villain."

Jed would come for the first reading with the actors and he would be brilliant in talking about that story to the cast. He would then leave and I would do all the directing and the blocking of the action and so on. The day before we went into the studio, he would come back and I would do a run-through for him.

He was hard of hearing, because of a nerve loss that evidently makes people speak very quietly. They hear themselves very well internally, so that they think that they're shouting if they talk loud. It was very, very difficult to hear him.

I would tell the cast ahead of time that Jed would be asking one of them to "step out of your role and watch from the front," while Jed stepped in to play the role. I'd say, "He doesn't know the lines, so he's only going to mime it, while you say all of the lines. Don't look at the other actors, just look at him."

He would go into the scene and, my heavens, he was brilliant. He was the best actor — the best non-speaking actor — I have ever seen. It was not the conventional way of directing actors, certainly, but he would do that for Walter Hampden — and Walter Hampden, the great Shakespearean actor, would step aside very gladly! The only way you can get away with it is if you're good, if you're really great. And Jed was really great.

The next day, I would go into the studio and set it up on cameras. The first two shows, he came around early in the morning to see all of that happening. The third show, he certainly didn't do that, because it was very boring — just stop and go, and the camera's getting into position, and the cables. I think he was aware of the cameras, but not terribly.

It ran twenty-six weeks — half a year, exactly. After that, for a short time, I went on staff at NBC, while I did *The Somerset Maugham Theatre*, and I began to alternate on *Robert Montgomery Presents*, the big hour drama anthology.

The first show that I did for Robert Montgomery was *The Farmer's Hotel*. It was adapted from a John O'Hara novella, and it was, I think, a terrific show. It got marvelous reviews. Thomas Mitchell was in it, and Faith Brook, and a man who's now a producer, John Newland.

*The Farmer's Hotel* was very successful. The next show that I had to do for Robert Montgomery was a script that I absolutely loathed. It was, I thought, a very right wing, Fascist piece, and I remember going back to read the novel to see if there was something about it that would be mitigating. It was called *The Tender Men*, or something like that. There was a problem in the script about a white and a black rooming together, and continuity acceptance at NBC called me protesting about that.

This was 1951. I called Mr. Montgomery to tell him about this difficulty but I didn't get him. The secretary was very cordial and pleasant, though, and she said, "I think he's over at his club."

I called him at home, and his wife said, "No, he's at his office."

Well, I didn't want to blow the whistle on him and say, "I just called his office, and he wasn't there," so I said, "Oh, I'm sorry! I thought he wouldn't be there yet. I'll call him there."

I made about five calls to Montgomery. Then the question became academic because the script was going through some changes and that scene where you saw the two guys actually rooming together was no longer in.

The morning after the show, I was called in by Robert Montgomery, who said, "Mr. Petrie, you told me that in the matter of the continuity acceptance thing, you called me on several occasions."

I said, "Yes, I did."

He said, "Well, my secretary keeps a log on all incoming and outgoing calls from this office, and there is a record of one call from you last week."

"Oh," I said, "Call her in, and she will tell you that I had at least four other conversations with her."

He said, "I don't think that's necessary, do you?"

I said, "No, sir, I don't."

He said, "Do you see any reason why we should continue our relationship?"

I said, "Well, when you phrase it that way, Mr. Montgomery, no." And I got up and left. My time at NBC as a staff person was six months or so, and I left by virtue of being fired by Robert Montgomery.

He was just unhappy with me. It could have been chemistry. Norman Felton, who directed the show for a number of years, had a good relationship with him. It was the only time in television that I ever got fired — I've been fired from theatre shows — so it left a kind of indelible mark. I think sometimes those things are also good for you, in that they make you perk up and take notice how you are dealing with the people around you, and learn a little of the politics of the situation. I was, I suppose, pretty feisty, and felt that I knew everything. Maybe I gave those kind of vibrations to him, and he said, "I just want to take this kid down a peg."

**Paul Bogart:**  It must have been in 1952 when I start working on *One Man's Family*. I'd only been in television for a year and a half. One night Eddie Kahn, who was the director of *One Man's Family*, came by while I was the floor manager on *The Aldrich Family*. He stood in the corner watching me, and when we went off the air, he asked if I wanted to work with him as an associate director. I told him that I didn't know what the job was and he said, "We'll give you fifteen dollars under the table every week in addition to your salary." I told him that I was already getting fifteen dollars under the table on *The Aldrich Family*. Campbell's Soup was the sponsor and they used to salt the crew a little bit here and there to get better work out of them. Then Kahn offered me twenty-five dollars. I couldn't refuse twenty-five dollars!

I went on to *One Man's Family*, which was like a soap opera, but my being hired resulted in a delicate situation. There was a wonderful girl working there named Elenor Tarshis, who had been Eddie's assistant. When I moved in, she felt I was moving in on her job, but I managed to be nice about the whole thing and not step on Elly's toes or anything like that.

The producer was a wonderful guy named Richard Clemmer. Since the show broadcast every week, Eddie Kahn took every fourth or fifth show off. A week or two into the show, Clemmer decided that the associate director would direct the show during Kahn's week off. I didn't know which end of the camera you shot out of yet!

I said, "I don't think that what I know is really going to help me. I don't understand the job."

Clemmer said, "Don't bother me! We're very busy."

At the end of the fourth week, they gave me a script and said, "It's yours. Do it."

Even though I protested that I didn't know how to direct, they said, "Please. Eddie has to rest."

The show aired live for a half an hour every Saturday night, at seven-thirty. Prior to that, we rehearsed for three or four days, then on the fifth day, we went into the studio for the run-throughs and camera blocking. We then did the dress rehearsal and went on air. We only had the crew for that one day and maybe for the last run-through on the day before we came into the studio.

I was learning how to direct, not just how you shoot something, which is the first terrifying hurdle, but what the story was about, how to work with actors. The first few shots I did on *One Man's Family* really scared me. When we got off the air with the first show, I felt I had just shamed myself in front of the whole country. The phone rang. It was Kirk Browning who was a staff director at NBC and is still an esteemed director of music shows and opera. Kirk was laughing hysterically. I said, "What's the matter?"

He said, "Don't you know you can't do that, dear boy!"

We met a few days later and Kirk went to a lot of trouble explaining certain basic rules of cinema. The rules of geography, for instance, and not confusing your audience by displacing the objects in the frame. I didn't know any of this. A lot of people were good to me and took time to help me.

After that, I directed *One Man's Family* during Eddie's break. NBC hired me as an outside director, while I'd take a leave of absence from my regular job as a stage manager. I was scared to death of losing that job because I wasn't a staff director.

In the beginning, my most paramount fear was how I would cover the action. If there's a camera on you and there's another one on me, the action is covered until one of us stands up. Then you have to figure out how to cover that. I wasn't at all concerned with content because I figured that would take care of itself. But it doesn't! On the fourth or fifth show, I suddenly realized that shooting is quite easy as long as you follow the rules and don't let the actors walk off the stage or behind the scenery. The important thing is what the actors say and do and if what they're doing is right. Shooting television hasn't bothered me since. Of course, it's a whole different story in film.

After *One Man's Family*, I started to get a few more directing jobs. TV was all black-and-white and then NBC decided to institute color. They put together a six- or eight-episode show that was to air once a week during the summer of 1954 called *The Marriage*, starring Jessica Tandy and Hume Cronyn. These were ex-radio scripts which had been rewritten for television. NBC decided to invest their entire color budget in that show. Because the idea was so new, they didn't have a sponsor. [This was the first network show to be regularly telecast in color.]

I worked *The Marriage* as the assistant to the director, Jack Garfein. Jack had a big falling out with Hume. I don't know what it was about, but Hume was very gentlemanly about it and let him go. After experimenting with a string of other directors, they decided to let me direct the show. I had a wonderful time doing it. They were wonderful people and very kind to me.

I was directing the last two episodes in that series when someone from Wheat Chex Cereal asked me to work on a live commercial for them. I didn't know anything about doing commercials, but I would have directed anything, so I went to work for them. I was on shows like *What's My Line?* At the end of the act, I would sit down in the director's chair and direct the commercial. When it finished, I'd get up while he sat down and continued with his show. On more complicated, bigger shows, the commercials came from the next studio. But they were usually live.

Somehow, I'd gotten a kind of reputation from doing *The Marriage*. The next series I worked on was called *Ethel and Albert*, written by a wonderful woman named Peg Lynch who was a very funny and original woman. The scripts from that show were also ex-radio stories adapted for television.

Peg Lynch wrote and played the lead in them. She was the first actor whose technique astonished me. I could see her at work, see what she was doing, and understand why she was doing it, although I couldn't articulate it. She let me direct a couple of shows when her director left to do something else.

By then, a lot of people knew my work as a director, and David Susskind, who had been involved with Revlon commercials, wanted to represent me. I said terrific. David then said, "I also have a show I would like you to work on." So, he turned out to be not only my first agent, but also my first steady employer on *The Armstrong Circle Theatre*, when it was a half-hour, live television show. [This was 1950-55. The show was an hour from 1955 to 63.]

David was a talent agent, who had just started to work as a packager. He had a foot in both camps. The only disadvantage to me was that I never knew how much money I was going to get paid. My wife would say, "How much you gonna get?"

I'd say, "Gee, I don't know."

She would say, "Ask him!"

When I asked him, he'd say, "Don't worry kid, I'm gonna take care of you," and four hundred dollars would come in the mail. I didn't get paid much, but I learned an awful lot during those years. They would hand me the script, I would look at it and die in terror, because the topics were about things I knew nothing about, like a mutiny at sea.

Working with Susskind's organization [Talent Associates] I got to know all his people very well. David surrounded himself with a lot of women, more than any other outfit I ever worked in. Jacqueline Babbin was story editor, Ethel Winant worked in casting, Audrey Geller and Anita Gonzales — a lot of women who did everything. They were his casting people, his production people, and his story people.

I did *Armstrong Circle Theatre* for a long time with Susskind. Then I alternated with The Theatre Guild, who did the *United States Steel Hour*. They were a little more austere, and were not as warm and friendly as the Talent Associates group. But I had season contracts with them to do a certain number of shows. There was an art director and a scenic designer who met with the director to work out the plan for the set and whatever effects we needed. There was an associate producer who handled the money and made sure that things were where they should be. There was also a producer. Producers in television were very deeply involved in the show. In fact, they were close to the show in the same way that producers in the theatre are. If you rehearsed a show for a week, they would see the run-through and tell you what they damn well thought of it, and where to fix it.

After a while, it became less a matter of taking what they handed you and more "This is not for me," or "What else have you got? Do you have something lighter?" Sometimes I was able to get with a writer and talk about the script and work on it for a little bit.

During this entire time, I kept my floor manager job at NBC. It was five or six years later when, after going on leaves of absence from NBC, they finally said, "You'd better make up your mind." So I quit. I've been a freelance director ever since.

**Adrienne Luraschi:**  After *Philco*, I went to *Mr. Peepers*. It started out as a summer replacement, and we got inundated with so much mail! Just a roomful of it! The network kept it on, and we went three years.

Fred Coe was the producer. He was wonderful with the writers — on *Mr. Peepers* as well as *Philco*. They were Everett Greenbaum and Jim Fritzell. Jim was a little paranoid, because every once in a while when we tried to get him to make some changes in those scripts, we couldn't find him, so we'd ask Everett, "Where's Jim?"

He'd say, "He's not looking at the typewriter today. What do you want? I'll try to do it."

There was another quirk about Fred that took me quite a while to figure out. When we were doing *Mr. Peepers*, he would come in to see a run-through on the day before the show. He would ask me, "How's it coming?" — with a big smile on his face — "Good? Funny show?" I might say, "Fred, it might be missing me. I think it's lacking laughs. I mean, I have a feeling I'm going to need more script because I don't think I'm going to need all that padding time. I don't think it's that funny."

If I said that, he'd roll on the floor. Happy. The best show. I'd think, Well, he knows better than I. He's the genius. Then we'd go into the studio the next day, show day, block it and have a run-through. He'd say, "Oh, my God —" and of course that's no time to make the changes. Twenty million changes and making sure everybody got them. I tried to figure what all the changes did to the timing. I used to think, Oh, for gosh sakes, Fred.

That kept up until I finally caught on. I learned to play games with him. When he asked, "What do you think?", if I didn't think it was very funny, I'd say, "It's a pretty good show, Fred." Then, when he had watched the run-through, he would say, "No, no. We've got to make…" — just the opposite of what I'd said. I couldn't understand it. Why would he have such a plot? Why would he ask me what I thought and then dismiss it? It was very strange.

I think the only thing that kept me from getting an ulcer is that I would take just so much and then explode. For instance, after a run-through, or even a dress rehearsal, he'd be screaming, "You've got to change all the music."

"We can't change the music! We're going on the air! And I've still got all these notes to take care of!" I'd shout, "You are a son-of-a-bitch!" and then start to cry. Everybody in the control room would freeze — not a peep out of anybody — as Fred and I went at each other. "You're wrong! And I'm right! You shouldn't have yelled!" Eventually, his voice would go up so high it was like only a dog could hear. I'd get hysterical, start crying, and leave the control room. I'd think, "What am I doing to myself?" So, when the show was over, I'd quit.

And yet, I did love working with him. I learned so much. Every time I would quit — which was quite regularly after the first year — and we'd be down in Hurley's, the bar on the corner of 49th Street and Avenue of the Americas, he'd come over, put his arm around me, and say, "Hey, baby. Someone told me you're unhappy on the show. You know I can't do a show without you. I love you." So I'd come back. I did stick up for myself. Things would calm down for a couple of weeks, then it would start up again. He was never aware, apparently, of his behavior in the control room.

It seems to me we rehearsed three days. The show was done live with an audience every Sunday night at the Center Theatre, across 49th Street from NBC. A large theatre. Because it was a half-hour show, we blocked it, had a run-through, and a dress rehearsal on that same day.

Hal Keith directed. Hal was a sort of bombastic, very positive person, like a head cheerleader. I thought that he didn't have a nerve in his body.

Before the show went on the air, I had to be very concentrated and go over in my mind and with the script just what I had to do to open the show, get through the opening titles and first commercial, after which Hal would take over.

One day I came into the control room after giving out notes. Hal said, "You know, for those first couple of minutes before we go on the air, I am in an absolute dead state. Because if I don't have it all focused in, it's going to be a big blank, and I know I'm going to do something wrong. So forgive me if I seem morose and don't talk for those few minutes before we go on the air."

I said, "Oh, Hal. I always thought you just came in without a worry in the world and ran it with such ease. I'm glad you told me because I have to do the same thing!" We were just so pleased that we found that out about each other. Once we got into the show, we were fine. We could handle most any emergency. It was just those first few minutes.

Hal was the first director who took time to teach me — to explain what he was doing and why. I'd say, "Why are you shooting it from there?"

He'd say, "Because you've got to remember where the cables are coming from — if you're not careful the camera cables will get tangled and you'll come to a standstill."

I found it so *interesting*. After a bit he'd say to me, "You've got the script and floor plan. I've marked where the cameras are coming from. Why don't you sit down and figure out how you would shoot that scene?" And I would do that. Most of the time I would already know what the blocking was, so it wasn't too hard to figure out the camera shots. But, some days I would think, I wouldn't have had him walk there. I'd have had him walk over there. And I was doing my own creating. Hal would say things like, "That's not the way I would have marked that scene, but it doesn't mean that it won't work another way." He was never, "Only one way, my way."

After a while, I did understand more about the cameras so that I felt very secure by the time I got to working with George Schaefer. I will always be thankful to Hal for teaching me, for showing me how and why and what to do, and where I went wrong. He was a darling man. I loved him a lot. His wife Bee was a former dancer. I was very close to them.

That last spring, before I went on my first trip to Europe, they gave me a big party. When I came back from my vacation, *Mr. Peepers* had been canceled. I believe it was that winter when Bee called to say that Hal had bone cancer and wasn't expected to live long. About a week after I had been to see him, Hal died.

Albert McCleery had been in the theatre before the war, had risen to the rank of major in the armed forces during the war, had become a professor in the Fordham University drama department after the war, and had joined NBC as a director in the spring of 1949. In May of 1950 he created and produced *Cameo Theatre*, an innovative, low-budget, anthology dramatic series, noted for using black backgrounds with set pieces and furniture for scenery, while emphasizing intimate action and close-up shooting. After running until September, it came back for three months in June of 1951, and for a similar period in January of 1952. It was revived again for the summer season in 1955.

Having won the big fight over which color system would be adopted, RCA was eager for as much color programming as possible. Therefore, although NBC quickly began converting the prime time schedule, the parent company pressed NBC to add color to the daytime schedule so that dealers would have something to demonstrate during shopping hours.

Although it seemed like an impossible undertaking, NBC decided to produce a one-hour, Monday-to-Friday dramatic show for the afternoon schedule. Because of his success with the limited production required by *Cameo Theatre*, McCleery was appointed producer of *Matinee Theatre*.

* * *

**Walter Grauman:**  I began to drive everybody that worked at NBC crazy, saying, "Look, I'm a director, I'm a director. Here's my résumé. Here's what I've written. And now I'm stage managing. I want to direct. I want to direct."

Fred Wiley was a vice president of NBC. I went to his office so often that he called Albert McCleery. He knew that McCleery was going to start a new series, called *Matinee Theatre*. He said words to the effect, "I've got this kid here who's driving me crazy. Give him a chance. I don't know whether he can do it or not, but get him off my back."

So Albert McCleery made a deal with me and with Boris Sagal. On a try-out basis, we directed a summer replacement show that Albert was doing on the network called *Cameo Theatre*. This was at Burbank studios, in 1955. *Cameo* was really a half-hour version of *Matinee Theatre*. Albert said, "Okay. You passed. You can do one with an option for another, and then an option for another."

Boris and I were Albert's first two directors on *Matinee*. I did eighty-one, Boris did close to that many, I'm sure. Lamont Johnson, Arthur Hiller, Lawrence Schwab, Alan Cooke, Sherman Marks, and Allan Buckhantz became directors. Livia Granito was Albert's assistant before she was moved to directing. Livia I love dearly. Dennis Patrick was an actor who conned Albert into letting him direct.

We didn't really have a choice of material, because it was such a highly organized, mechanical operation — five shows a week. Scripts came in, and Albert or Winston O'Keefe or Darryl Ross would assign them. But we didn't have to do anything we didn't want to do.

We each directed one a week, alternating between two stages. We didn't have a lot of time. We'd have a reading, then we'd lay it out on the floor with tape or chalk in a rehearsal hall. I'd rehearse with the actors, and I'd be the camera, running from one angle to another. All of us became much more adroit with cameras, with cutting.

We'd work with the art director, who'd be building whatever sets there were, and the prop man. Then we'd go out to Burbank, for camera blocking, a rehearsal, and a dress on one day; a run-through, a dress rehearsal, and air the next day. The color was maybe a little bit richer than it is today, a little more vivid, but it was beautiful.

Albert was dead set against using sets. I liked to use as much of a set as I could get, but he wanted tight, close, and forget the background. On a marvelous play, *Autumn Crocus*, I had the art director build a little hamburger stand. It had a couple of boards and a little counter and what have you. I started on the hamburger being fried on the grill, the camera pulled back, and I kept pulling back until I saw the full stand. Suddenly I hear this voice behind me saying, "God damn it, you're crucifying me!" I looked, and it was McCleery. He'd come into the booth and it wasn't his *Cameo* technique. Oh, he was mad, but whenever I could, I tried to get a sense of the environment.

The night before we aired a show with Sarah Churchill, I took my wife, Sue, to the hospital, went in for a run-through, went back to the hospital, went into the delivery room, saw my wife and my daughter —

who's now twenty-four — saw they were okay, went back to Burbank, did the dress rehearsal and the show.

McCleery was an organizational genius. I had enormous respect for him, and I liked him a lot. He could be tyrannical, he could be tough, but he was really something special. However, when things didn't go well for him, a lot of the people wouldn't give him the time of day. Damn shame too.

*Matinee Theatre* was a great blessing for many people. I was thrilled that I was lucky enough to be involved in it. It gave a lot of us opportunites that we couldn't have had any other way, and some very good talents came out of *Matinee Theatre*. I think that we were, fortunately, in on the birth of a new creative business.

**Allan Buckhantz:** I stayed with CBS, and color began to appear. NBC had guaranteed that they go on the air with color, producing so many hours a day of programming. There was not enough of a marketplace for color, and sponsors wouldn't back it, so RCA had to come in and sponsor *Matinee Theatre*, which they did for a long time. They did a hell of a job on it, too.

I told my agent, "I would like to do that."

He said, "You're crazy if you want to go to color. It's a brand new thing. They're going to pay maybe a hundred fifty or a hundred twenty-five dollars."

I was already earning about two hundred or two hundred fifty a week, but I said, "I don't care." It became a real challenge, and, again, I was already involved in a love affair with live television.

Albert McCleery decided that after everybody got a crack at two shows, he'd make the final selection. He put out a call for directors, and I was one of them. Then, I got a letter from him stating, "We regret to advise you that your application as a director for the NBC *Matinee Theatre* cannot be accepted." I had a deal for two shows, and I had never *put in* an application. I didn't know what the hell that letter was talking about. What happened was that he found somebody he wanted to give a chance to, and he thought, Well, then, who can we get rid of?

I asked my agent, "What is this application business?" He got very upset and called NBC, not McCleery. There was a big scandal. I got a telephone call from McCleery, asking me to come in to see him. It was a very pleasant conversation until he said, "Look. You're causing me a lot of trouble." This was the beginning of a relationship mind you.

I said, "Mr. McCleery, I'm sorry. I never gave you an application. What are you talking about?"

He said, "Look. Let's cut through the bull. I'll give you one show. And that's all I have."

Most of the people involved were with NBC. They would come in and start creating on the stage, which is fine if you can do it. I, for one, can't. I have to think it out.

Everybody was finishing their rehearsals at nine, ten, eleven at night, but they still weren't ready. Finally, someone called and said pull the plug, that was it. McCleery was going out of his head because the overtime was staggering.

I came to NBC very well prepared, just as I always did at CBS. Two nights before the show, I moved into a motel right next to NBC and stayed up the whole night, got all the traffic worked out, and made sure that the boom didn't have to be moved twenty feet and hurry back real quick. I came in with camera sheets and the whole bit. I went into rehearsal and finished at five minutes to seven. The telephone rang at about four minutes to seven. It was McCleery. He said, "Well done." This was after the argument in his office.

I was only supposed to have one show, but McCleery called me in afterwards and said, "You're staying with the show." Didn't ask, didn't say anything. It was as if, "All right. You made it. You're now one of us." He never again mentioned that incident concerning the application.

As time went on, whenever a guy would fall out, they'd say, "Get Buckhantz," because I knew how to pick it up. TV directing becomes sort of a mechanical thing after awhile.

I don't know how many shows we did all together on *Matinee*, but I know that I'm number one. I wound up directing approximately one every ten calendar days. By the ninetieth show, I was pretty damn tired, and the show itself wasn't really all that hot.

I was notorious for having a lot of shots. I used to average three hundred shots an hour.The interesting aspect is that in the shows I had directed up to that time, I never had an error. Now, that doesn't mean the show was good or bad, but there was never a boom, a boom shadow, or a camera in the shot. It was about the ninety-third show that I finally did make an error. I was tired and not very impressed with the show I was directing. It was a split-second mistake, and I forgot about it.

I went over to the offices on Vine Street. Everybody's smiling, and Albert McCleery is standing in the corner at the end of the hall with a big smile on his face. "Allan come here. Let me shake your hand."

I said, "Albert, what is this? The show wasn't all that good. It was just another lousy show."

He said, "It's nice to know that you're human."

I must tell you, that was probably one of the most traumatic moments for me. Here's the man that I'm working for, waiting for me to make an error — the "Infallible Buckhantz." It's nonsense. There's nothing infallible about me. I make the same errors everybody else makes.

I said to myself, "If that's what McCleery feels, how does a propman feel? How does the electrician feel?" They used to say, "He comes in with a script marked with three hundred shots. He'll get three hundred shots." Everything was a critique. It was positive, but it also was negative, which I didn't know about until that day.

I realized that my cameramen didn't talk to me because if I said, "It's day," they wouldn't even bother to look out a window. They'd think, "Buckhantz says it's day. It's day even if it's midnight." And that was wrong, very wrong. Well, as of that day I purposely put in four or five mistakes, so that during rehearsal I could say on the microphone — so everybody could hear me — "I don't know what happened to me last night, fellows. Sorry. I apologize." Bull. I knew exactly where those errors were put in. I was looking for some sort of conversation to modify my "infallibility."

There's an interesting story about the scripts we were given. We did three-act shows. There was a director who used to go on the floor and rehearse two acts during blocking and rehearsal. He never got to the third act, which was always the best, because he simply used to over-rehearse the first two. His shows weren't good.

One day he got called into McCleery's office, and McCleery said to him, "Hey, what's going on with you?"

The director said, "How can I do good shows when Buckhantz gets the best scripts?"

Now, I never got the scripts that I wanted because we were given a script and that was it. So I did the best that I could. I'm not going to say my shows were great, but I did do some very good ones and won awards for some of them.

Every time this director walked by my office, he used to say, "Hey, Allan, how's the script?"

And I'd say, "Great. Great," even if it was a piece of crap. Why should I go and publicize that I got a rotten script?

Albert called me in. "Hey, so-and-so was in here, and he said you get the best scripts."

I said, "It's bull. Look. Walk by the office tomorrow, and I'll be sitting, reading this script. When he says, 'How's the script?' I'm going to say, 'Great.' You come in and take my script away from me. I'll put on a big act and give him a *Buckhantz* script!"

The next day, sure enough, the guy comes in, and Albert waits for the cue. The guy says, "What are you reading?"

I said, "It's my next show. It's sensational."

Piece of crap. Then Albert says to me, "I meant to tell you, I'd rather he does that show."

I say, "How can you do that? I've put in two days' work?"

Albert says, "Allan, there's no point in talking about it."

So the guy got my script and went out and did a horrible show. I mean, I'm not so sure that mine would have been any better, but he again rehearsed two acts, while the third act got lost in the shuffle and was the best act.

Only once did I argue about doing a show. McCleery called me in one day and said, "I want you to do *Jekyll and Hyde* live."

I said, "Albert, that's impossible. They tried to do it on *Playhouse 90*, and it didn't work, so they had to use film."

Albert already had an actor in New York he wanted to use. He said, "Allan, that's what we're going to do, and you're going to do it. Technically, I have nobody who can do it. If anybody can do it, you can."

I was very upset about that because I was very familiar with the subject matter, and I distinctly knew that I couldn't make hair grow on a live television screen. I spent a couple of days thinking about it, and, finally, I came up with an idea to do it in a different way. Indeed, it would be a different *Jekyll and Hyde*, creating sort of an organic development, rather than a physical development.

I saw McCleery and said, "Albert, I think I have the answer for *Jekyll and Hyde*."

He said, "Of course, I knew you would."

I said, "What would you think if we took the organic approach?"

Instead of asking me what it means, he said, "Just a moment." He then calls this actor in New York. I'm sitting there, waiting for him to listen to what I've come in with, while he says to this actor, "I just had a brilliant idea. I got the answer on *Jekyll and Hyde.* We're not going to have the hair grow. We're going to do it in an organic way. Talk to you later." Boom. He didn't even know what I meant by it. He said, "Now Allan, what is it?"

After the actor took his potion, or whatever it was, he'd go, "Oh!" He had cotton in his hands which he'd put in his mouth. I'd distort the image with lenses, and it was viscerally more scary than if he'd had fangs, hair, the whole bit. It did turn out to be a sensational show.

Albert used to assign me the job of helping actors who wanted to direct. I helped Lamont Johnson, who was wonderful. On the other hand, there was an actor, who is a very prominent actor today, who was given an opportunity to direct, but he certainly knew nothing about the technology. I took a very special liking to this guy, and I still like him a great deal. I told him what needed to be done then came out and blocked it with him. I told him what he had to think about, the cameras, the cables, the whole bit.

At Schwab's on the Sunset Strip, he showed me his script the night before camera blocking, and none of it worked. He simply didn't comprehend the mechanics. I told him, "Look, this isn't going to work."

We closed Schwab's that night, working on his script. We laid out the stage and the set, put in the cameras, then I redid his whole book with about two hundred plus shots. He said, "Allan, you've got to stay in back of me. Just in case something happens."

I said, "Sure. I'll be in the control room." I stayed with him, and he finished three minutes early.

We had a spot at the end of the show where John Conte [host of the program] interviewed one of the actors, but in this instance he said, "Let's interview the director. Allan, would you take over the directing console while he's downstairs?"

The first question John asks him is, "Well, how does it feel?"

He says, "Oh, it feels wonderful."

John said, "Do you find directing difficult?"

He said, "My three-year-old son could do it."

I'd laid it out for him!

**Livia Granito:** In the summer of 1955, Albert was starting *Matinee Theatre.* He needed at least ten directors, so I knew I had a fighting chance. He was hiring in New York and Los Angeles, and he only came to New

York for a week or two. Once he offered me the position, I spent my whole week's vacation on Fire Island trying to decide, "Do I really want to go back to that place?"

I had sworn that I would never come back to California, as I hated it with a vengeance. I was one of those really, really provincial, distasteful New Yorkers who thought everything in Los Angeles was terrible and everything back there was perfect. I wanted to have a personal life as well, but I just knew I would never find anything in L.A. I mean, everybody was always behind their house and on their patios. There was never anyone out on the streets. There weren't any places to mingle with people, and as a young woman, I was looking for more than just work.

But I wanted to direct so badly that I just thought, Well, screw it. If I'm in the studio working and doing something I love, what difference does it make where I am? I'd better take this chance.

So I went to Albert and told him that I really wanted the job. He looked at me and said, "You're crazy. You hated Los Angeles." But I told him that this time I was serious, and that this was a whole different ball game. So he said, "Well, let me see what I can do."

Albert was a many faceted man. He did many hateful things that people still remember, but he did marvelous things that I don't think many people remember quite as well. He was always for the underdog, he was always looking for a chance to change things, and I came under that heading. So he went to NBC with the request that I be given a chance.

This was 1955. There were no women directors at ABC, and it seems to me that ABC was the most recalcitrant of the networks. Lela Swift and Gloria Monty were both directing at CBS. I was the first woman director on staff at NBC. They gave me a chance, but there was a slight bit of male chauvinism that went along with it. NBC was having the prospective directors do two kinescopes as trials. They were going to be aired, but they were test shows, pilots in a sense. They would chose the directors from those two pieces. I was only allowed one show. In addition to that, the men who came from out of town were given expense money while I had to do it on my own, and I had a lot less money than those men who were already directing. It was like blackmail, in a way. The only way Albert could get me through was to do it their way. I had to sink or swim, so I took whatever odds I was given, which were none.

Because I was busy working at NBC in New York and had to dismantle an apartment, I came out here very late. By the time I arrived, there were hardly any scripts left. In fact, Arthur Hiller had the choice of the last two, and I took the one he didn't want. I think I arrived an hour later than he did, although he also got there late because he was coming from Canada.

The move from the AD chair to the director's chair is a lot farther than from this chair to that chair. Albert used to like to quote me on that one. While you're in the associate director's chair, you are not making the decisions, you are not making the choices, and you are not having to get them done as the leader.

I knew a lot of men in the business — stage managers, ADs, and other directors — and there were those among them who badmouthed me, and others who came to offer their help. The surprising thing was that some men that I really expected to be delighted for me went around saying, "What business has she got doing such a thing?" But those men that I thought would be absolutely against me, came up and said, "Livia, can I help you with this script?" Some of them were a little too pushy, but I told them, "Well, I want to do it myself. If you want to look over and see what I've done when I've prepared my script, it's all right then. Please do." This approach seemed to work fine.

As a director on *Matinee*, sometimes the crew would make things difficult for you. It wasn't so much that they wouldn't do what you wanted them to do, but they would make you explain yourself even when they knew what you wanted, or they would be slow about performing the task. They would take an opposing point of view just to see how serious you were about what you wanted. Whether that happened more because I was a woman or because I was new, I don't know. But the other directors went through it to a certain extent as well.

One of the advantages that I had was that Albert had the same cameramen, TDs, and crew that he had been working with for a couple of years. I had to prove myself in terms of directing, but these men knew me, and we got along very well. They were out to help me, not hurt me, and that I felt was a great blessing.

Fortunately, I knew a lot of the actors, too, but the woman that I got to play the lead in my test show was someone I did not know at all. She was scared stiff. Later I was told she had a physical problem that made her appear drunk and always forgetting her lines.

As a neophyte director, I had two problems that I later understood to be of my own making. One, because you're new, you feel that you must make everything work. You say, "Maybe if I do this she'll come out," or "I'm not eliciting this because I don't know how to get it from her." You don't say, "Replace this actor." It took me a long time to realize that this is often the better thing to do. I shouldn't have put up with her. I should have just replaced her right away.

The second problem was that, as a woman, you feel that you have to prove that you don't give up right away. So you slog through situations you have no business doing! It was dumb. Your mental set is different when you start out as a director.

Albert was very keen on organizing tasks in military style, so our three supervising producers worked in army fashion. One was in charge of casting and under him were several casting directors. The second producer was in charge of the production and crew, while the third was in charge of scripts. Albert was really fanatical about using military conventions. In fact, I remember him writing a letter to the NBC brass for me when I wanted a raise as an AD. He referred to me as his "valued lieutenant."

The whole thing was live to New York at three in the afternoon. Since there were so many shows to begin with, we couldn't just stay within a certain genre, so we did all kinds of things, including remakes of classics. It was up to the producers and Albert to decide who would be best for this show or that show. They would program shows to give variety to the anthology, and when your turn came up, that's what you got. I think I got a lot of the quote "women's shows," although there were so many of that kind that the men got them, too.

Basically, I had one every two weeks, and sometimes one every three weeks. But there was one period where a lot of the men got sick, and I did one a week for a month, meaning that I did four in a row. Generally speaking, I did fewer than the men did, partly because the men who had families wanted to do as many shows as possible since they got paid per show. As for me, I was working on staff and getting a salary no matter how many shows I did. Even the week I wasn't working, I still got paid.

I guess it was to my benefit to be on staff because if anything happened to the show, I would still be working. Albert may have had something to do with that. He was always very conscious of his budget, and putting me on staff may have saved him some money in the long run.

We had five days of rehearsal with just the actors. A reading on the first day and four days in the rehearsal hall. The last two days were always difficult because rehearsals were scheduled to start at two p.m. at the earliest. McCleery liked to rehearse at night, so generally we'd have the first rehearsal from two to five and another from eight to eleven.

The night before the show, you would go in for the camera rehearsal and set the studio up. You could be there until the early hours of the morning depending on the complexity of the show you were doing, and then you had to be in at five or six the next morning. The actors came in at about nine or ten a.m. the day before the actual show and at five-thirty a.m. on the day of the show.

When I was directing the show, the stage was divided into two. One show would be rehearsing while the other one was airing, and then the cameras would just pull over. In the afternoon they would rehearse the show for the next day, so we had two shows going on continuously.

One time, I was on the side of the stage that was rehearsing. The show that was running was short, so John Conte dragged me in to interview me as a woman director. I didn't like the way I was dressed and my hair wasn't fixed, so I ran into makeup because I insisted on looking at least as good as I could. The whole thing was informal, and everybody knew everybody. We were very much like a family in that sense.

Another interesting thing was that Ethel Frank, our producer in charge of scripts, was in New York. She was very good at her work, and everything went through her. The feeling was that most of the talent and most of the creativity was in New York, and with the writers, that was very much the case.

It was a special show in that we were allowed to experiment, to try many things. We had a lot of chances to fail that we just never had in the same way after that. Directors came and went on their own, or by NBC's and/or Albert's decision. I stayed with the show until it was over, from 1955 to 1958. I did about seventy-five shows in that time.

**Arthur Hiller:** I decided to send McCleery *The Swamp*, because it illustrated how involved a live show could be. But when I went up to the library at the CBC in Toronto, that show was missing, so I ended up sending a half-hour Mickey Spillane-type mystery. It had no sets, just a black cyc. If we wanted to show that it was a lawyer's office, we would put a bookcase in the background. If you wanted to show somebody walking, you'd shoot at the person past a candelabra. Because the shooting style of this kind of detective story called for close shots, we never used anything looser than a waist shot. We used the idea that, "If it's a two shot, and you're not touching, you're not in the shot." Everything was done very close.

It proved to be exactly the kind of thing to send. The person who was assisting McCleery in the production told me, "Ten minutes into that show, McCleery was ready to marry you." If I'd sent *The Swamp*, it would have been entirely wrong.

William Shatner takes credit for my being in the United States, because the reason that I couldn't find *The Swamp*, was that Bill, having starred in it, had the kinescope under his arm in New York showing "Bill Shatner, the actor."

McCleery and his people phoned and offered me a two-show trial. If those two shows worked, I'd have a job. It's interesting how you think to yourself, "Yes, I want this," you do all the interviews, send the kinescopes, and then somebody says, "Okay. Come to Hollywood." All your friends are saying, "Sure, sure, Hollywood. Yes, you've got to go," but you're thinking about leaving your home, your friends, and the job where you have security. What did I know about Hollywood? Only what I'd read in the magazines, which left me quite weary. Finally Winston O'Keefe, who was the producer I was in contact with, called and said, "Wednesday at one o'clock our time, I want a yes or no."

I phoned and said, "Okay, I'm coming."

By that time, I'd had three weeks of no sleep. My wife and I were quite nervous, so to calm down and relax, we decided to go for a quiet dinner and to a movie. Halfway through the movie I was paged, by a cousin who was living with us. She said that Winston O'Keefe's secretary had called from Hollywood. When my cousin had told her that I was at a movie, she said, "Have him paged." I went back into the theatre, all the while thinking, "I'll be damned if I call until this movie's over." I lasted ten minutes.

I went out and phoned O'Keefe. He said, "Arthur, this morning when you called and said you were coming, I forgot to ask you what it's going to cost to move your family down? I have to put it in the budget."

After that conversation, I seriously thought about not moving to Hollywood. They page you in the middle of a movie to ask what it's going to cost to move a family down? That didn't sound like the kind of life I wanted. Later, I discovered that O'Keefe didn't ask to have me paged. He simply said to his secretary, "Get Arthur Hiller," and she was going to get Arthur Hiller no matter what.

A few weeks after my conversation with O'Keefe, I came to Hollywood. I had to take a connecting flight, and on the way from Chicago to Los Angeles, I experienced a bout of fear and panic. I was just terrified. If I could have turned that plane around, I would have.

We landed at about four in the afternoon. It was one of those gloriously perfect, eighty-two degree days with a smog-free sky. Suddenly, the tension was gone, and I felt much better. I took a taxi to O'Keefe's office, where they welcomed me and handed me a script. I took a room at the Plaza Hotel, read the script that night, and hated it.

The next day I went into O'Keefe's office, "I hate this script. I'd rather not do it."

He said, "Well, if you'd gotten here sooner we could have given you some choice, but all the other directors are here, and they've chosen their scripts. This is the only one available for you."

I knew that there were fourteen other directors on trial, so I reluctantly agreed to keep the script. I went down to the little office they'd assigned me, where I read it again. I thought, "No, I'm not going to do it. If I've come from Canada to do this, I might as well go back right now."

I went back to O'Keefe, "I'm just not going to do this."

He said, "Well, we'd better go in and see McCleery."

We walked into McCleery's office. O'Keefe said, "Albert, this is Arthur Hiller, the young man that you brought from Canada."

McCleery said, "Oh, so pleased to meet you. Welcome." Simultaneously, O'Keefe was saying, "He doesn't want to do the first script."

In an angry voice, McCleery said, "What do you mean he doesn't want to do the script? I mean, welcome. What do you mean he doesn't want to do — ?"

I interrupted him, "Look, you brought me on a two-show trial. I don't feel that I have to do scripts that I love, but I shouldn't have to do one that I really hate, and I really hate this one." Then I said, "If I have to do it, I'm going back to Canada."

McCleery said, "That's fair." They gave me three others to choose from.

I usually like to work wearing a shirt and tie. I don't know if that's from my Canadian upbringing or what. In the middle of the first show I was sitting in the control booth, while McCleery was sitting behind me watching.

I thought, "Oh, boy, it's really going well." The actors were wonderful, the cameras were moving well, and I felt so pleased with everything. Suddenly, I thought, "Why isn't he saying something? Is it not as good as I think? I'm not directing well? The actors aren't good? I'm using the wrong camera?"

All of a sudden, everything felt wrong. Finally, he leaned over and whispered in my ear, "I'm really terribly impressed." I puffed up. Then he said, "You're all dressed up." There I was in a tie when everybody else was in a tee shirt or an open sport coat. After the show, he told me that he loved my work, and not to worry about the second show. Just bring my family down.

Because there was no money for sets, and we wanted an outdoor-indoor look, we settled on using frames for full-length windows and doors. In addition to the sets, I initiated what you would call "normal shooting." I still remember the look on Albert's face when he came on the stage — he turned red! He was so furious with me that he couldn't even speak, because it wasn't what he called the *Matinee Theatre* style.

I said, "We're just trying it once, that's all."

Because *Matinee Theatre* consisted of five full-length shows every week, we couldn't always find five "safe" scripts, so we did some interesting, first-rate material in addition to the second-rate stuff. *Bottom of the River* was originally written for the *U.S. Steel* program. Because it dealt with juvenile delinquency, they considered it a little too controversial, and decided against producing it. Somehow it was picked up for *Matinee Theatre*.

**Lamont Johnson:**  I was moving back to New York after four very unhappy years in Hollywood. I had my little girl already enrolled in a school back there and I had a deposit on an apartment. I was doing more interesting work in live television and theatre in New York.

While I was on one of my eastern forays, I read in *The New York Times* that Albert McCleery — for whom I had worked a great deal as an actor, on *Cameo Theatre*, *Hallmark Hall of Fame*, and a number of other things — was going to do something called *Matinee Theatre*. McCleery was auditioning directors by having them do kinescopes, which were very bad 16mm films that could be put on the air in case somebody dropped dead.

I called McCleery, who said, "You're an actor, you're just about to become a star. For Chrissake, what are you doing trying to get into directing? It's a terrible game, and very hard in live. Don't do it. No, I won't let you try out. I've got people who are emotionally equipped for it. But come on out and do my last *Cameo Theatre*, and you can watch the big boys play in the next studio."

I did that. I played Thomas Wolfe in *Look Homeward Angel* for him, with Thomas Mitchell as my father. I spent every single second that I wasn't in McCleery's studio watching them make these kinnies in the next studio. Boris Sagal, Arthur Hiller, and Alan Cooke were among the directors, and these were the people who were pretty well already in the McCleery set.

I went to him over and over again as I was working with him as an actor, and said, "Hey, I can do just as badly as they're doing, for Chrissake. Let me have a chance to prove it." He laughed and was very amused. I did the *Cameo* show for him, and was almost packed up to go back to New York, when he called me in the middle of the night and said, "One of my guys just had to be carried out of the booth. He was going to do the next show, *Wuthering Heights*. Do you want to do *Wuthering Heights*?"

I said, "Sure." I didn't give it a second thought. I just was so arrogant and so relatively young, that I thought, "Why not?"

I called my friend, Richard Boone, with whom I had worked in the Actors Studio, and with whom I had an acting group in California — we called ourselves "Actors Studio in Exile." I asked Dick to do Heathcliff and he did.

I put in a score that had McCleery's teeth chattering. It turned out be quite exciting with harpsichord and bagpipes intermingled, and sometimes a roulade, to get a sense of the period. I suddenly got very turned on with the whole idea, and didn't sleep for like five days, just worked constantly on what I was going to do. McCleery loved it. I saw a kinnie of it somewhat later when it went on the air and just was appalled at how awful it was.

He put me under contract, and for two years I ground them out at the rate of one every ten days. I did seventy-seven more, and I would say maybe three or four of those shows probably were pretty damn good. Although there was great material occasionally, you usually took very inferior plays and the only actors you could grab at the moment. I did two Biblical pieces, I did Shakespeare, I did Dickens, I did Shaw, I did a Gore Vidal that I was very proud of — one of his very first teleplays — and a Paddy Chayefsky. There were some very early, exciting playwrights who were just proving up, whose work one could do because everybody was working for next to nothing. I was getting, I think, three hundred dollars a week.

Ethel Frank was our head of properties. She was always encouraging new people and established playwrights. She had a whole staff just digging for material.

We made suggestions. I brought in several writer friends. An actor friend had dramatized a short story, *The Children of Papa Juan*, on which I gave Herschel Bernardi one of his first starring roles.

John Conte was in the series the whole time, and he built an enormous following. My God, his fan mail became almost movie star fan mail.

We all were very fond of McCleery, but he was a tyrannical boss and had a terrible temper. We would have awful fights with him. I would fight and quit and so forth. But I got around it and he loved what I did. And, because he had a sort of perverse Irish temper and humor at the same time, he would relish somebody who had enough invention and wit to come around and do something better. He could still always take credit for that.

I did a production of *The Courtship of Miles Standish* based on the Longfellow poem, with no scenery. I said, "I'll show the sonuvabitch."

Against a naked cyc, I composed the first shot which looked like a great glob of a headland in the dawn, just with back light. It looked quite marvelous in color, on the monitor at least. Then, as the poem, the narrative, began, the spotlight picked up something in this glob that looked like a long-shot of New England, Plymouth Rock seen from the sea, with a face in the middle of it. Then the face separated from the others, and the glob turned out to be a bunch of actors that I had clotted in a group. That's the way I did all the transitions. I would get the actors back in and they would become a ship, they would become a house, they would become a glade with trees, then they would become animated and go into the scene.

I loved that technique, and I adapted it in other things that I've done since. And McCleery loved it too. He said, "That was good *Cameo*."

There's something to be said for his point, in television. However, about that time, never having seen it on a big screen, I saw *Stagecoach* on television. I was spellbound with John Ford's incredible panoramas of Monument Valley, and my eye immediately adjusted to the great scale of Monument Valley on my little set. I simply scaled down my imagination and my focus to the point where it made great sense. I felt that one didn't have to eliminate long shots, and once I got out of a live studio, I never shot a single television show that didn't use extensive, very wide shots. In *The Execution of Private Slovak*, for instance, I did a considerable amount of the execution in very, very wide courtyard shots filled with soldiers and people and snow and landscape. I love to do a whole scene sometimes, three and four minutes, with no cuts, no intercuts, simply move actors appropriately and organically in a scene to the camera, or the camera to the people in such a way that you make your own coverage as you go along, but you're not cutting it up. That works very well in certain scenes, not in all.

I took the cameras outside on a couple of occasions but it was not very successful. Mainly because I simply did it as a stunt, and hadn't thought it through and was sort of trying to tweak McCleery's nose. He hated the idea — television was like the theatre, you're not trying to kid people that it's real. There's a point there, too, with the techniques that were available to us at that time.

When I was an actor, I paid no attention to technical things. I never much liked machinery, so I let the technicians do that. I just worked with the actors and the text. I infinitely preferred live television to film — I hated film. Live was more like the theatre. One rehearsed, went on the air, and played it through. It was a terrific experience. I got to work with great work as well as dross. It was an enormous opportunity to just do everything, to get in the big Mixmaster and work. I had a great deal to unlearn, because you learned a lot of wretched tricks while just doing the work that fast. It was a marvelous, marvelous thing, and I miss it today.

Matinee Theatre was a very good idea, but it wasn't refined in any way. There was just a tremendous euphoric, headlong rush into grinding out this material, and, because it was such a great strain on our nerves, there was a mutual congratulation that we were all surviving.

We had a severe problem when we did a more or less affectionate, twenty-fifth year recollection of Matinee Theatre. We survivors banded together and did a memorial tribute to Albert McCleery, our boss, who had taken the great chance of hiring us. As we sat at UCLA and looked at these kinnies — Arthur Hiller, Walter Grauman, and a few of the others — we'd say, "Jesus, what are we going to put on? There's nothing here that we want to show. They're terrible." Arthur Hiller had one that was pretty good, but on closer examination we all agreed that it wasn't so hot either. Wally Grauman had a pretty good one. I couldn't find anything of mine that I wanted to do, and embarrassingly enough, we couldn't really find much of McCleery's that wasn't downright embarrassing.

Aside from events like championship boxing matches, series programming was the most prevalent form until Sylvester "Pat" Weaver became the head of NBC Television. An innovative programmer, Weaver inspired the shows known as *Today*, *Tonight*, and *Home*, the first two of which are still on the air. He also brought forth the weekly *Wide Wide World*, taking cameras all around the nation to broadcast live images. Seeing actual events and scenes in real time was so startling that it was not necessary to do much in the way of script or story — merely jumping from the Atlantic coast to the Pacific thrilled and satisfied the audience. Weaver also fostered the idea of special programs, with large budgets and big-name casts, which he called "Spectaculars."

In 1952, Hallmark Greeting Cards sponsored a half-hour summer series, produced by Albert McCleery. That fall, they picked up on the idea of special programming and began what turned out to be the longest running series of quality dramatic fare in television history, the *Hallmark Hall of Fame*.

\* \* \*

**Livia Granito:** I worked for Albert McCleery when he did the first *Hallmark* [called the *Hallmark Summer Theatre*]. It was a half-hour historical drama that was done in Los Angeles [in the summer of 1952]. In fact, the show was his idea, and he sold it to Hallmark. We started with Sarah Churchill as the hostess. I was the associate director. I really enjoyed doing it because I got exposure to different types of shows.

The first *Hallmark* was done in Studio One in Burbank, which happened to be the first studio built for color. It wasn't really finished then, so we directed from a mobile control booth outside on the parking lot. The show was done out here because there was more room and a bigger pool of actors to draw from. Even though people were in the movies, they still needed work.

**George Schaefer:** In early 1953, Maurice Evans decided to do a production of *Hamlet* for television that would be a record-breaker in many ways. It was to be a two-hour show, done live on a Sunday afternoon, and sponsored by a single sponsor, the Hallmark greeting card company. Mildred Alberg, who had been working with the Evans office, had gotten the idea of packaging it and helping sell it. The feeling was that if we could catch the kind of playing excitement of *The G.I. Hamlet*, it might make a good television show.

Maurice and I did the script together. I cast it and directed the actors, but did not direct in the full sense of the word, because the cameras were still very new to me. Albert McCleery, a wonderful pioneer in television who had been doing a half-hour Hallmark program regularly, served as the director in the control room, planned the camera work, and did all the shots. As is always the case on such split authority, it's not very satisfactory and it does not last very long.

Having once sensed what can happen with the cameras, I knew right away that it was something that I liked and thought I'd be very good at. The following year, the second production was *Richard II*, done under the same auspices, with Maurice Evans and Kent Smith. I not only directed the actors, but was much more involved in the camera work, although I still was not a member of the Radio and Television Directors Guild and was still not actually calling the shots in the booth. Again, Al McCleery worked on it. The third production of that trio of Shakespeares was *Macbeth* with Maurice Evans and Judith Anderson. That I directed in its entirety, both the camera work and the actors.

All three of the Shakespeare shows were so successful that Hallmark decided to go into television in a way that no one had done before, which was to do a series of six or seven special programs plotted at different times over the course of a year, all of them live, with the world's finest actors. Maurice Evans agreed to be the sort of overall artistic supervisor and I agreed to direct the entire lot.

That was in 1955. We then began — I guess one should say not immodestly — the most successful series of live television shows that existed, with the *possible* competition of *Playhouse 90*. *Playhouse 90* was quite remarkable in its own way because it was dealing with new material, but we went a good many more years than they.

A great many of the shows were classics or modern plays, but more and more as it went along we began to delve into original writing. Classics weren't necessarily my preference, actually. It was the Hallmark people who liked that. They had a slogan for their greeting cards: "When you care enough to send the very best," and they felt that way about doing the very best of plays. These are typical Hallmark shows: *Alice in Wonderland, The Devil's Disciple, The Corn is Green,* Molnar's *The Good Fairy, The Taming of the Shrew, Cradle Song,* Martinez Sierra's beautiful play *The Lark, There Shall Be No Night, The Yeoman of the Guard, The Green Pastures, On Borrowed Time, Dial M for Murder.*

We began to get a little team. I was very blessed with *Hallmark* because I had Robert Hartung as my associate producer. I would trust him with my life. He worked with many of the adaptations. In general, I would talk to the actors myself and let him talk to the extras, because time was precious and every minute counted. Adrienne Luraschi, who's still with me and was with me through all the shows, was the associate director.

After the first couple of years, I used, in general, one set designer, Warren Clymer, who I felt was incredibly brilliant. Noel Taylor did our clothes for almost all of these shows. The technical director was, at first, Robert Long, and later O. Tamburri. The cameramen would in general be the same; it saved a lot of headaches. Usually I'd have four cameras, sometimes five. The head cameraman, Don Mulveany, a brilliant cameraman, did almost all the shows in Brooklyn.

I used to be able to lay out an entire year's work ahead. I'd say, "Well, these are the seven shows we're going to do and these are the dates they go on the air." I'd work backwards from there and block in my time. In order to get them delivered, I'd have to be cast and designed by this point. Casting would frequently overlap, and we would very often have leads cast for the whole series.

In those days, the rules were different. You could build a momentum that was much better than the system today, I think. On a ninety-minute show, we paced it so that we covered just a three-week period. From the time I started rehearsal until we went on the air, I would allow nineteen working days. We would rehearse [without cameras] for fifteen days. The last two or three days we'd spend entirely in run-through because I'd have to get an "opening night" playing for the company.

Then we would go into the studio for four days. The first day would be spent entirely in just blocking shots, because most of those scripts would have three hundred to four hundred shots. I would always have a scheme in the back of my mind of the kind of relationships that I wanted. I'd know the places where I wanted to get a line-up so that, with four cameras, I could get the right close-ups in relationship to rights and lefts. I'd know where I'd want to follow the entire scene on one camera. I have a great personal aversion to cameras moving around. I don't like it when I see it in other people's work, so I try not to do it in my own. In general, I only have the cameras move with people.

The morning of the second day we'd finish the blocking; afternoon of the second day we'd do a first sort of a rough stop-and-go, hoping to get through it. The morning of the third day we would do a smooth stop-and-go, and late that afternoon we'd try to get as close to a good dress as we could. By that time we had it all costumed and made-up.

That would be the performance where I would have to judge my changes, so I would be calling the shots and watching it very carefully. I would go home that night, usually get three or four hours sleep because I'd be exhausted, then get up and spend another three or four hours going through the show in my mind, shot to shot, and making lists for each cameraman with the changes for the air show that day.

There would always be things I'd like to try. I'd say, "How can we do this? How can we try that?" I'd say, "Camera three, on shot 247 how about letting that be a close-up instead of an over-the-shoulder, and we'll eliminate shots 365 and 368."

Following rehearsal, I would go to the actors while they were getting in costume and make-up, then they would have a good, hopefully smooth, final dress rehearsal. There'd be quite a break between that and the air because they needed two full hours to get the color camera tuned up, and even then they rarely held for the entire show. It was another world with those huge cameras.

While the engineers were doing the test pattern, the cast would be able to take a break and I'd get together for last-minute notes. On some things, such as with *Green Pastures*, we held a genuine prayer meeting because we were really fighting all the odds on that one, but my goodness, that cast came through.

Then we'd go on the air, when I would only be watching the technical things. I'd be cuing up the music and constantly talking to the floor manager. There was nothing I could do about the performance. I would snap my fingers for the shots and be talking to Adrienne Luraschi, talking to the cameramen, talking to the technical director. I know there was a jurisdiction problem at one time, but I've always been very close to my technical director and the cameramen and we've always talked.

Once we were on the air, it was like being up in an airplane — if we lost a motor, we had to keep flying. A camera would conk out, or some little unexpected element would go wrong, and we'd have to improvise. With maybe two hundred people locked in that studio for ninety minutes or two hours, there's no way that all two hundred, being human, would perform to perfection. Those were the little things you had to bounce with. But it was a tremendous excitement, a tremendous high, actually. You'd find by the end of the program you were absolutely sailing and didn't want to come down.

There was no post-production. Once it went off the air it was completely finished, so we could collapse, take two or three days or a week off, and then start over again.

In the early live shows, a wonderful fellow, named Bernie Green, who'd been in radio and television all his life, but who is unfortunately dead now, came around and said, "Listen, instead of playing old records, you should be having original music for these things."

I said, "I can't afford it."

He said, "Well, I'd do it for fifteen hundred dollars for a score" — a ridiculous price.

Bernie would take the black-and-white kinescope, study it, time it with a stopwatch, work with about four musicians in a small recording studio, and end up with really wonderful scores. It was the first time that we could use real music. The combination of getting better sound plus the Bernie Green scores brought an element of production to those shows that was a major breakthrough. Jerry Bock is an old friend who did a score, and one show had Richard Adler's music and lyrics. On *Cradle Song* we used just simple guitar music, but Tony Mattola wrote it and played it, live.

We did *The Green Pastures* live, a very exciting production. It was all crowded into the one studio and it worked like a dream on television. It got rave reviews and very few listeners. It turned out to have been scheduled the night of a huge gala party that Mike Todd gave at Madison Square Garden for the opening of *Around the World in 80 Days*. Liz [Elizabeth Taylor] and everybody was there. Nobody knew about *Green Pastures* until the next day when they were just killing themselves at Hallmark. They said to me, "Oh, we'll just have to do it again."

Nothing existed except for my script and the idea, but the following year we got the cast — a very huge cast — together and did it again. It was a tremendous success, watched by everyone, a very huge rating.

Maybe because it was the second time, but I don't think the second production was quite as exciting as the first. It sounds very immodest but it would be very hard to do it any better than we did it the first time.

We did *The Taming of the Shrew* in '55 or '56 with Lilli Palmer and Maurice Evans and Diane Cilento. *Shrew* was a lovely production. It was one of the first startling color productions. It had a completely white set, cyc, floor. Everything was white, but the clothes were brilliant colors. It was done commedia dell'arte style. It's breathtaking to look at, because you had this sea of white faces with the Italian masks and all the commedia figures were very clever, would vary in color adaptation. Rouben Ter-Arutunian designed it with this flair. My kinescope has been worn to a frazzle.

*Berkeley Square* was live, *Winterset* was live, *Doll's House* was live, *Christmas Festival* was live. The commercials were live, too, of course. They were done in Chicago, cued in by Adrienne Luraschi.

*Little Moon of Alban* was an incredibly beautiful original. The reviews were spectacular. We did a very successful second production of it later, although Christopher Plummer and three other members of the cast weren't available. We were very fortunate that Dirk Bogarde was willing to accept the challenge of playing the lead, because Chris had been quite extraordinary and Dirk was equally extraordinary in his own way.

When we did it the second time, we were able to do it on tape. Partly because I had tape, I was able to do a few things that I couldn't do the first time. That was also true of *Cradle Song* when we repeated that on tape.

However, in both cases I think something was lost — that wonderful thing that live television did that you don't see anymore. When you got a group of the best actors and actresses in the world together and rehearsed them with great care so they were relaxed and confident and knew what they were doing, suddenly a performance would start and the ball would begin rolling and it would gel, the way a great opening night on Broadway does. If that happens, and at the same time the cameras are just where they should be and you are experiencing it in close-up, it probably is the most exciting form of dramatic entertainment that exists. That sudden excitement of great actors and actresses really living their roles accumulatively, not just in one little scene after another. There were a lot of little mishaps, you saw some booms and some boom shadows and occasionally a camera, and yet it didn't really matter.

Another show that looked quite amazing was *Give Us Barabbas*. It was all done in one studio and it was incredible. It was an Easter play, and we used these little models that we could shoot through in perfect perspective. You'd swear you were seeing the crosses up on Calvary with all the soldiers running around.You look at it today and you can't believe it. The show was repeated four times. We just reran the tape.

It's very hard to do musicals on television. Occasionally for *Hallmark* we used to do a little Christmas thing that had music attached to it, but book musicals on television aren't very successful. The best musical that I did was the Gilbert and Sullivan *The Yeoman of the Guard* which did work, beautifully, I thought. I also liked my production of *The Fantastiks*. It was a very imaginative, magical production, and we had a lovely cast. Bert Lahr and Stanley Holloway were the parents; John Davidson, little Susan Watson were the kids; Ricardo Montalban was El Gallo.

The book musical is a creature of the theatre. You have to see that orchestra sitting there, see the conductor waving his baton, to get the proper relationship. Nobody's ever succeeded, but I think Bob Fosse has come as close as anybody. He understands the problem. In *Cabaret*, Bob managed very successfully to bridge, for me at least, the fact that musicals on film don't have an orchestra. You keep wondering why all those silly people are singing instead of talking.

I must say in all fairness, sometimes shows didn't work. We did a production of *There Shall Be No Night*, with Katherine Cornell and Charles Boyer playing the leads. Ray Walston was in it and the whole cast couldn't have been better. Miss Cornell had real opening night nerves. Although she had perfectly splendid run-throughs and dress rehearsal, on the air she was so nervous that she almost couldn't hold the coffee cup in the first scene. We used to run in three acts, which doesn't happen much anymore. She settled down and was really warming up by the second and third acts. Those acts are as exciting as anything I ever did, but the first act was very rocky. There's a case where if we could have gone back and started over again, it would have been better.

An early, live production of a play that we later did on tape was *Blithe Spirit*. It was a crackerjack cast. Mildred Natwick was Madame Arcati, and I believe it also had Claudette Colbert and Lauren Bacall. Noel Coward, himself [author of the play], who could do no wrong, directed it, played the lead. We did it live. Somehow he thought it would be good with an audience. And it was awful! The actors were playing to this audience who could only hear them part of the time. Suddenly the camera would be on somebody doing nothing and there'd be a laugh in the audience.

Noel Coward was a smart, amazing man. About three months later on CBS he did a production of *This Happy Breed*, no audience, just cameras. It was one of the great television productions of all time. He learned very fast that you cannot serve both. If you ask the actors to act as though the audience wasn't there and then have the audience sitting out there yawning and bored, it doesn't accomplish anything. It's all right for sitcoms. It works very well with *All in the Family* and stuff like that.

Several times we did plays such as *Dial M for Murder*, where we used members of the original cast. It was always a great problem because you'd have to keep saying to them, "What are you waiting for? Why don't you speak?"

"Oh, that's where they always laugh."

I said "Nobody's laughing. They may smile at home a little bit, but no one's laughing, you've got to make it real."

Those shows could be done on television even though the film was still around. Live television rights to a great many of them had not been sold to movies. They were the property of the author.

The most interesting story of all was *Pygmalion*, which we'd wanted to do for a long time. We had touched base with the Shaw estate or the Society of Authors in London, because we'd worked with them a lot. They kept saying, "No, it's all tied up with a musical and nothing can be done."

We said, "Well, if it ever does become available, let us know." At long last, after five or six years, when *My Fair Lady* closed, we got a call from the Society of Authors. They said the rights were available again and did we want to do it on television. We said, "Great," and bought it for fifteen thousand dollars for a single showing of it, live.

You've never heard such a roar, because Jack Warner had just paid five million dollars for the rights to *My Fair Lady* and he suddenly picked up the paper to see that *Pygmalion* was being done on *Hallmark* that year. He threatened to sue, but the Society of Authors were wonderful. They just wouldn't budge. They said, "You didn't have enough sense to tie up the rights when you bought the musical. You don't have the rights and these people do have the rights."

I had no sympathy at all. I said, "You should be paying us for doing it. It's going to be a coming attraction for your movie. I hope your movie's half as good as our production."

It was a great company, Julie Harris, James Donald, John Williams. George Rose was the father, absolute heaven, and it twinkled. Gladys Cooper played the mother, which she had never played before. They saw her and used her in the movie.

It was really a wonderful, wonderful, wonderful performance. We did it pure Shavian style. I was so proud of that production. But they did say, "You cannot make any copies of it." I had a kinescope of it, but the tape had to be destroyed with witnesses there and the Shaw Society had to promise they wouldn't allow anybody to do the play for I don't know how many years thereafter.

Maurice Evans and I produced *Teahouse of the August Moon* originally, on Broadway, and like fools sold the movie rights. It was made into, not a bad movie, but not really as good a movie as it should have been, with such a great play. I'd always wanted to do it again. Nobody, least of all the film companies, wanted to press the legal case to see whether so-called live-on-tape was really live or film. If it qualified as film, we didn't have any rights to do it, but if it was considered live — if it had merely been put on tape for the convenience of the viewers — the rights reverted to John Patrick. That was the position we were taking. They let us do it if the tape was immediately erased and destroyed, so it would never be repeated. That was a shame because with Paul Ford and David Wayne and John Forsythe and all my original cast, and design by Warren Clymer, it was such a brilliant, stylish visual production. It was all the things the movie was not.

*Shangri-la* was a musical, not one of our triumphs I regret to say. It was a musical version that had been done on Broadway where it had flopped, but we felt we could lick it. It was a tough one, but it had some lovely things in it. Richard Basehart played the lead. Claude Rains was just wonderful as the old High Lama. Marisa Pavan, Gene Nelson, Alice Ghostley, Helen Gallagher — a nice cast.

*Shangri-la* was all in the studio, except the last part of it, where they run around the mountain in the snow and she turns into the old lady. That whole section we taped, because of the make-up problem and the snow. We did it live from the beginning, rolled in that eight- to ten-minute tape piece, and ended up live again with Basehart delirious in the hospital. There was this legal problem again when all you had were the live rights, but at that point you decide if there're eight minutes of tape and the rest live, you can't lose.

On *Hallmark*, the standards of design, of casting, of acting, were as high as I've ever had in my life. Not unnaturally, with all of that going for us, we would sweep the awards year after year. Our original production of *Little Moon of Alban* won five Emmys. They used to have an award at the Academy, after everything else was all over, for the single most exciting show of the year. We won it with *Macbeth*. The following year we won it again for a production of *Victoria Regina* with Julie Harris. We redid *Macbeth* as a film, which I think won five or six Emmys. There was a lot of competition, we weren't all alone by any means. DuPont had a series of such specials, Ford produced a showcase.

And the public was incredible. We built a corral of roughly fifteen million homes that would tune in and watch those shows and look forward to them. *Hallmark* became a major part of their lives. Fifteen million homes today are not very many and the ratings would probably be considered quite a failure by the networks, but in those days, it was a triumph. In fact, the *Hallmark Hall of Fame* has gone on and is still a very active force in television.

The only record of all those early shows is black-and-white kine-scopes. It was always a trying moment, but I enjoyed that first look at the film when we ran it to see what we had. I'd wince at things that went wrong that had happened right in dress rehearsals, but you sacrifice something for the excitement of it. I wouldn't give up those days for anything. In fact, if anybody were still doing live shows, I would probably be fighting to do some.

Once or twice I would withdraw from *Hallmark* and let another director take over. For example, we did *Born Yesterday*, and Garson Kanin [author of the play] himself directed it. I just faded into the background because I was doing a play at the time. I still loved the theatre and I didn't want to get that far away.

Roughly five years into the ten on *Hallmark*, most of my friends who were directing the kind of live shows I was doing — that's John Franken-heimer, Sidney Lumet, George Roy Hill, Franklin Schaffner, Fielder Cook, and all that gang — one by one gave up on New York, because the edge was off the excitement of shows there. They came out here and signed movie contracts.

I did at one point, about '59, decide that maybe I should make that change. Mildred Alberg and I had formed a company to package the shows, but we had certain artistic differences. I thought it would be better to let her continue to do the shows and go her way, so I signed a contract with MGM, to produce, direct, and, theoretically, write — although I can't write at all. When that was announced, the Hallmark people were in great shock. They came to me and said, "You're out of your mind. You know how much we appreciate you and want you to stay and what do you want?" A very complimentary approach.

In the meantime, the people at MGM, once we'd agreed on the deal, hadn't even sent me a penny postcard saying "Glad to have you." Everything was sitting in limbo. I thought, Why am I really doing it? Just because the other people have done it? So, I changed my mind. Hallmark and I set up Compass Productions. It was a very active corporation in producing the shows, and it exists to the present time. MGM was very upset. They claimed we had a verbal contract, but they were understanding, and said, "Look, if you're just doing it to stay in television, okay, no legal action. But if we find you're working for any other movie company, we're going to really throw the book at you."

My change of heart was a very genuine one and I've never regretted it. I think, had I come out here at that time, I probably would have had a completely different career in features, for better or worse. But I would have missed five of the greatest years of my life, continuing doing those shows. I left *Hallmark* after some sixty or sixty-five productions.

**Adrienne Luraschi:** *Hallmark* had been on for a couple of years doing hour shows. When they went to an hour and a half on Sunday night, the producer was Mildred Freed Alberg and George Schaefer was the director. Bob Hartung was George's AD. Bob eventually won a number of Writers Guild awards for adaptations of plays that he did for *Hallmark*. He hated being the AD — made him too nervous. So, after working on two or three, he told George, "No, I can't do that. But I know a perfect person for you. You should meet her."

Bob called me. It was in the hot, hot New York summer, and I was working on something — the *Home* show, I think. He said, "It would be wonderful to see you again. Could you come over to meet George Schaefer. He's looking for an AD."

I said, "Oh, fine. I'll be over." I kept thinking, Hartung? Where do I know Bob Hartung from? I don't even know the name Bob Hartung. I was sweating, I was running late, and I had my perpetual scarf around my head. I always had a scarf on in the summer because any curl in my hair would end up drooping from the heat and humidity. I just looked a mess, but in I went. There's this person coming and hugging me. "Hey, it's so good to see you." And I had never seen him in my life before.

I said, "Who are you?" It's a wonder he didn't show me the door right then.

He said, "Bob Hartung. We worked on *Philco*." He had worked with me for a couple of weeks, when he was a summer replacement for the stage managers, and he had been very taken with me, he said. I still didn't remember, but I played along. "Oh, for heaven's sakes. Well, you have to forgive me. I've been running around, and I really shouldn't be seen by anyone, not even my family. I look so awful."

He said, "No, no, no. George is looking forward to meeting you." I'm sure he wasn't. I met George, and he must have thought, Well, what is this thing the cat dragged in? The next thing you know, I got a call. I'm pretty sure Bob said, "Oh, no. She's fun. You'll love her."

Months later I told Bob I had no memory of our first meeting. He took it very well, and to this day with people we meet he'll say, "I'm a memorable person. Even though we'd worked together, the next time we met she didn't remember me at all."

I learned a lot from George because he's the most organized man. Most directors' rehearsal schedules read:

10:00 to 1:00 - Rehearse
1:00 to 2:00 - Lunch
2:00 to 5:00 - Rehearse

George would break it down, so we could also make arrangements for costumes or hair or publicity, whatever. His schedule would read:

9:00 to 9:40 - Block Scene 1 - (and actors needed).
9:40 to 10:15 - Block Scene 2 - (and actors needed).

We'd look at that and say, "Oh, sure. Certainly we will." But we did! He'd go a little over, but eventually he'd get back on time. So the actors could leave and know that they had an hour and a half before they would be working. It was really good use of an actor's time.

After the blocking, which took several days, he would review the blocking. Then, after a couple of more days, he would say, "All right, the next time without the script, please." Those were called work-through days. Then we would start to polish the performance. We always called it "Polish" — "Now we are doing our 'Polish' session."

Meantime he'd be marking his script. He had a stamp that made a square block like a TV screen. He would stamp several of these blocks on each page. Then he would sketch in two noses — or heads or whatever

— for a person in the background and a person in the foreground, so I could be sort of ahead of him. I would have to determine who the people were in each of the shots.

By the time he did his rough script, I could grab it away from him at lunchtime to make up my script. Then, the night before the technical crew came in, I made Tamburri's script — a darling, lovely man. Then I made up shot sheets for each of the four cameramen, a script for the sound man, and put all the cues in the stage manager's script.

Quite often, there would be a number of spots in the show where I would write in, "Move the flat after this shot. The flat has to get back in by this shot." The stage manager and cameraman involved had to be alert or we couldn't take the shot.

George knows exactly what he wants. He knows how to talk to the actors. He's like big daddy, which is very comforting, and which a lot of actors need, especially the women.

It wasn't until I was working with George Schaefer that I could be a part of a production from the beginning of the project — when the script first came in, through the casting, script changes, shooting, editing, mixing until I put it on the air. It was a wonderful time.

At first I was too shy to make suggestions. I would discuss some ideas with Bob Hartung, who was now the associate producer on the *Hallmark* shows. If he thought they were worthy, he would tell George. I was thrilled when George accepted them. Finally, he encouraged me to speak out and not feel I had to go through Bob. George never put me down — he took ideas he felt he could use and ignored the rest.

Budgeting's one thing I always kept out of. I didn't want to know anything about the money, but I was always involved in the preliminary casting — making up lists for the star parts and feature parts. I had an excellent reference library, all kinds of books and bios. We eventually signed up a casting director to do the negotiating and final casting.

In the live and tape TV days, we would set up a limit, a top for the actors. Gradually, when we were able to get some real film stars, who hadn't done television, the agency said, "Pay them." Well, once you start doing that, the word gets around. The agents always know, and there was no way to stop the climb. You couldn't have a top anymore because the top was meaningless. Look what's happening in the screen world now — an actor works three days and gets five million dollars.

A couple of actors asked me if I had any desire to direct. I think I could do it as far as the mechanics, but I was too shy and too intimidated by the actors to have the courage to tell them what I wanted. Any director I've worked for who's not been "in charge," sort of falls apart. It's all right to listen to everybody and his mother, but don't just take everybody's advice. That was what was so good about George. He was a very secure person in what he knew and how he arrived at it.

When we were doing *The Lark*, one of the main cameras broke down and George had to continue the show making do with the remaining three cameras. Watching him, I wanted to sing my theme song again — "There's no business like show business." He would say, "Take two — three, you're released to the cell — one, you're going to get ..." He thought so fast, didn't freeze or panic.

It was in a crisis like that when the propmen forgot they were just in charge of props, and people didn't say, "That's not my department." They all worked together. That teamwork's a wonderful thing to see — when it happens.

After I worked with George for a long time, I began realizing that at the beginning of every show, he would be saying things like, "I don't know. I think it's time I retired. I'd like to go to Hawaii and retire. Why am I doing this job?" And I'd think, What is it with him?

That was his way of showing nervousness, I believe. And yet, once he got started, all of that would disappear. He was very gung ho. And it made me feel better because I wasn't the only one to be nervous and worried. I really think George was just wonderful. To this day, he's a friend, not just somebody I worked with. A dear, dear man. A dear person.

# East Coast-West Coast: 1955 to 1963

DuMont produced shows through the early years. In 1949 they launched Sid Caesar and Imogene Coca in *Admiral Broadway Revue*, which later changed into *Your Show of Shows* on NBC. In 1950, Jackie Gleason became the headliner on *Cavalcade of Stars*, where he developed all his great characterizations and sketches, including *The Honeymooners*. The show was a hit but was lured away from DuMont by CBS in 1952.

By 1955, the DuMont Network proved no longer able to compete and closed down. The company later merged with a local radio station, WNEW, to form the Metropolitan Broadcasting Company, operating the old DuMont television station in New York, Channel 5. In 1957, Metropolitan Broadcasting was bought by John Kluge, and merged with several other entities to become Metromedia.

Television had become firmly established as a big business and a major factor in American home life. Shows that are now considered classics dominated the schedule. Although CBS had risen to where it had ten of the top fifteen shows in the Nielsen ratings, ABC had finally broken into that charmed circle, thanks to Walt Disney. *Disneyland*, which ranked sixth in the 1954-55 season, was fourth in 1955-56. Rounding out the top five were *The $64,000 Question*, *I Love Lucy*, *The Ed Sullivan Show*, and *The Jack Benny Show* — all on CBS. NBC's highest show, number seven, was *You Bet Your Life*, starring Groucho Marx.

\* \* \*

**Buzz Kulik:** I never worked with McCleery, but his show at NBC, *Matinee Theatre*, was designed to work with a really sparse set. We used the same *Matinee Theatre* technique on earlier shows that I did. If you're prepared to accept that "the drama isn't about having a big house," I think it makes for a wonderful, interesting, different kind of theatre that we just don't do anymore. We were younger and willing to take more chances and make more concessions.

In 1955, I went under contract to CBS, where I stayed for five years. I did a season of *You Are There*, which was a dramatization of a historic moment with modern day reporters. It was modeled, once again, after a successful radio show, and it really worked well on television.

Then, for three seasons, I directed *Climax*, which was an hour show every two weeks. With *Climax*, as with *Lux*, each production had its own problems. Each show had to be approached on its own merits.

The producer had to be aware of the fact that when he had fifty-two shows to make on a budget, he had to be able to rob Peter to pay Paul. He knew that if he agreed to do one show with a greater number of sets, a greater number of actors, it was going to be more costly. But if he did another show with fewer sets and actors, it'd even itself out. That's pretty much the way we did it until things went crazy at the end. John Frankenheimer led the way and off we went, trying to top each other. In my opinion, that really was not what the live television era was all about. It played better as "kitchen drama."

Production started to get very, very big in live television and go beyond the bounds that it should, from the standpoint of good drama. For example, I did a *Playhouse 90* dramatizing the death of Benito Mussolini, where I took the cameras outside and shot up in Franklin Canyon. The show, which was produced only eight years after the *Kraft* show, cost about three hundred thousand dollars for an hour-and-a-half show. I did several *Playhouse 90*s, and after that I left CBS. I started moving over to film and essentially stayed there. That was around 1960 — just about the end of the live tape era.

**Fielder Cook:**  I came back east for some *Kraft Theatre*s. Then, in 1956, Franklin Schaffner, George Roy Hill, Worthington Miner, and I formed an independent production company called Unit Four. We did, every other week, a prestige, live, hour drama, on NBC on Tuesday nights called *The Kaiser Aluminum Hour*. It lasted for about a year.

It got its Emmys and awards and marvelous ratings. Kaiser [Henry J. Kaiser, president of Kaiser Steel and Kaiser Motors] would review some of these programs in Hawaii. The old man fired us all because he thought that we were a little too radical. We did a production of *Oedipus*, and one or two others, that he felt were exceedingly unkind to American womanhood.

Then we all went freelance. We went to *Playhouse 90,* the first hour-and-a-half, and the last of the long shows, and did those out here.

**Franklin Schaffner:**  Our first Unit Four show was broadcast out of NBC. The network feed was still principally by kinescope. Because of this, there were delayed broadcasts from place to place in the country.

There is always a certain inherent difficulty when you have three different producer-directors, but none the less we tried to vary the content show by show within our own schedule, so that it was tasteful, provocative, and entertaining. It did not matter whether it was a light comedy or *Antigone* so long as it represented what the producer-director thought was a fair presentation of his individual taste.

Our understanding with NBC was that we had creative control of the show. Of course, NBC had also given Henry Kaiser the understanding that *he* had creative control over the show. Because of the delay, we must have done eight *Kaiser Aluminum Hour* shows before Henry Kaiser found out the program content. Kaiser took the position that when we formed this company and agreed to do this dramatic series, we were supposed to do programs about motherhood and America! That was the first we had heard of this. Eventually, this misunderstanding led to a falling out that resulted in Kaiser canceling the series. So, we were paid off and then bumped.

When *Playhouse 90* started, I spent two or three years on that. Martin Manulis produced it for two years, after which there was a series of producers. My first experience with tape came in the second year of *Playhouse 90* — not that it went to tape, but we did use tape sequences.

Around 1960, I moved to Los Angeles, where I signed a three-picture deal with Twentieth Century-Fox. The first project had the rug pulled from under it, so I went back to television. It wasn't until 1962 that I did my first film. Somewhere between 1962 and 1964, Fielder Cook and I formed The Directors Company and did the *DuPont Show of the Week* for three years, but by 1967 I had gradually phased out of television.

**George Roy Hill:**  Except for their length, *Playhouse 90* used pretty much the same technique as *Kraft*. Generally, I was allotted about six weeks to do a *Playhouse 90*, including the preparation and everything. Rehearsal was pretty much the same as on hour shows, except there was a little more time, perhaps an extra day of camera blocking in the studio, and an extra couple of days of rehearsal.

The difference was that you didn't have to do one every three weeks. You'd do, say, three *Playhouse 90*s a year and they weren't always back to back, so you had more time to prepare and work on a script.

**John Frankenheimer:**  Martin Manulis called me to see if I would direct a show called *The Best of Broadway*, which was plays, staged for television. He only wanted me to do the camera for that, and I wouldn't just be a camera director.

He said, "Well, the director is Alfred Lunt."

I said, "I'm sorry, not even for Lunt would I do that. I'm not just a camera director."

It turned out that what he really wanted was an interview with me, because two weeks later he was sent out here to California to do *Climax*, and he brought me with him. That was CBS's big, expensive, hour-long dramatic show which was in terrible trouble. We came out in February of 1955, and we won the Emmy for Best Dramatic show. I had a choice of which scripts I wanted to do — the things I didn't want were done by the other director.

Then I did a movie in the summer of 1956 based on a television show that I had done on *Climax*. The movie was called *The Young Stranger*, the television show had been named *Deal a Blow*. Both were written by the same man, Robert Durocher, and both had the same actor, James MacArthur.

I hated the experience of doing the movie, but I knew that it was only temporary, because I was going back for the new hour-and-a-half dramatic show that CBS had, *Playhouse 90*. I did the first one, the last one, and every third one in between. It was one every three weeks during the season, and then we got two days off. I don't know how the hell I did that, but I did it for three years — over fifty *Playhouse 90*s. The quote that Sidney Blackmer used, that I rather liked, was, "It was like summer stock in an iron lung."

We were live at six-thirty to the East Coast, kinescope on the West Coast. I had the same assistant director, the same script girl, the same crew, all those people. Most of the time, we used four cameras, sometimes more. We couldn't get some actors that we wanted — we couldn't get Cary

Grant, we couldn't get John Wayne. But we got very good actors because they wanted to appear on that show, its prestige was tremendous.

On *Playhouse 90* there were certain things that didn't quite work out. Nineteen fifty-six was the opening of the series, and I was supposed to direct *Requiem for a Heavyweight*. I cut that show from a hundred-ninety-page script down to what it was, and, in fact, even cast it. Then CBS decided it was to be the second show of the series rather than the first show, so Ralph Nelson did it.

**Ralph Nelson:** *Requiem for a Heavyweight* was in the big CBS studio at Television City. The first show, *Forbidden Area*, was adapted by Rod Serling from a Pat Frank book, and directed by John Frankenheimer. It was not a success at all, but with *Requiem, Playhouse 90* just exploded.

The procedure was that the star of the succeeding week would host the current one. Eddie Cantor introduced *Requiem for a Heavyweight*. I had never met him, but he came up to me after the dress rehearsal to tell me we really had something remarkable.

In *Playhouse 90* there were six acts. If you got through the first act and it went well, you just prayed that there'd be no breakdown in the second act and so on. The great advantage of live was that everybody's adrenalin was working overtime. Also, the audience was very forgiving, because they knew it was live.

Marty Manulis did two or three years of *Playhouse 90*, and then he was burned out. They brought in a number of different producers — I did one for Herb Brodkin, *Out of Dust*.

**Arthur Penn:** I worked with Paul Newman a couple of times in live TV. I did a Korean War piece with him, and I did a show with him called *The Battler*, in which he played a punch-drunk prizefighter.

I did one experimental *Studio One* as a summer replacement. After a while I did a lot of other stuff at NBC. When NBC decided to go to color, they kicked it off with a number of dramatic shows that were big and very expensive.

I did a couple of *Producers' Showcase*s, including *State of the Union*, for Fred Coe. He was the premiere producer at NBC by that time, so we had an awful lot of freedom. It was produced here in New York at the Brooklyn studio, the one that's still used today. *Peter Pan* was one of the scripts that they did.

Fred and I also did another series, called *Playwrights 56*. It was done mostly out of New York, but a little bit was done in California. I did anything that Fred Coe was involved in, up through '55.

Around that time *Playhouse 90* went on the air, paying ten thousand dollars a show. For us, who had been working for four hundred dollars a week, that was huge money. Martin Manulis signed up a whole bunch of us and asked how many shows we could do. I just signed on to do four, and *The Miracle Worker* was one of them. Those four were enough for me.

**John Frankenheimer:**  *The Last Tycoon*, if I recall, was in March of '57. It was written by Don Mankiewicz, and starred Keenan Wynn, Peter Lorre, Viveca Lindfors, and Lee Remick, who'd just done the Kazan picture, *A Face in the Crowd*. She was beautiful.

*The Comedian* was a terribly difficult show, technically, because all the shots showing a show within a show were planned. It wasn't just a random "Take this, take that" — everything was staged.

I got out of my CBS contract, moved back to New York, went freelance and did some shows for NBC. I did *The Indian Who Raised the Flag at Iwo Jima*, about Ira Hayes, with Lee Marvin; I did *The Turn of the Screw* with Ingrid Bergman; I did all the Hemingway stuff for CBS; and then I came back and did the last *Playhouse 90: Journey to the Day* by Roger Hirson, produced by Fred Coe.

I did about seventy-five, maybe eighty shows with Martin Manulis, and only four shows with Fred Coe. They were both superb producers — Manulis much more of a politician than Coe, Coe more of a creative artist than Manulis. Manulis was good on script, and wonderful in crisis situations. He had an emergency every week, and he'd bend and roll with the punches so well. Manulis pulled that thing off for three years, doing a show every week. It was unbelievable how he did it, how he got all those elements to work. It took three men to replace him when he left *Playhouse 90* — Coe, John Houseman, and Herbert Brodkin.

Coe couldn't do as many shows as Manulis, because he got much more involved. He worked harder on the scripts; Manulis left much more to the director. People had problems with Coe, but I never did. I really liked him a great deal, and I think I did my best work with him: *Days of Wine and Roses*, *The Old Man and the Sea*, *For Whom the Bell Tolls*, and *Journey to the Day*, and all of that work was really superb.

By that time James Aubrey had come into CBS, and had decided he wanted no more live television as we knew it. The television management wanted bigger and bigger shows. They sent us out to Mulholland Drive to film *Korea*. The budgets were going up, it was coming to end, and I just decided that really wasn't for me, there was no future in it.

About that time I was offered *Breakfast at Tiffany's* with Marilyn Monroe. Then Marilyn Monroe fell out of it, and the producers cast Audrey Hepburn. Audrey Hepburn quote "never heard of me," so I was paid off for not directing it. Then my agents got very guilty and got me another picture which turned out to be a thing called *The Young Savages*. I think I did *The Birdman of Alcatraz*, which was my third movie, because I knew they couldn't call it *The Young Birdman*! I was just thirty when I did the movie with Burt Lancaster, and that was in 1960. I've been doing movies ever since.

**Ralph Nelson:**   It has always bridled me that you work with a great many producers, and so many of them don't know their job. For one reason or another they get the title "Producer," and, as the director, you found that you were doing a lot of their work as well. This held true later in motion pictures as well.

I wanted to leave *Playhouse 90*, because they were giving me all the comedies. Comedy is the hardest thing to do on live television without an audience, so I was not too happy. I spoke to Hubbell Robinson, who was then head of production in New York, overseeing the entire network, and he agreed to allow me to take over the producing of *Climax*.

I had a couple of directors working for me. I had to exercise restraint, because, naturally, I would have done it differently, but I wanted to encourage them to do the best that they could.

I had two standbys — Paul Nickell and Buzz Kulik. Paul had a strange career. When I first went to CBS, he was on the staff there, and then later he moved out to California, as we all did. Then he went back to teaching, I think, at the University of North Carolina, because the stress had gotten too much for him — he broke out in shingles. He just retired entirely from directing.

I produced the *Climax* series for a while, and then CBS kept sending me back to New York for all their big specials. I was hired to direct *This Happy Breed* with Noel Coward, *Aladdin* by Cole Porter, and *Cinderella* for Rodgers and Hammerstein. Julie Andrews was Cinderella, Edie

Adams was the Fairy Godmother, Howard Lindsay and Dorothy Stickney (husband and wife) were the King and Queen. Alice Ghostley and Kaye Ballard were the two ugly sisters. We did it in tiny theatres that were converted to television stages. With a live orchestra hidden behind some scenery, we deliberately hired thin extras because we were that crowded for space! That was about 1958. Later it was revived, but they couldn't get Julie Andrews, so they used Lesley Ann Warren. I had nothing to do with that production.

Another was *The Nutcracker Suite*, with the New York City Ballet Company, as a Christmas show for *Playhouse 90*. In rehearsals, the program assistant had told me we were five minutes short. I went to George Balanchine and told him. He thought for a minute and said, "I'll tell Tchaikovsky to write more music!"

**Delbert Mann:**   After I left the *Philco* show and after Fred left it, we did the *Producers' Showcase* in '55 and '56. I did *Yellowjack* and *Darkness at Noon* in New York and then we came out here in June to do *The Petrified Forest* with Henry Fonda, Betty [Lauren] Bacall, and Humphrey Bogart. In September we came back out to do *Our Town*. They were both from the Burbank Studios.

*Our Town* was one of NBC's first dramatic shows in color. It was all live, even the music was not pre-recorded. The orchestra was piped in from another studio, our people sang to the orchestra's sound which they were hearing over speakers. It was an unusual show with a stylization of the sets that worked very well for us. A hit song came out of it, "Love and Marriage."

I was in New York most of the time up until about '59. I stayed with NBC almost exclusively until about '56 or '57. Then I went freelance and began to work with other networks. When you were doing a series like *Playhouse 90*, or *Philco*, you had a continuing staff, the same people, week in and week out, and only when you switched over to another network or another show, did you become involved with an entirely new set of people. For example, *Omnibus* had its own team of cameramen, designers, lighting technicians, and so forth. I did several of the *Omnibus* Sunday afternoon shows for Robert Saudek, but not very much else for CBS until '58, when I did *Playhouse 90* out here.

*The Plot To Kill Stalin* was the opening show of the *Playhouse 90* third season. It was one of the bigger shows that we mounted in that particular season, with a lot of production values, an unusual amount for that time. Luck was part of it, but it was an unusually smooth and error-free production.

**Livia Granito:** After *Matinee Theatre* went off in '58, there was nothing back in New York as a director. That fall, Albert McCleery got the *Ellery Queen* series to do, and there were four directors on that. He hired me, Boris Sagal, Alan Cooke, and Walter Grauman. It was a fun show, done one-a-week at night for prime time.

We were photographing it very much the same way as *Matinee Theatre*, but we had more production value. We did them like a live show, in the studio at NBC. Although it was tape, we didn't stop, because it was too expensive, and the budget mandated that we keep the time down.

The problem with the show, as with a lot of mystery things, is that they do not translate well. When it comes to whodunits, you can fudge a lot on the printed page, but the minute you have to see it, that's another story. It only lasted about thirteen shows, and I did about four or five of them.

I had a friend who had started working when I first did television, who was now an independent producer in New York. She and her husband were producing a series called *Play of the Week*, which was the very prestigious sort of thing you'd find now on public television. Their emphasis was on Broadway plays and classics. I worked on the first three, in the spring of '59. I was associate producer when they did *Medea* with Judith Anderson. Jose Quintero directed it. It was all very top drawer material.

All kinds of people who later went on to do other things were just starting. Bob Rafaelson was working in one of the offices as a script editor. I was working for Louis Friedman, who was a producer then, and who went on to big things in public television.

The story gets a little personal here. I had been dating one of the script editors in Los Angeles. In the fall of 1959, we got married in New York because both our families lived there, but we came out to Los Angeles to live because he was working out here, and at that point the business was really out here. A few months after I was married, I got a call from CBS to direct a soap. I said "yes" right away and then had misgivings because I was three months pregnant. I thought, how can I do this without telling them? So I told them, and Larry White [a network program executive] said, "Well, you won't be on any closeups, so what difference does it make?"

It was every day, and there was too much work to do. You couldn't do a show every day. Physically, there wasn't the time to rehearse and put it on camera. We had two directors and we alternated.

I must say that it was another very wonderful time where everyone was just delightful to me. I worked on the show until two months before I had the baby. Then they got somebody who had worked on *Matinee* to replace me and do the show until I came back. I stuck until it went off the air, which was the end of that season.

**Walter Grauman:**  I had directed Patricia Barry on *Matinee Theatre*. She played the Bette Davis role in *Blind Victory* with John Baragrey. She liked my direction, and we became friends. Her husband, Philip Barry Jr., was producing in New York. When she got back there, she touted me to Phil, who brought me to New York to direct *Alcoa/Goodyear*. I did *Your Every Wish*, with a big cast. It was a comedy, written by Albert Goldsmith. I'll bet we rewrote the third act five times, until we got what was the best we could do at the time. When we went on the air, old Tom Burry, who was a brilliant technical director, was as busy as he had ever been. Phil said, "I have never in my life seen so many cuts in one show." I think I had four hundred twenty-five camera cuts in the hour.

**Fielder Cook:**  *The United States Steel Hour Presents The Theatre Guild on the Air* was the only show left that was live. *Theatre Guild* had the longest history in television then. It was a very well-financed and prestigious show, not just some of the productions of The Theatre Guild. They did mostly classics, some of the prestigious O'Neills, like *Anna Christie*, but very few modern playwrights.

In the late fifties, because everything else was tape, I'd choose a couple of scripts a year from them, just so I'd have a chance to do a live show. The only reason they did it live was because the last year or two it was cheaper than tape. By the time it was over, the show was being milked to death for every nickel they could get out of it.

I really was the mortician of the end of live television. I did the last *Playhouse 90*, the last *Philco*, the last *Studio One*, and the last *Theatre Guild on the Air*.

# Writers and Actors

Although New York actors appeared overwhelmingly in shows produced in the east, Hollywood talent showed up very early. In 1946, Helen Parrish, who had been featured in a number of movies (including two hits starring Deanna Durbin), was the host of *Hour Glass*. Johnny Downs, star of a host of college musical films, appeared with Kyle MacDonnell in a musical series, *Girl About Town*. With the proliferation of drama, more and more stars and featured players made the hegira to New York.

At first — because they were essential — there was a moderate amount of money allocated for actors, but there was little or none for writers. However, as soon as budgets became somewhat more generous, writers were sought after and nurtured. The flowering of the Golden Age began.

\* \* \*

**John Frankenheimer:** I think every medium's a writer's medium. No one can do anything unless it's there on the page.

**Paul Bogart:** Live television was a direct descendant of the theatre. It was centered mostly in New York, and was written and acted by theatre people, actors who were working in the theatre during the day and on television at night. The writers were also trying to get into the theatre, so the scripts were very theatrical. They were based entirely on ideas, on dialogue, and on feelings. Not on car chases! The stuff that came out of Hollywood was almost all film series.

**Fielder Cook:** Basically, I do everything for myself and out of the writer and the actor. My personal care is telling a story and getting actors to become characters. In the theatre, if you don't do that you have nothing, because there's nobody on the stage but an actor. I would make it almost a condition that a writer be at rehearsals because I love working with them. If a line is wrong or the balance is wrong, the best person to help is the writer. He should be there to see it, because he's going to fix it better than a director or the actors, who don't know how to write. But there were some directors who didn't want writers there at all, because they would make changes themselves.

**John Peyser:**  On *Suspense* and *Studio One*, we used brand new writers, we used radio writers, we used theatre writers, we used everybody. All the names from the Golden Age, people like Tad Mosel, were dug up out of the woodwork. We found them, agents found them, universities turned them out. There was an outpouring of tremendous talent.

**Martin Ritt:**  I was mostly my own producer and developed my own material. We stayed mostly with adaptations. Very few originals were used because there's no time to fix those and you could be in serious trouble if they didn't have some fundamental structure that worked.

I worked with Abe Polonsky and with Walter Bernstein, with whom I did two films. I worked with a lot of other people too, because of the time factor in preparing a show a week.

**George Roy Hill:**  We tried to find our shows two ahead at least. Then we'd have a couple that would be in longer-range planning. We'd get one original to every adaptation.

There were a lot of very good writers who were writing exclusively for television. Reginald Rose was one, and the fellow that did *The Twilight Zone*, Rod Serling. We worked with the writers and I always invited them to come to the rehearsals. I find them more often helpful than not, and I can't remember ever having any hassle with them.

**Buzz Kulik:**  I worked with a number of writers. It was absolutely mandatory that the writer had to be with us at all times, from rehearsal through shooting, because we really used to rewrite. The writers got paid a nominal fee and were not given another salary, which was terrific for us but not so hot for the writer, because that was a time when he could be writing something else.

It was the most extraordinary experience when I went into film, because I'd always had a writer with me. Some writers today say they'd be more than willing to be on the set, and I've worked with a number of guys who do, but many more just give lip service to it. I don't blame them — they've got to earn a living.

**Fielder Cook:** *Philco Playhouse* came in under Fred Coe and blew the horizon off for writers. Worthington Miner was creating original forms technically, but Fred set up the challenge that the hour should belong to the human heart; that we should get the best drama that we could and return to the mode that the television tube is the best for, which is its intimacy.

What Fred did, for the first time, was to create original forms, to turn over a massive amount of television time to writers. He developed them, nurtured them, and gave them a home. He was a brilliant editor, a brilliant producer, and a good director.

He created the nucleus — the Chayefskys, the JP Millers, the Tad Mosels, the whole box of writers; and the directors from Vincent Donehue to Arthur Penn to Delbert Mann. They blended, so that between the writers and directors was a symbiotic relationship. Fred was the big daddy on top of it all, blasting out these marvelous things on Sunday nights. My memory is that Fred's writers were intensely loyal. I can't imagine them being on any other program in those "Golden Days." Each might write six or eight shows a year.

**Delbert Mann:** Fred Coe gathered together a group of young writers and inspired them to work for him and with him. He never, to my knowledge, really told them what to do. He would explore things with them, he would pressure them, he would guide them, or he would make suggestions in a way that inspired them to do their best work.

It's very hard to articulate exactly what he did, but my clearest memory of it is when we were doing an adaptation of *Yellowjack* on the series *Producers' Showcase*, in the winter of 1955. It was the first show that I did for them, produced out at the old Brooklyn Studios, an hour-and-a-half show in color — one of the network's first dramatic color shows. JP Miller did the adaptation of the Sidney Howard play. We had a marvelous cast — Lorne Greene, Wally Cox, Jackie Cooper, Phil Abbott, Eve Marie Saint, Rod Steiger, Dennis O'Keefe.

The evening of the first reading and rehearsal, Fred called JP and me to his office in the RCA Building. We sat up there for about two hours as the sun set over the Hudson River, Fred talking about the script and what could or should be done with it. He ripped it apart. His premise was, "Don't be too slavishly adherent to the Sidney Howard play. That's what you have done. You have just cut this play, really. Now, television can do more than that. Television needs different sorts of things, and we can make this something special." Fred probed that with JP, while I sat there and listened. He absolutely destroyed the script in front of the writer's eyes, and yet, in two hours' time, sent him out of there full of energy, full of enthusiasm for rewriting the whole damn script — which he did. Each morning at rehearsal we would wait for JP to arrive on the subway from Queens with the next scene, which he had sat up all night writing. He did a wonderful job with it.

Fred's writers — Paddy Chayefsky, David Shaw, Tad Mosel, and Horton Foote — all tell essentially the same story. They would get an idea, come to Fred, and outline it in four or five sentences. If Fred thought it was valid his answer would be, "Okay, write it." They would set off, charged up to the skies to do the best work they could possibly do for this man who had such faith and such trust in them.

Writers were always there during rehearsals. They had to be, simply because of the pressure of time, and the necessity to cut to fit the air time. Scripts would be long, scripts would be short, things would have to be changed. Scenes would not work. It was a bonanza for the writers to have that experience, and for the directors, such as myself — who were learning our craft, growing up in the business — to have the opportunity to work with the writers on a day-to-day basis. It was the routine way to do it, but it was the best training ground for all of us to learn to work together. People like Paddy, who went off on his own for theatre and film, always said that kind of experience was the best thing that ever happened to him. I think all the writers feel the same way, and I noticed the directors do.

Each time that I have done a film or a television special, I have re-found, over the years, that the gathering together of the cast around the table for three or four days of reading rehearsals with the writer there — similar to the first rehearsals of a live television show, similar to the first rehearsals of a stage show — is the most valuable thing that you can possibly do. It's the way that I just insist upon working, if the script is such that it allows for it.

If you're doing an action script, obviously it does you no good to sit around the table and talk about the car goes over the cliff at this point. But when you have actors who have enough master scenes or emotional scenes played together, it's just essential. To talk through the scenes, to work through them, to rewrite them, as the writer has the opportunity to listen, to hear, to participate in the discussion, and to take the problem off and bring it back the next day with work redone, to hear that, to change it again. To have the writers present and to participate in those discussions, is a joy, and a rare experience.

**George Schaefer:** Having come from the theatre, I treat the writers intelligently, as I do in film too, for that matter. I rehearse when I'm shooting, and want the writer there because one makes good changes in the course of rehearsal. I would always have the writers around for the final run-throughs.

I think television was a co-mingling medium because the basic material was obviously the writer's in the same way that it is in the theatre, but one of the tricks of the director's trade was making it appear to be less restricted than one would suspect from locking a small cast in a studio at the same time it was being done. Delbert Mann mentioned that he ran some kinescopes, like his original *Marty*. There'd be a taxicab coming down the street, and his kids would say, "How did you do that? I don't believe that was live. You must have been out somewhere." It was quite amazing how much visual breadth you got from the shows.

In the theatre the writer has the final authority and can say to the director or the actor, or the producer for that matter, "These are the words. This is the way it is or you can't do it." That is not true in television, and certainly isn't true in film, but I think by treating the writers the way one does in the theatre — yet with the writer instinctively knowing that in the final analysis the producer/director has the decision — you get a kind of give and take that is terribly healthy. I've never had any problem with writers. Perhaps I've tended to use the same ones over and over again because we work together so well.

*Little Moon of Alban* was written for television [by James Costigan]. Following the second production, it was done as a play. Mildred Alberg wanted to do it in the theatre and wanted me to direct it, but I couldn't see it. I love that play, and it would make a great movie, but it's a camera piece. It needs to be done with infinite realism and the wonderful Irish verbal poetry that comes out of it. Instead, they did it in the theatre with the same star, Julie Harris, and a Mielziner set that was all kind of symbolism. It just didn't work. I was glad that I hadn't done it because I have such happy memories of it.

James Costigan and I have done a whole series of things. He wrote *A War of Children* for me, a movie we shot in Ireland about two Irish boys, that is still completely topical. It won the Emmy for the best show. He also wrote *In This House of Brede*, the screenplay of the Rumer Godden novel that we filmed in England and Ireland, and he did that brilliant adaptation of Scott Fitzgerald's *Last of the Belles*, that we filmed down in Georgia. A great writer, James.

Hallmark had a contest for original writing and *The Joke and the Valley* was one of the three winners. It was Jerry McNeely's first script.

**Ralph Nelson:** Rod Serling was so prolific, the stuff just poured out of him. He was an incredible man, because he got to where he could dictate all the scripts. Carol [Rod Serling's wife] said that as Rod was dictating, he used to play all the characters. He was not a terribly good actor, but he became a good narrator on *The Twilight Zone*.

Rod had done me a favor by appearing in *The Man in the Funny Suit*, so as a return favor, I directed one *Twilight Zone*. It was with Phyllis Kirk and Keenan Wynn as a writer who dictates people and they come to life. Then he made Rod disappear at the end. I suggested that, and Rod didn't want to do it at first. So we shot it, and then later, in the editing, he agreed to disappear.

Rod won about five Emmys in a row. *Patterns* was his big hit. It was done on the *Kraft Theatre*, directed by Fielder Cook. Rod was afraid of being a one-shot writer, and then *Requiem* came along, and later *The Comedian* and *A Town is Turned to Dust*.

With *Requiem*, Rod was living in Westport, Connecticut, and he had to go back there. I needed some final changes, so I phoned him and said, "This is what I'd like to do."

He said, "You go ahead and do it yourself."

The average writer, particularly working for television, is just interested in going on to the next assignment. I had one notable exception, and that was Sterling Silliphant. Sterling's even more prolific than Rod, but he prostitutes himself. He writes some of the worst material in the world — and he will agree to that. On a film called *Charlie*, he attended the rehearsals, then he went to Europe. While we were filming in Boston, I called him because we were running into a very sticky problem. He came back immediately. We finished filming at the MGM studios in Hollywood, where he had an office. He would come down to the set to watch and to make additional changes that I wanted. In the editing process, I was really stuck, so he would come in and try to help me. I'm surprised that he didn't get an award nomination, because that was superior writing.

**Paul Bogart:** The writers were on the set if you wanted them. If you didn't, they were just as happy to take the money and run because they were glad to have sold a script. Writers knew how to get the actor from one scene to another and give him a chance to change his tie or whatever. Sometimes the writers stayed with a particular show, if they made a good connection with a producer who liked them and developed scripts with them. Most of the writers for television were learning their craft as well. The Paddy Chayefskys and Sumner Locke Elliots were not everywhere.

A lot of television was ex-radio stuff that made the transition, like *The Aldrich Family* and *The Goldbergs*. On *One Man's Family*, the characters all predated the director. They were invented by Carlton Morse who did that story for years on the radio. Each week, we had to invent a whole new life for the characters. These half hour shows were done in five days. We would read on the first day, then start rehearsing as soon as possible, while trying not to fight about the content, which was usually weak.

**John Peyser:** You were dealing with actors from three different areas — stage actors, radio actors, and the occasional screen actor. All three techniques were absolutely different. The radio actors were wonderful at the readings. The stage actors were very good at acting, but their projection was wrong. If they had no stage experience, the screen actors had tremendous difficulty trying to sustain a performance through an hour or a half-hour program. You had to merge these three different kinds of actors into television acting. It was a school of acting that flourished and disappeared, because it has no place to practice any more. Some tremendous talents came out of it — Paul Newman, Rod Steiger, Ernest Borgnine. A lot of ladies came out of it, too — Eva Marie Saint, Grace Kelly.

**George Roy Hill:** It's awfully hard to make a generalization because there are so many exceptions to the rule, but I would say that New York actors who were active in live television were more used to the form, because not so many live television shows came out of Hollywood, until *Playhouse 90*. Here in New York, there was almost a repertory company of actors who did all the live shows: *Danger, Philco Playhouse, Studio One, Kraft*. Most actors would fly from California to New York if you wanted them for a specific part.

You develop your own style of working with actors. Directing them is such a personal thing that the form of communication you have with them is individual. Some directors are very *laissez-faire*, and will just give the actors the general situation, and will encourage them to improvise and make things out of the moment. Others will let them block themselves. Others are very specific in what they want, down to line readings. I tend to be more specific than not. That's just the technique that I've developed, and it's not necessarily the best.

There were tremendous foul ups. There is one story that Paul Newman tells. He was standing in front of a fireplace playing a scene with a leading lady. One camera was there taking a waist shot, another camera was out on the terrace where they were going to end the scene. In the middle of the scene, she was to go out and he was to follow her. On the air, the camera on the terrace failed. They were still standing in front of the fireplace and if they left the scene, there wouldn't be an end to the show. The floor manager got on his hands and knees just out of camera range. He put his arms around both of their legs so that they couldn't move. They had to pretend that nothing was happening as they went through the end of the scene.

I remember a show where an extra came out of a saloon too early. He ran into an actor who was supposed to go through the door and get shot inside. As a result, the sound effects man shot him before he got inside. He went in and realized that there were no shots so he had to clutch his breast and fall in silence.

I did a thing with Paul Muni where he could not remember his lines. I had him play it as a deaf man and put a plug in his ear with the floor manager's receiver on him. If I gave him the first two or three words of every line, he could finish it. He was a marvelous actor, with marvelous concentration, but he had such a slow playing pace he would drag things out endlessly.

**George Schaefer:**   I like working with actors and I like to make them feel that they're doing it all themselves. My idea of a well-directed cast is one where all the actors think they've had no direction at all, so everything they're doing is full of conviction, as though that's the only way it could possibly be.

I practically never give readings as such, unless I am really desperate or I have a real klutz. I'll deal with ideas, with emotions and interplay, experimenting, striking out in different ways, asking questions and letting them come up with the answers, so that very often, at the end of two or three hours of rehearsal, even though I've had a scheme to begin with, I will have altered that scheme considerably.

Something else you learn working with people: some actors and actresses have good first instincts, but some good actors and actresses have terrible ones. If you let them follow their own first instincts, it will be disastrous. Yet, with just a little guidance, and saying, "Oh, look, want to try that? All right, try that once ... Terrible, no, it didn't work ... Were you happy? No, of course you weren't happy, all right, go back and do it this way ..." you kind of push them around and mold them and then they end up giving tremendous performances. Unfortunately, it is not true that sensitivity and intelligence always go hand in hand with acting ability. In the great ones, I guess they do. In the Julie Harrises of this world it all comes together.

We used a great variety of people but, nonetheless, an awful lot of them we used over and over again. For one thing, when we were live like that, we were so dependent on them that they had to deliver. We couldn't shoot around them, we couldn't protect them with extra takes or any of that. They were either perfect or they were no good. It was a very strong discipline.

The wonderful thing about live, or even taped, television is that you're not locked in, because you have a rehearsal period not unlike that in the theatre. You work a long hard day, and at the end of it you say, "Ehhhh, there's something not right." You come back the next day and say "All right, just for fun let's just play that same scene as though you really *hate* each other. You're playing it too much love story."

You run through it and rehearse it that way, and the actors bring things to it. And you say "Look what happened. See what you learned here." Then you start to put those pieces together and it grows from day to day and the only thing that matters is that final performance on the air.

Everything else leading up to that is by way of growth and experimentation and solidifying a certain kind of a pattern.

With multiple cameras you can do so much — in movies it's much more rigid. In the first day, if I've shot half of a ten-minute scene, it doesn't matter what inspiration I may get overnight, I can't go back. Whatever's on that film is final. It forces the director to be much more arbitrary.

I rehearse films in order to get the input of the author, to get rewrites, and to get the actors to understand what it is about. I'm really just approximating the final performance because when I finally break it down and film those three or four minutes a day — or whatever it is I'm lucky enough to get in the can — I want to be sure that the freshness and life of the performance is all happening in front of the camera.

Live is like the theatre, except you have that wonderful thing of not having to project. When I work in a theatre now I get irritated, because I sit in the back sometimes and say, "I can't hear it, can't see it. It's got to be bigger." Yet I know that basically what the actor or actress is doing is true and would look wonderful if I had a camera that could get right into their eyes.

**Paul Bogart:**   Actors were very busy in New York hopping from show to show. The best people in the world were working in television — Maureen Stapleton, Grace Kelly, Jason Robards. God, those actors were wonderful. I learned more from them than I have in the last twenty years.

It terrified some of them that millions of people would be watching them. If they pulled it off, it was an enormous sense of gratification. If they messed up, there was an enormous sense of disgrace. In one of those early *Armstrong*s, there was a five-minute teaser at the beginning to make sure the audience didn't switch to the next channel. George Grizzard was making his first appearance on television. He is an enormously solid actor, very certain of what he is doing. We rehearsed the scene where he is to meet this drug pusher on a street corner. The young boy who'd been sent in by casting — who was to appear only in that teaser scene — read the scene well. You could hire actors who had under five lines for a lower rate if you didn't bring them in until the day of the performance. Most actors can handle that. We go on the air, fade up on George waiting under this lamppost, and I cued the boy on. He came on and George said his first line which was something like, "Where've you been? I've been waiting."

And the kid said, "Heh, heh, heh," That's all he did. He just laughed. He could not think of what his first word was. George thought about that for a second and then made up some kind of line that encompassed the guy's line. He gave him yet another cue, and the kid went, "Heh, heh, heh," and giggled some more. It was hysterical. I thought it was the funniest thing I'd ever seen. I knew it was a potential disaster, but what can you do? George finally invented some speech to cover everything that had to be known — as any good actor would.

After we got off the air, I went up to George and thanked him for doing that. This kid had been hiding in a phone booth, where nobody could see him. As I was leaving the studio, on the third floor of the RCA Building, he came up to me and apologized. I said, "It's all right." He swore he would never act again in his life — and he didn't.

Once, I was on the air as an assistant on a show when an actor had an epileptic fit. Peg Lynch and Alan Bunce improvised a whole scene around this actor who had to be dragged out and put in an ambulance and sent to the hospital.

I did a show in which a leading actress was playing opposite her husband, who was solid as a rock. This was the wrap-up of the show where she explained the whole story. She forgot her lines so he kept inventing things to give her a cue that she might remember. Never came out of her. We came off the air early with no resolution to the story.

There were some actors who would leave little bits of paper around on the set with their lines on them to remind them of what they had to say. Some actors you can tell right to their face what their line is and they won't hear you, see you, or know you're there. That happened to Maurice Evans one night on live television. He said to me, "I'll never remember this passage, dear boy." He was wearing a headset at the time, playing a man defusing a bomb, who was supposed to be getting instructions over this headset. I said, "Don't worry. I'll cut into your headset and tell you your next line." He said, "Oh, that would be wonderful."

Well, as advertised, he forgot the passage. I said to the audio man, "Cut me in." Then I said, "Maurice, this is Paul. Your next line is — " and I gave him the line. Forget it. He didn't hear me. He only knew his panic. The other actor in the scene, Nicolas Coster, helped him out of it. All the information he was supposed to have gotten from Maurice, he made up himself.

I did a wonderful scene with George C. Scott and a girl named Angela Fountain, where George had been really solid throughout the entire rehearsal process. On the air, we were on tight close-ups back and forth between the girl and him. He lost his last line, and she said something to give him a little hint. I said to the cameraman, "Watch him. He's going to get up and walk to the fireplace, cause that's where the prop is and he'll associate his next line with the prop that's on the fireplace" — which he did. After we got off the air, he was gone like a shot. I went to Angela to thank her for having helped him get through the bad moment. She said, "Do you know what he did?" George had been smoking a cigarette and he put it out on her lap. She showed me her skirt where she had this large burn hole. I don't know if he even remembered that he had done it. But that's what happens.

After realizing that they were the ones that mattered and not me, I spent all my time working with the actors. What we're doing is communicating feelings and emotions, and that's what you have to capture. The camera became secondary, always secondary.

I would try my very best to make the actors feel secure. When we went on the air attempting an awful lot in a very heavy production, no matter how I felt, I tried to make the actors feel as though everything was just wonderful and going to be marvelous. Often, I would be in a state of great excitement and apprehension, but five minutes before we went on the air, I would visit the studio, go around to all the actors and the crew, and calmly wish them well. As we were counting down to two minutes, I would still be on the floor walking very slowly up into the control room, as if there was no hurry and that it was all under control, because I wanted them to feel good. After the door closed, I'd hyperventilate.

I never panicked. There was a lot of hollering in the control room — shouting orders and things like that. Sometimes I would be picked up on the microphones through the headsets. You could hear that little telephone-like voice when the cameramen wore their headsets loose because they hurt their ears. When we got off the air, I'd call my wife and ask, "How was the show?" She'd say, "I heard every word you said."

**Livia Granito:**   Of course I had problems with actors  from time to time, but I never have been afraid to say I didn't know something if I didn't know it, and I never was the type not to take suggestions from actors, if they were good ones. It's true though, that when actors work with a new director, they have a feeling of "show me" unless you come in with a reputation, in which case they'll swallow almost anything.

I must say also, the bigger the name of the actor that I worked with, the less trouble I had. One of the shows that was the most delightful to do was one in which I had an all-star, English, male cast. I had people like Reginald Denny, John Abbott, Philip Tonge, Alan Napier, and Lumsden Hare. I had never seen such amiable and charming men. It was a wonderful experience.

I had more of a problem the last year I was an AD for Albert. At that time he was producing and directing several of the *Cameo* shows, and he would get bored with rehearsal. A great deal of the rehearsal was strictly technical, in that the actors had to learn their lines and positions. He would have me take over those rehearsals, and that was good for me because I got to work directly with the actors.

One actor refused to work with me. It was more hurt pride than anything else. Since the director did not come to the rehearsal, he refused to rehearse. Finally, Albert had to come in and tell the guy, "You're either on this show the way I run it, which is she's taking the rehearsal, or you don't work for me." The actor decided to keep the job, and then we got along okay.

The *Cameo* technique, which McCleery had devised, was something that I used. It made many special demands on actors. In *Cameo* there were no sets, just pieces against black. We would put the furniture up on blocks and have people stand unnaturally close to each other, which did present problems to the actor. It necessitated very arbitrary positions where they would have to look into the camera when they didn't want to look into the camera; where a big move was two inches instead of two feet. Unless you had people who had worked the technique before, you could have lots of problems. Most of them hated it, and I can see why.

**Arthur Hiller:** I got into live television through *Matinee Theatre*, and into film through Ray Sackheim, who was a casting director on *Matinee Theatre*. Ray's brother, Bill Sackheim, was a producer at Screen Gems, and Ray told Bill how much he liked this young Canadian director. Bill told the head of Screen Gems, Fred Briskin, about me. What fascinated Fred Briskin was that he heard I talked to the actors! On their half-hour shows, they were not used to directors working with actors. They thought they'd just take their pictures and that was it.

I would say that most of the live television directors worked with the actors because most of them came out of the theatre, and the early film television directors were basically "B" directors from film who were into action.

Fred asked if he could come and watch me work. In a live television booth, even if you don't know what they're doing, it's terribly exciting and impressive. That's especially true for somebody who's never been in there before.

He was very impressed with what he saw, so he asked if he could listen to me give my notes to the actors between dress rehearsal and the show. He also wanted to watch the dress rehearsal, but I thought a stranger sitting in might disturb the actors. I said, "Just a minute, let me check with them."

I explained the situation, and they said it was all right, it wouldn't bother them. The actors asked me every question they'd asked me all week. They made me really sound good.

I loved *Playhouse 90*, because I had three weeks of rehearsal to work with the actors and to start my staging, which was very satisfying and really like doing a play in a sense. Then there was the added fun of the four days of camera blocking.

You didn't have that long rehearsal period in film. One time I was told that I could have a half-day rehearsal. In a sense, that pressured me just as much as live television. I turned it down, because in working with the actors, I would break down the characters, but I didn't have the time to bring it all back together. In film, quite often, what you really did was to go on the actors' instinctive approach to their characters. The level may not be as high, or you may not get as interesting a performance as you could get on a live television show.

Sometimes you got a surprise. I worked with Geraldine Page, and when we had our first read-through, if I hadn't known it was her, I would have said, "Out you go!" I would have thought I could do better just bringing somebody in off the street. She gave nothing on that reading. Then, in the first rehearsal, I saw little things happening. Every day it got better and better, until very soon, it was past what I was looking for. She was an exciting actress.

Generally, the scripts were written to allow for set and costume changes. On one show, I think it was *Bottom of the River*, there was a sequence with a scene and costume change. It started on a waist shot of this guy and the action going on behind him. I wanted to do a time dissolve to another set that was built at a right angle to the one we were on. This allowed me to pan the camera to that set instead of having to cut to something.

The actor was to run off and then appear in the next set. I did a dissolve to a head profile of the actor, and then followed him with that shot until we were looking into the other set. Because I was following him in such a close shot, he was able to change his jacket on the way to the next set. There were many items like this.

That dissolve technique is something I learned while watching Delbert Mann in action. I remember thinking, How is that possible? It just fascinated me, because I could see that he had done something that I had never done. I then realized that he had built the sets adjacent to each other.

I want to tell a story about Herschel Bernardi. He stayed out on the West Coast for a while, and he worked with me a couple of times. He called one day and said, "Arthur, is there something for me in your next show?"

I said, "There really isn't."

He said, "Oh. I need money, I'm going back to New York."

I said, "There is a small character, but it's only the part of a reporter. It's not big enough."

He said, "I'd like to play it."

I said, "Fine, if you'll take the money we can pay."

At the end of the show, I said goodbye to him. I was sorry that things hadn't worked out for him, and that he was going back to New York.

A few weeks later, I went to the movies on Hollywood Boulevard, and just as I was heading to the box office, I saw Herschel walking towards me. I couldn't believe it.

I said, "Herschel!" He paid no attention. As we got closer, I said again, "Herschel!" Then I realized that he had these huge dark circles under his eyes, and he was very spaced out. I thought, "My God. He didn't need that money to go back to New York. He was on dope and he needed it for that." It was the strangest feeling. I shuddered a little and I put my money down to get my ticket when a voice said, "Hi, Arthur. How are you doing?"

I turned and it was Herschel. He said, "Couldn't talk to you because I was shooting a scene."

I had walked right by cameras and lights, and I didn't even notice. He'd been to New York and was back working. It was so embarrassing because he was just playing a part. I felt so silly.

**Ralph Nelson:**  The best story I recall of those days was of a character actress named Josephine Hull, who was a delightful, little, plump lady, who had been in *Arsenic and Old Lace* and *You Can't Take it With You.* In the middle of the *Studio One* in which she was appearing, suddenly that glazed look came over her eyes. She turned, looked directly into the camera and said, "I'm sorry, I've forgotten my lines."

The stage manager who had a script off camera, fed her the line. She said, "Thank you," and continued with the play. A little bit later, she looked at the camera and said, "I've done it again." Well, from her, it was totally charming.

Later I wrote and sold the backstage story of *Requiem for a Heavyweight* to the *Westinghouse Theatre*. *The Man in the Funny Suit* was an hour show. All of us, Rod Serling, Keenan Wynn, Ed Wynn, Red Skelton, and I, played ourselves. The only exception was Martin Manulis, the producer. We had an actor for him.

It was the story of how we had tried to fire Ed Wynn. The title was prompted by the fact that Ed Wynn, was always after Keenan to inherit everything that he had built up in fifty years as a headliner — his funny costumes, funny props, and so forth. Keenan would argue back and say, "Pop, I don't want to be the man in the funny suit. I'm trying to make a career as an actor."

Keenan was in Japan making a film. Martin Manulis said to his secretary, "Get me Mr. Wynn on the phone." Ed was at Keenan's house, babysitting. Ed answered the phone, and Marty said, "Mr. Wynn, we're starting a new program called *Playhouse 90*, and I'd love to send you the script."

Ed said, "Fine." He was hungry for work at the time.

Keenan came home from Japan, and his father came over to see him. Keenan said, "Pop, I've just been offered a great part in a new show called *Requiem for a Heavyweight*."

Ed said, "Well, I'm going to be in it, too."

Keenan said, "You're kidding."

Ed said, "I don't know if the part is big enough."

Keenan said, "I'll swap parts with you, Pop. It's a great part."

"Well, will I be able to wear my funny clothes?"

Keenan said, "No, Pop, this is a drama!"

Well, that's what we had to combat. He always wanted to put in a lot of his old schtick.

It was the first drama in which Ed Wynn had ever appeared. Ed was so bad at the readings and the first rehearsals. Because he had Parkinson's disease, he couldn't control his head — it was bobbing all the time — and his voice would crack. It was just a disaster.

While we were in rehearsal, Marty did accede to this: we had hired a very good character actor, Ned Glass, to play the bartender, and to also understudy Ed. We had rehearsals with Ned after Ed had been dismissed. One day Ed came back — he'd forgotten his script — and saw us all rehearsing. We all went to Martin Manulis. Keenan Wynn said, "I cannot let my father disgrace himself in front of twenty million people," and Rod Serling said, "If you keep the old man, take my name off the script."

Since *Playhouse 90* had been announced to go on the air, Marty didn't want to say that one of the major stars had withdrawn from the cast. He insisted we go through with Ed. Faced with this edict, we all went to work, teaching the man the mechanical things to do. There was one scene where he was supposed to break down and cry, but he couldn't cry. I told him to go home and practice in front of the mirror. He came into the rehearsal hall the following morning and said, "Ralph, I did exactly what you said, but every time I looked at myself, I got hysterical."

So, eventually, I said, "Ed, on this phrase, let your voice crack,and on the next phrase, take a handkerchief from your pocket, and on the following phrase, turn your back to the camera and let the audience do the crying for you. It's an old trick."

He said, "Where does somebody like you learn something like that?"

I said, "George M. Cohan used that in *Ah, Wilderness*! He wasn't going to cry every night."

The show opens with shooting up toward the boxing ring. We could never go into the boxing ring, because we couldn't afford that many extras. Then, the winner and all his hangers-on come down the ramp into the camera, talking about what a great fight it was. After they've cleared, from around the corner come Mountain [Jack Palance] with his arms draped over the manager [Keenan Wynn], and Army, the trainer [Ed Wynn].

The first day of camera rehearsal, I was standing on the floor, blocking out the shot. When I cued them in, Jack and Keenan came on, but there was no Ed. I gave everybody a five minute break and said, "Keenan, where the hell is Pop?" which I was calling him by then.

He said, "I don't know, I don't know."

Then I heard that he was in Red Skelton's dressing room. Red Skelton was in the adjoining studio for his show. Came time for another break, and I was furious by then. I was on my way to see Ed in Red's dressing room, when Red stopped me and said, "You're going to burn up the old man."

I said, "I sure am. He's going to ruin my show."

He said, "Let me tell you what happened. The old man was so nervous that at four this morning he had not been to bed at all. He doesn't drink, but he'd had a number of shots of bourbon, and he drove down Wilshire Boulevard. He was determined he was not going to miss the rehearsal. The only room he could find open was my dressing room, so he went in there, and crashed. If you want to go tell him off, go ahead." Naturally, I didn't.

On the air, I sat there concentrating on the drama of the piece and giving cues for camera shots with my fingers crossed that the old man was not going to go totally haywire. It wasn't until I went home and watched the kinescope performance on the air in Los Angeles that I realized what a good performance he had given. Ed gave me a large photograph of himself, autographed, saying that I had given him a whole new career, because then jobs kept coming in for him as a dramatic actor. All this is in *The Man in the Funny Suit*.

**Franklin Heller:** When Johnny Carson retired, I was reminded of another story. I directed *To Tell the Truth* for the first five years, and one of my other duties was to book the panelists.

In a political maneuver, I was transferred as director to *I've Got a Secret*, which I didn't much like, but I continued to book *To Tell the Truth*. Like *What's My Line?*, we had three regular panelists and a rotating one. During this period, in the fifties, I was looking for bright, good looking, young people, to be panelists.

I saw this fellow, Johnny Carson, on a daytime show on ABC called *Who Do You Trust?* It was an ordinary afternoon quizzer, but he seemed to me to have some personality elements that other people didn't have. I used to go to Goodson with a list each week of who might be the fourth panelist, and I put Johnny Carson's name on my list. For some reason or other, I never knew why, Goodson hated him. He would say, "No, no, no, not Johnny Carson." Occasionally I would have to leave the list for him, and there would be a line through Johnny Carson's name and "No!" by it. This went on for months. Then Goodson got married and went off to Europe, for something like a six-week honeymoon. During that period I had no supervision booking the panel other than Gil Fates, and Gil usually went along with what I suggested. So while Goodson was away, I booked Johnny Carson on the panel. And by the time Goodson got back Johnny Carson was solidly established on *To Tell the Truth*. Everybody loved him. There had been critical comment. There had been columnists writing about Johnny Carson. They would say things like, "Fellow from daytime, shining out on this prime time show." And then, of course, Goodson couldn't fire him, because he liked success, as everyone does, and Johnny Carson was a success.

When Jack Paar left *The Tonight Show* and NBC was looking around, they didn't have to look very far. There was Johnny Carson on a prime time network show, and he went from *To Tell the Truth* and *Who Do You Trust?* to *The Tonight Show*. And I must say for Johnny that he never forgot that.

When I was doing *Snap Judgment*, with Ed McMahon as the emcee, Johnny was on it a couple of times. He used to come by occasionally just to say hello, and he never failed to say, "You know Frank, if it wasn't for you, I would never have made it. If you had not put me on *To Tell the Truth*, I would still be on in the daytime on ABC."

The climax came some years later, in the seventies. After I retired from television, the very first book that I agented had been written by my great teacher, B. Iden Payne. I arranged with Jack Klugman, also a Payne disciple, who was starring on *The Odd Couple*, that if I could get him booked on the Johnny Carson show, he would plug Iden's book. Iden had died before this book was published.

I called NBC in Burbank and asked for Johnny Carson. Much to my surprise, I got through to him. I said, "Johnny I am no longer in television. I'm a literary agent." I told him about the book and about my great teacher and about how he was dead. "I'd like you to book Jack Klugman on your show. I'd like to get this distinguished Yale University Press book about a Shakespearean scholar mentioned on your program — and it will give your show some class, too."

He said, "Absolutely."

Jack got on the show — didn't sell any books, but that doesn't matter.

When television started up after the wartime hiatus, it was almost entirely sustaining. There were only a handful of commercial programs, such as Jon Gnagy's *You Are an Artist*, which was presented by Gulf. The artist delivered the commercials himself, drawing an illustration, such as a Gulf service station, as he spoke.

At first, sponsorship replicated radio. There was spot-buying during station breaks, with commercials ranging from ten to thirty seconds. Advertisers also bought quarter-hour, half-hour, or one-hour chunks and sponsored the entire program. Commercial time could be split as the client saw fit. On *Philco Television Playhouse*, for example, the allotted six minutes were divided into a twenty-five-second opening, two act breaks totaling approximately four and a half minutes, and a closing spot of about one minute.

Pat Weaver brought about a major shift when he announced that he was going to break the stranglehold of the advertisers and agencies by fragmenting sponsorship, making television advertising as available to Adolph's Meat Tenderizer as to General Motors. Programs were sold on a participating basis. At first, advertisers bought minutes, but gradually shifted to the smaller and smaller segments that are commonplace today.

\* \* \*

**Buzz Kulik:** John Reber's big idea was "sponsor identification." He wanted *Lux Video*, *Lux Radio Theatre*, *Kraft Music Hall*, and he was very successful. However, when you had multiple sponsors, there were problems.

**George Roy Hill:** We always had to clear the material we were going to do through John Reber. That clearance would come through the script department, which served all three directors — or six directors when they finally had it on twice a week. I don't remember much interference.

**Fielder Cook:** The network had no say-so over screenplays; the advertising agencies controlled most of commercial television and took the responsibility for it. On the *Kraft Theatre*, the vice president at Kraft in charge of television and radio did not want to read the scripts. He said, "If you can't do them good, I'll get another advertising agency. What am I reading scripts for? I'm not a showman." Kraft didn't know what was going on the air until it got on the air, except their continuity acceptance had to check it out for profanity.

**Martin Ritt:** Television was considered a small thing. I don't think we went any farther west than the Ohio River. It still wasn't big enough to attract institutional sponsoring, but, as it began to grow, they came and took over.

It was fun until the agencies got involved and it became a commercial enterprise. After that, you had to deal with a lot of people who didn't know anything about television, in addition to sponsors and their taste. It really signified the beginning of the end of that artistic kind of television.

The only interesting work was done in the area of sex and psychology. All you had were little kitchen dramas that were truthful and worthwhile. And, that was a safe recourse. I don't mean to minimize live television, but you couldn't do a piece of material with ideas that challenged anything.

**Franklin Schaffner:** Censorship existed in terms of the standards and practices of the television station or the television network. Those rules and regulations were well known to everybody. One hoped to work effectively within those standards, knowing that they would change radically from year to year. You can actually chart a time when the standards-and-practice codes loosened. If you thought a particular project might not be approved, you knew that the next year it might have a fighting chance of getting on.

**George Roy Hill:** There was the obvious censorship, where you couldn't even say "damn" or "hell." But once you got used to the fact that it was a very strict taboo, you just didn't fight it. You found that the swear words were not as necessary as you thought they were.

I think that the censorship today is in some ways more onerous than it was then. When I'm asked to edit a film for television that has been released theatrically, I find the cuts that Standards and Practices demands are much more distressing than any of the censorship in the days of live television.

**Buzz Kulik:** Standards and Practices had always been there, and it's always been a problem. It really came into its own after the first scream from Congress in the early fifties.

**Franklin Schaffner:** It was assumed that before you commissioned a screenplay, you would submit a synopsis to the agency. It was standard practice to make the synopsis look as acceptable to them as you could. Then, once you got the okay on the synopsis, you'd go back to what the script's original intent was. Later, when you submitted the script, you hoped that while reading it they weren't as alert as they might be.

I recall instances when, after they saw the thing on camera on the day of rehearsal, they would demand changes that might run from two or three words to the meaning of a scene. But it was not a deliberate attempt to violate someone's intentions. If they didn't understand you, or if you did not understand what they intended, then obviously certain adjustments had to be made. At that point, you sat down and had an eyeball confrontation with them. Because of the pressure of putting the show on, the producer won more than he lost.

**Paul Bogart:** The United States Steel people and whoever the agency was that represented them were the worst people I ever worked with. In one show, the dialogue read, "What makes you want to seduce every woman you meet?" They held the firm position that "seduce" was a dirty word and had to be changed.

I said, "To what?"

They suggested, "What makes you want to 'make' every woman you meet?"

I said, "That's dirty!" We had terrible fights all the time with those people. The battles were continuous. They'd start at the beginning and they ended when we were off the air.

The sponsor and agency people eventually had a sponsor's booth; a little comfortable place where they could sit and watch the show, usually behind the director. The objective was to get them out of the control room so we wouldn't have to listen to them talk.

The commercials were done by different directors. They came from another studio, while we were re-routing the cameras to the next positions and the actors were changing their clothes.

**John Frankenheimer:**  Lots of network interference. Lots of sponsor interference. There were rehearsals that they could see — they had monitors in their offices. It was a very Big Brother type of thing. A network executive'd come down with notes, and you did what they said. In my case it was usually William Dozier, who was a friend of mine. You fought up to a degree, you fought, you fought, you fought, but when you lost, you lost.

You had arguments about the cleavage of women's dresses and the length of kisses, all that kind of stuff. We lost three affiliates with *Winter Dreams* because John Cassavetes and Dana Wynter kissed too long.

We wanted to open the second year of *Playhouse 90* with a show of Rod Serling's, *A Town is Turned to Dust*, about what happened to the man who killed Emmet Till, a black man who had been hanged in Tennessee. I'd done a lot of stuff of Rod Serling's.

Rod wrote a brilliant script, but at the last minute they said we couldn't do it. They wouldn't have any part of it. We hunted around madly for something else and came up with a terrible thing called *The Death of Manolete*. It was dreadful.

Finally, there was a terribly compromised version of *A Town is Turned to Dust*, which I did as the last show that year, with Rod Steiger and William Shatner, and for which all were nominated for the Emmy. At the end of this version, Rod Steiger gave a long speech to the town, and then they said to him, "All right, Harvey, what are you going to do now?" Because he was guilty, guilty as hell.

He said, "The right thing. The right thing." He's supposed to turn and go into the courthouse, while we held outside the courthouse and we heard a shot — BOOM! — and you knew that he'd killed himself, and that was the end of it. Well, at the last minute, three days before we went on the air, the insurance company that was sponsoring the show said they refused to allow that ending, that nobody was going to commit suicide on an insurance company-sponsored show.

Well, there was consternation. I refused to do it, Rod Steiger refused to do it, but it all ended up that they won. I had to invent the cockamamie ending where, when William Shatner was shot, a bullet came out of his gun, and hit Rod Steiger in this near fatal wound, however not fatal enough to where Steiger could not give this long Wagnerian type of address to the crowd, and then conveniently die at the end of it. It was a very contrived ending and compromised the show terribly.

They definitely could stop you from doing things. If you were under contract to them, or if you wanted to work for them again, and you did some stupid thing like defying them, you wouldn't work. It was that simple.

**George Roy Hill:** I was doing *Judgment at Nuremberg* and had researched a lot of film that was shot by John Ford and George Stevens when they were in the Signal Corps. They went into Germany, were among the first to enter the concentration camps. They took horrifying films of the inmates and the mass graves. I used that in a scene where the defendants in the Nuremberg trial were forced to look at these films, and I showed them looking at them.

A few days before we were to go on the air, I was handed the commercials, and right after that particular scene involving the concentration camp was an American Gas Association spot. It said, "Nothing but gas does so many jobs so well." It was really a ghoulish kind of thing.

I immediately brought it to the attention of the producer and the agency. They still wanted the American Gas Association to sponsor the show. There was something in the contract that said that gas could never be used in a derogatory way, so their solution was to say that we couldn't mention gas in the show. So you can't say that six million Jews died of apoplexy.

There's no question that it was handled badly. I would not tell the actors to delete the word "gas" because it just made no sense. I would have had to change every reference to gas and gas ovens. So, we went on the air and every time the word gas came up, the sound was cut. You would have somebody saying a word and, suddenly, they'd fade out and they'd fade back in again. You could see from their lips, even if you were not an excellent lip reader, that they were saying "gas." This was picked up by a number of newspapers around the country, and CBS was furious about it. I think they took the blame rather than laying it on the sponsor. I was never asked to return to CBS, and that was the last live television I did. It was quite an experience, but I'm glad I handled it the way I did. I can't really say that it put a dent in my career because by that time, I was pretty much more interested in movies and in the Broadway theatre.

**Livia Granito:**  The network and sponsors trusted Albert McCleery a great deal, but Ethel Frank and Albert did a lot of arguing with the network over continuity acceptances. At NBC we were censored even in terms of the sponsor having something to say about things, but I don't remember having any show pulled because of the content.

**Arthur Hiller:**  Even though Albert would get upset about some things, he could also be very supportive. We had a cigarette sponsor. Their attitude was that they were not the ones who got young people to smoke, despite the fact that all their ads were always pushing them to. On *Bottom of the River*, we got into our final camera rehearsals the day before the advertising people came. They were very disturbed because our young characters were smoking. The sponsor decided to withdraw and pull out their sponsorship entirely.

Albert called me and said, "Arthur, if you can change it fine. If you tell me you have to have it, that's what it will be. The sponsor will pull out."

I said, "I do have to have it."

He said, "Well, that's it."

About ten minutes later, I called him and said, "I have an idea. We'll only have the bad kids smoke. How's that?"

That's the compromise that we reached with the advertising people, but Albert was prepared to lose the sponsor.

I did another show once where Addison Richards and Richard Jaeckel played a father and son who were both doctors. It was an old-against-young story, and the young doctor had another doctor friend who was a black man.

This was 1955, and at that time you didn't have professional black people on television. Everybody said, "No, you can't do that. The network will object."

I spoke to Albert, who said, "If that's what you want Arthur, do it. If the network objects, we'll hear the objection."

We hired a black man to play the doctor. The actor brought me clippings from the black press, and you would have thought that Jackie Robinson had broken into baseball they found it so different from what they were used to. He told me stories of people asking him, "What are you doing?"

"I'm working on a television show."

"What are you playing?"

"I'm playing a doctor."

They said, "Oh, a witch doctor." It just never dawned on them that he could play a medical doctor.

Nobody ever complained. Nobody made a comment. Everybody is so fearful of what might be the response, that nobody initiates anything. You've got to take chances. If you believe in something, you have to hang in there for it.

**Ralph Nelson:** On *Playhouse 90*, with a number of sponsors involved, they would be invited to one rehearsal in the rehearsal hall. All over the studio, we had tapes on the floor showing where the sets were, so the actors would have some kind of orientation when they got to the real set. We played it very low key, and dialogue would not have to be projected as in the theatre. The sponsors would all sit against one wall, so they couldn't hear anything over there at all.

On *Requiem*, it got to be ridiculous, because one of the sponsors was Ronson Lighters. They got after Rod Serling, because Keenan had a stub of a cigar and was always saying, "You got a match?"

They said, "Couldn't he say, 'Have you got a lighter?' "

Rod got furious. He said, "Well, at the end, Mountain is in a wrestling match — should we change that to a wrestling lighter?"

There was another terrible example, while I was producing *Climax*. The first show I did was the *The Andersonville Trial*, which was the trial of Captain Wertz, the infamous commandant of the Andersonville Prison in Georgia during the Civil War. Chrysler was the sponsor of *Climax*. We were not permitted to use the name of the then-president of the United States, because his name was Lincoln. Because we knew we would have to trade off some lines that they would object to, we'd deliberately put things in the script like "We've got to ford the river," or "That's an old dodge."

**Arthur Penn:** Before television began making an awful lot of profit, commercially it was not terribly important to the sponsors. But they did some studies on their cost per thousand and began to be aware that television was a very powerful medium. That's when they began to send guys from the advertising agency to start interfering with the scripts and with the casting.

There was silly, name-brand stuff. No competing product could be shown that could be identified. But it was much more than that. There was also the content of shows, and it was also a very difficult period politically. They began to say, "Well, you can't say that. People will be politically offended."

**Delbert Mann:** Fred Coe ran interference for us. Fred took that on his own back and we only got a reflected view of the pressures from up above. The pressures were not particularly from the network as they are today. They were from the sponsors and their advertising agencies. We hated it, we felt it was absolutely dreadful, and we fought their edicts as to what they wanted and how they wanted it done and who they wanted to cast.

They were terrible pressures, but they were nothing compared to what one feels from the network today, in terms of insensitivity, of grossness of casting ideas. The network's only interest seems to be in casting someone who is on one of their series to help promote the series. They also make it difficult to do worthwhile material.

**Arthur Penn:** Something happened that was very different for those of us on *Philco* who had been used to working with a great deal of freedom, with very good writers and actors. The interference that Fred Coe had been able to run was being diminished. All of us were beginning to get very flattering offers from movies and elsewhere, so that within a period of a year, Del Mann had gone to Hollywood and Vince Donehue had gone to Broadway. I was getting ready to make a move to Broadway and Hollywood because suddenly I thought, "Who the hell needs this anymore?" It had been a marvelous medium up to that point, but when we were suddenly having to deal with these fellows from the advertising agency, that was just plain nonsense.

**John Peyser:** Censorship of the material that we were doing didn't start until the McCarthy period. Then the businessmen, the agents — people not from the artistic community — stepped in and never let go again. It all changed after that. The networks were becoming afraid that they might offend somebody, so censorship, broadcast control, became a part of the network.

In that same period, audience research came in, and they started telling us what the demographics said. The minute you started doing demographics, you started dropping the quality of the material. *Studio One* disappeared. Its place was taken by the hour-and-a-half show that emanated from Hollywood, *Playhouse 90*. Some of the material on *Playhouse 90* was very good, but it started going, I thought, in a different direction. It started looking for sensationalism, for thrills, for murder mysteries, instead of the kind of stuff that had been done on *Studio One*.

**George Schaefer:** Early in the year, I'd go to Kansas City to meet Mr. Hall [Joyce Hall, President of Hallmark] and the Hallmark people and the Chicago agency. We would agree on the six or seven shows that were going to be done that year. Then we'd go back to my office in New York, cast them, produce them, and direct them. They would go on the air live, Mr. Hall would phone me afterwards to tell me what he thought, and that was it.

The network was only responsible for getting them on the air and for helping to promote them. The network did not think of interfering or making suggestions. The agency would be around for the final dress rehearsals. If they felt that a gown was a little too low-cut or there was some salacious dialogue that might not sit well in Kansas City, they would speak up.

There was something about the power of a director, because the show was live. There was no time for silly things. If a sponsor objected to something and took ten minutes to discuss it with you, you weren't going to make the air. You'd say, "I'm sorry, it's got to go the way it is." So, for better or worse, you went ahead, and usually it was better.

Hallmark had six minutes of commercials to the hour, and there wasn't all the station break folderol. However, in a ninety-minute or two-hour span, it's really hard to come in on the second. Sometimes the shows would run under, but I don't think I ever had to tell anybody to slow down. The general tendency was to run long. The first *Little Moon of Alban* kind of grew and extended, and ran so late they had to drop their last commercial completely. We weren't even able to run the credits on the air. We had to take an ad in *Variety* with the credits listed.

It was nice to do new things. The first film for television was ours. I think most of the shows budgeted at three hundred, three-fifty, maybe four hundred thousand, and Adie wanted to use some of the Hallmark money to do a movie in Europe, show it on television, and hopefully show it in a movie theatre later. No one had ever done that before.

We wanted to do *Captain Brassbound's Conversion*, the Shaw play, because with all the camels and the deserts, we thought it would make a great visual thriller. It wouldn't have been hard to make a deal with the Shaw people — I'd done a lot of shows with them — but somebody'd just bought the rights to make a musical out of it, which never came about.

We were very depressed, but said, "Well, why don't we do *Macbeth* again?" This was '60, '61, and it had been a number of years since we'd originally done it in '53. We went over to London and combined the roughly three hundred fifty thousand dollars that we got from Hallmark, with a modest advance from British Lion, which was going to distribute it as a feature. I — brave — put up the rest of the money myself, and we did it for under six hundred thousand dollars, at the Birnam Wood MGM Studios, which are now torn down. The cameraman was Freddy Young; the editor was Ralph Kaplan; the sets, Teddy Carrick; and the cast was a Who's Who of the English theatre. It turned out to be really a major experience. It was the first film of that sort that I'd done.

Before the first commercial, it ran fifty minutes without a break. It won all the Emmys that year, five or six of them, and was repeated again. It's now shown at schools, at the Shakespeare festivals. It's the only Macbeth that ever made money, and it still turns in a sizable profit every year. That was one of the nice things about the Hallmark relationship. You could think freshly and do things that hadn't been done before.

Hallmark couldn't have been more agreeable. I understood their objectives, and fortunately they were my own. They were really just reaching for quality. I think Mr. Hall personally was happier going to his club the next day in Kansas City and have people say, "Oh, what a great show last night," than with any report of large numbers. The ratings didn't mean that much. It was a much happier atmosphere than it is today.

In terms of program content, there were a few areas that they didn't like. I had an original written for them by Loring Mandel, called *The Odyssey of Peter Sherman*. It was a beautiful script about following an old man through different kinds of old people's homes and coming to terms with himself and his children. I was very disappointed, because they just didn't see it. Maybe it was Mr. Hall, himself, an older man, who was so successful and so in control of his faculties and his life that the problems of such a person did not appeal to him. It was dropped but it had a very happy ending. When CBS opened *CBS Playhouse*, Loring retitled it *Do Not Go Gentle into that Good Night* and I was able to do it. It won all the awards. It was a perfectly beautiful show that should be repeated, it was so wise.

After the Lunts had done *The Magnificent Yankee*, we became very dear and close friends. We wanted another show for them, and they were eager to do another show with me. James Costigan, who was probably the finest writer that we had with us during those years, came up with an idea for an original that I just was crazy about. Lynn and Alfred read the first act and liked it, so we went ahead and got the whole thing written. However, whether it was Alfred's health or whether they genuinely didn't like it, they decided they wouldn't do it. They had turned down almost every great success of their career originally and then reconsidered, so, maybe we could have waited them out, but they were getting on a bit.

You could have cast it with dozens of stars and I begged Hallmark to let me do it, but they felt that if the Lunts didn't like it, it couldn't be very good, so we lost the rights. Unfortunately, at the time it was done I was so busy I couldn't have directed it if I'd been asked. George Cukor directed it. It was *Love Among the Ruins*, that Laurence Olivier and Katharine Hepburn did so successfully.

I finally broke with Hallmark and decided it was time to do other things because of the Lunts. They wanted very much to do *The Visit*, in which they'd been so brilliant in the theatre. William Self, who was head of Fox, couldn't have been more helpful and managed to get the rights released for me. I was roaring to go, and went down to Kansas City. When I left the Hallmark people I thought we had a deal. The next week the agency called and said, "No, we're not going to let them do it because you can't sell Mother's Day cards with Durrenmatt's *The Visit*."

I thought, If it's come to that, it's time for me to look elsewhere. I took it to Mike Dann. When Mike was at CBS, I guess he was really president of my fan club. He read it and said, "Great, great, great, we should do it." Then he checked with his bookkeepers. They'd just lost a fortune on the beautiful production that Alex Siegal did of *Death of a Salesman*, so they said, "No, we can't get it in this year." Public television didn't exist at that time, so it's gone forever and it's a great loss.

The management at Hallmark was still the same, but I think the agency became more influential. Mr. Hall retired. His son, Don, runs the company now. A wonderful man, Don, and very much involved in continuing the series. They had a thirtieth anniversary party at UCLA and showed some of the old takes and a lot of the old gang was there. It's a most remarkable company and lovely people.

**Marc Daniels:**  When I went back to New York during the Golden Age of Television, the networks were beginning to take control. However, the agencies were still much more active than the networks in terms of setting budgets, and still had a fairly powerful control of the programs. I think they wanted the shows in New York, where they could keep an eye on them. Also, the production companies were in New York, and I noticed that there was greater proficiency and skill exhibited by the crews.

Single sponsors, like Ford, had a lot to say about the program. For example, I interested Paul Muni in doing a play by a very famous American playwright, Sidney Howard, who had written *The Silver Cord*, among others. The play that we were interested in was *They Knew What They Wanted*. It's the story of a middle-aged, Italian man who runs a vineyard in California. He advertises for a wife. The girl comes out from Chicago and they get married. He has a ranch hand who is a young, sexy guy, and the wife is a young, sexy girl — pretty soon they're sleeping together. The wife gets pregnant by the ranch hand. The husband tells her, "I want the baby. You two can have each other, and go away together." That's why the play was called *They Knew What They Wanted*. Everybody gets pretty much what they want, and it ends on an up note. Muni wanted to do it, and it would have been quite a coup to have him on the *Ford Theatre*. But, the Ford Motor Company said, "We can't do that play. That's indecent."

They were probably right. I don't think the great American television public was ready for that kind of thing, and you had to remember that television was being paid for by these people. Sponsors know better than we do what their particular customer relations are, and the images that they want to portray. If we're not happy with that, we shouldn't be doing television, we should be doing films or plays, where you don't have sponsors.

# The Blacklist: 1948 to 1959

The blacklist era began in earnest in 1950 when several FBI agents left the Bureau to begin publishing a newsletter titled *Counterattack*. After naming alleged Communists, they confronted sponsors with threats of retaliation for employing them. These same people later published *Red Channels*, and still later went into the lucrative business of clearing the people they had previously denounced.

Television got a bit of its own back with the Army-McCarthy hearings in 1954. Carried in full, these dramatic proceedings captivated millions of Americans. The spectacle was instrumental in destroying the power of the senator, and foreshadowed the impact of the Anita Hill-Clarence Thomas confrontation of the nineties.

\* \* \*

**Marc Daniels:** We felt the blacklist as early as 1948 or 1949. In fact, *Ford Theatre* didn't use Judy Holliday the second season, even though we had a wonderful project for her, because they got complaints. They would never admit that there was such a thing as a blacklist, except that once you decided who you wanted to cast, the list had to go to this man working somewhere in the office who okayed all the casting. This applied to leads as well as actors who were playing relatively minor parts.

**Fielder Cook:** I was doing *Kraft Theatre* when McCarthy was going on. We didn't know affected writers because all of our writers were twenty-one years old, and I don't remember ever having any problem with the screenplays. McCarthy's thing had nothing to do with content of scripts, it was just about hiring people who were pink, as they called them. It affected the moral climate of the time.

We had a lot of young actors and young directors starting out. The television people that were hooked deepest were the character actors. The Philip Obers and Zero Mostels who had been active in the thirties and forties were the ones who were really not allowed to work.

**George Roy Hill:** It was a terribly ugly period, but I'm not that interested in politics, because that is just not my nature. The blacklist was always denied, and I was one of those who denied it because it was never presented to me as a list. However, I found that when I would want a particular actor, the word would come back to me that they would prefer that I use somebody else. I remember being told that if I wanted to hire someone, to let John Reber check it first. He was very helpful, and got an awful lot of people passed.

There was a big hassle with this up-state New York merchant, [Laurence] Johnson. He had absolutely no power, but he had the networks absolutely buffaloed. Johnson would threaten to keep the product off the shelves if we used any of the actors listed in *Red Channels*. I never read *Red Channels*.

**Arthur Penn:** On *Philco*, we were pretty bold, and we were able to break much of the blacklist. Fred Coe was a terrific producer in that respect. Unintimidated. But there was some pressure, and it began to get bad in that period.

**Delbert Mann:** Walter Bernstein did *The Rich Boy* script for us in 1952, before the full effects of *Red Channels* and the whole McCarthy era. It was a terrible, dreadful time. We had constant battles with Fred, and Fred with the sponsors and the advertising agencies, to use the writers and actors that we wanted.

The blacklist was one of the most frustrating things that I can recall, but my most vivid memory of it came just about the time its effects were beginning to loosen up and people were starting to work a bit. There were still actors and writers who were just forbidden. Judy Holliday was one of them, the greatest comedic talent I have ever worked with. Every year for three years, David Shaw wrote a script tailored for her. We submitted her name to the agency and were told we could not use her. We fought, we screamed, we battled — we could not use her.

It was about 1954, in the spring, when a Young & Rubicam account executive, who had the Goodyear account, was retiring. It was, by that time, the *Philco/Goodyear Playhouse*, alternating shows. The account executive had a lunch at "21" for the *Philco/Goodyear* staff — one of those three-martini advertising agency lunches — in the course of which he was saying very expansively to Fred, "Pappy, I sure would like to show you boys how much I appreciate you. You've been great. I hate to leave you. You've been wonderful."

Fred, taking advantage of the opportunity, said, "Well, look, you remember that script you've got on your desk. I'll tell you how you can really go out with one hell of a show, if you will get Judy Holliday for us."

There was a long pause and the account executive said, "You really mean that? You mean she's that important, she's that good?"

Fred said, "Listen, she is the greatest. The script is written for her, you know how many times we've tried to get her. Just get Judy for us, and we will give you the best show you've ever had."

We went back to the office, and within two hours a telephone call came, "Use her." It was that simple. I don't know what the manipulations were behind the scenes, but suddenly Judy Holliday was free to work in television, where she had been denied doing any jobs at all for three years and more. She was blacklisted from movies as well. A terrible tragedy. Other people left the country. Some people committed suicide.

**Paul Bogart:** I'd heard vague stories about the blacklist, but believe me, I was very naive about it. I remember working out a list of appropriate people with the casting director, and then they would take the list and say, "Well, we have to clear them."

I didn't know what that meant. I finally asked Ethel Winant, "Who are these people you're clearing the actors with?

She said, "You stupid jerk. Don't you know you wouldn't be here if you hadn't been cleared?"

When I became aware of what was going on, I would send in the same names every week just to see if they would get cleared by accident. Sometimes they would, but we couldn't use a lot of people for a long time. It really didn't loosen up until well into the sixties.

We were doing a wonderful show on *Kaiser* where the last act didn't work. The writer had the flu or something, so Audrey Geller and I went to David Susskind to ask him for a little more money to hire someone to write the third act. Susskind gave us five hundred dollars, which we took to Walter Bernstein, who had people "fronting" for him because he hadn't been able to work. He wrote us a marvelous third act which was actually a little better than the other two acts. Walter didn't get credit. The man who had been cleared got the credit.

I think the agencies closed their eyes now and again just to get the shows on the air. Nothing was said as long as the names of the uncleared people were not on the product, and if the agencies couldn't be attacked for using them, it was all right.

**Dan Petrie:**   I worked with Leslie Sloat for quite a while before I said I was very unhappy with him. He seemed to be mealy-mouthed, and he just didn't seem to be addressing himself to the problems of the script. David Susskind was the producer. I went to him and said, "David, this guy is driving me crazy."

David said, "What are you doing for dinner tonight?" which I thought was an inappropriate reply to my question.

I said, "Gosh, nothing."

He said, "Well, call your wife and tell her you're having dinner with me."

I said, "Okay." That night, when I went to his house for dinner, I saw Walter Bernstein — who later wrote *The Front*. I said, "Walter, what are you doing here?"

He said, "I'm the real Leslie Sloat."

**Walter Grauman:**   I worked with one marvelous, marvelous writer, who lived in New York. His name was Joel Carpenter. I did a *Naked City* with him, and I was working with him on a project that I was trying to develop myself. I never knew he had been a blacklisted writer. We were shopping at a department store, and when he charged a gift for his daughter, he said, "Abe Manoff."

I said, "What are you talking about, Joe?"

He said, "Oh, I forgot to tell you."

His real name was Arnold Manoff. He died of a heart attack, a number of years ago. His daughter is a very good actress — Dinah Manoff.

Jeff Corey had been blacklisted, but I used him on *The Untouchables*. We fought it through until the network finally said, "Yes, it's all right. Go ahead."

I, thank God, missed the height of the blacklist.

**Martin Ritt:**   There were many more actors and writers than there were directors, so there weren't that many directors blacklisted. Directors were not generally considered among the intellectual class. Most writers generally are, even by their own admission.

There was a very famous show on television called *You Are There*, which was narrated by Walter Cronkite. Every script in that series was written by a blacklisted writer at one-third the normal salary they would have had to pay a guy who wasn't blacklisted. Abe Polonsky, Walter Bernstein, and Arnold Manoff wrote every script that was done while I was there, and I was there most of the time. Everybody knew it. Cronkite. Everybody. Nothing was ever said. Edward R. Murrow knew about it a long time before he spoke out against McCarthy.

If you saw *The Front*, you remember that scene where the guy who acted as a front man for the writer said, "It's not up to my usual standard?" I was there when that actually happened.

**Dan Petrie:**  A writer could go underground, but a director couldn't, because a director was there in the studio. One of the jobs that I got was as a result of another man being blacklisted and removed from a show called *Treasury Men in Action*. I often felt that "there but for the grace of God go I," because, when I was in New York in the early forties, I was asked to attend rallies and contribute to causes like Russian war relief. They were our allies, and I would have, but I just didn't have the money. Therefore, I escaped being tarred by that kind of brush. It was a sad and tragic period in our history.

**Arthur Hiller:**  I remember wanting to hire Herschel Bernardi, and being told I couldn't have him.

**Lamont Johnson:**  That whole vicious period from 1951 to '56 was a terrible time, and radio and television was a hotbed of it. We had a very strict law about blacklisting that we followed on the West Coast. Matter of fact, we were able to break the blacklist with Herschel because Albert McCleery not only had the guts to hire a bunch of really untried directors, but did a number of very good and courageous things in terms of bringing people on who had been blacklisted.

It was so easy to attack actors and directors and creative people, because the advertising agencies were absolute sitting ducks for those bastards who compiled *Red Channels* and those lists of supposedly disloyal people. They could say to a national advertiser, "Do you seriously want to give work to people who threaten your way of life?" Any material that looked the least bit suspect in terms of what might be propaganda was viewed askance.

I had been blacklisted as an actor for almost a year, when McCleery and Hallmark broke it for me. This was long before I started to direct. After I had read for McCleery, he said, "God you're wonderful, you're going to do this."

I said, "Thank God."

I didn't hear, and I didn't hear, and I didn't hear, so, being totally paranoid about it at this point, I anxiously called the casting director and said, "I haven't received any rehearsal calls."

She said, "For what, honey?"

I said, "For the show. McCleery said I had the part."

She said, "Oh. You haven't read for me."

I said I didn't know it was necessary, McCleery had hired me.

She said, "Well, we can do it on the phone. Why don't you do something from the Declaration of Independence, or some patriotic piece?"

I just hung up, sick to my stomach. I went and threw up, because I knew what she was talking about. I called McCleery, and said, "What's going on?"

He said, "You got the part. Don't listen to that cunt."

Everybody was scrutinized. Marty Ritt was badly out of work for a while. He was a live director in New York, who suddenly was blacklisted and didn't work. I was one of those who were quickly reinstated, but some people died or killed themselves.

**Buzz Kulik:** It was not so much with CBS, but more with *Lux Video Theatre*, which aired from 1953 to 1954. I'd cast a show and they'd teletype the names of the actors I wanted back to New York. I don't know what happened back in New York, but the list would come back the next day. Every once in a while a person would not be acceptable. We could fight, and I did. I lost some, but I won a few.

When I did *Emile Zola* on the *Lux* show, I wanted Lee Cobb. Lee Cobb had been named in these things, but had cleared himself. Even after he met with the Congressional Committee, everybody was afraid to hire him because they thought somehow or other they would be tainted. His name came back, marked "unacceptable." I called him and said, "I thought you had cleared yourself?" He said that he had. So I raised hell and he played the part.

People were squealing on each other; people even came to hate each other. Lee Cobb and Elia Kazan had been great friends, but one of them had turned the other's name in, and they ended up wanting to kill each other.

I once had a fight about Mildred Dunnock, who had been in the original stage version of *Death of a Salesman*. Elia Kazan directed and Cobb starred. She was blacklisted for being in the play. Guilt by association! That's the kind of craziness that went on.

It was such a terribly fearsome time, that, unless you were there, it's hard to articulate. I'm sorry to say that I was there, and was a party to it. You had to sit still because it was in the air, and there was really nothing you could do about it. What could you say — "I'm not going to work"? Quit? What good would that do? The best that you could do was to try and fight it.

**Franklin Schaffner:**   The blacklist functioned for the most part while I was doing *Studio One*. It was during this time that CBS circulated that now famous document they wanted everybody on staff to sign, saying you were a "loyal" American, or whatever the phrasing. Certainly, there were a number of directors who suffered from it. Marty Ritt was one who, until the blacklist, had a promising career in television. Without question, it was an enormously obscene and inhibitive instrument, and everybody rejoiced when it was exposed and the whole issue was done away with.

**Ralph Nelson:**   I had a number of meetings with Joseph Reem, a vice president in charge of something, who was trying to persuade me to sign the loyalty oath. I went to see the American Civil Liberties Union.

I said, "The only thing they have on me, the only organization I've joined, was the Boy Scouts. I served four and a half years in the Army, and I'm doing a seditious show called *Mama*." I was prepared to publicize this as much as I could, because I did not want to sign, and I got away with it. I believe Martin Ritt and I were the only ones who refused to sign.

For a while, at the same time I was directing *Mama*, I produced the half-hour *Armstrong Circle Theatre*. David Susskind was the packager. We had to submit the names in advance, to be cleared, and we had terrible times trying to clear some actors. We were coming near rehearsal time, and no clearance had come through on this one particular actor, Rex Thompson. I kept after David, "We're going into rehearsal tomorrow."

"Well, we met with the advertising agency and they couldn't get clearance on him. They said there was something in his background that was questionable."

I said, "He is ten years old." They finally cleared him. His name was mixed up with somebody else.

In charge for Armstrong Cork and Tile Company was a man by the name of Beznoff, or something like that. In David's office, we had a meeting in which he said, "Certainly we want no Communists or Socialists, and even Democrats are questionable."

That's when I decided to leave that show.

**George Schaefer:**   I had to check everybody I hired with the people at NBC, but we managed to get an awful lot of people back on the air through Hallmark. Hallmark was not in favor of any kind of blacklisting at all and when the network had one sponsor like that, it was much easier than if you had multiple sponsors.

I wasn't conscious of it in terms of the writers the way I was with the actors. However, when we did an original about the last days of Napoleon, called *Eagle in a Cage*, Millard Lampell won the Emmy for the best television play, and, to my amazement, when he made his speech, he mentioned that this was his first job after having been on a blacklist.

Blacklisting is for those who are frightened... for the insecure and the stupid and, I must say, Hallmark always was secure and intelligent.

**Martin Ritt:**   When my contract came up for renewal, I was in a good position at CBS. I was very noticeable on the television scene because of my series, *Danger*, which was very hot at the time. I was kind of a troubleshooter actor and director around the studio, was on the verge of selling my own series, and had directed a rather famous television short adapted from a Mark Hellinger short story called *The Paperbox Kid*, which received very good press and a lot of notoriety. So when I had an idea for doing a television show about New York City, things seemed to be moving along nicely. Then the Cold War started, and that was it. They laid me off when they decided I was expendable.

I was called in to see a very nice man named Donald Davis. I went up to CBS headquarters, on the fourteenth floor, and was walking towards his office when I saw a producer who I had just helped out of a terrible situation with his show. He saw me and quickly disappeared. Since I know the kind of business we're in, and the kind of people that very often inhabit it, I knew what was coming. I walked in to see Donald. He said, "I don't understand what's going on Marty. How come you're not renewed?" I told him why and he said, "Oh come on Marty, this is America, they don't do things like that here."

I said, "Okay." That was it. I was out. The Block Drug Company was producing my show. They knew about the accusation and didn't care! It was CBS that insisted I be fired! They were known as the liberal network, consequently, they were even more frightened of the Communists. All the networks were as craven as hell. They fed us polite garbage. The point is that nobody has ever admitted that blacklisting existed — not the networks or anybody else.

After the trouble started, I didn't work for six or seven years. Absolutely nothing. Your name was on a list and when they ran down the list and your name was on it, you were not getting called. That was the united front. It has since become quite clear a lot of it was economic. A lot of people were blacklisted, while other people were getting those jobs.

Once a guy I worked with, who I knew was dead broke, came up to me, and said, "Jesus Christ, Marty, I need a job. I got a wife and a kid." I knew he wasn't too much of a writer, but I said, "Well, we can do something."

I sat down and worked with him. Later he fired me from a show that he was producing. His job was in jeopardy because somebody had made a mistake and I was hired. He was just another bum, common in every walk of life. He couldn't write and he couldn't produce. He only survived because other people weren't allowed to work.

As an actor, I was once removed from a show that Dan Petrie directed. Obviously, I had slipped by some of the flunkies who were supposed to check those things out. I was playing a thirty-five-year-old Jewish cab driver, which was about my age at the time. The official excuse was that I wasn't right for the part. The day that we were supposed to go on the air, they ran a kinescope. Petrie, a new kid from Chicago, couldn't believe that's why they took it off. People didn't allow themselves to believe it, because if they believed it, they would have to take a position, and it wasn't a stand most people were prepared to take.

Since I had not been subpoenaed or named, I went to a friend of mine at the actor's union for help. He said, "Marty hasn't been named. He hasn't been subpoenaed. Why don't you guys let up?"

He was told by this actor who was a bigwig and a very conservative fellow, "Look, you know Marty's not on our side, and unless he gives some concrete evidence that he is, we will do nothing to help him." That was the end of it, and I accepted it as a matter of fact.

A week after *Hud* opened in New York, I got a letter from CBS stating how they remembered with great fondness our working together in television. When I went to New York to make *The Front*, I wrote CBS and said, "Listen, you can be very helpful to me because you still have some period equipment that I'd like to use, which would save me sixty or seventy thousand dollars on my budget. If we can't borrow it, I'll have to build it."

I got an answer back saying, "We choose not to deal with that period in the history of television. We're glad that the film is in responsible hands, because we know that you and Mr. Allen will not falsify the facts."

CBS is, I suppose, still considered the most liberal network, and what the hell that means I don't know. Liberal until it costs, and when it costs you're not liberal anymore. Certainly they did not behave well in that period. They were guilty and should have been condemned and nailed to the cross, but they never were. Nobody has been. Networks behaved in a venal manner, but so did everybody.

**Delbert Mann:** The blacklist closed down that whole era of relative freedom of material, and I think it was one of the things that started the end of the time of live television. Increasing costs, the expanding network, growing sales of television sets, and the blacklist all came at the same time.

# The Advent of Tape: 1956 to 1965

Technicians and scientists at Bell Labs were the early experimenters who successfully produced video recording. They used paper tape that was undoubtedly too fragile to be commercially feasible. However, its biggest drawback was the speed at which the tape had to run past the recording head. A half-hour show would have required so much tape that the reel would have to have been at least several feet in diameter.

The breakthrough came when Ampex, in partnership with the engineering division of Bing Crosby Productions, devised the method of having the head revolve at great speed, perpendicular to the tape, rather than parallel to it. With that one stroke, tape recording for television became a practical tool.

For a one-hour program, the first machines used two-inch-wide, plastic tape contained on metal reels approximately eighteen inches in diameter. Recording was done directly from the electronic system, and dubs could be made from one tape to another, although noticeable quality was lost from one generation to the next. At first, it was necessary to play the tape using the same head that had been used to record it, but this limitation soon disappeared.

Early editing was a laborious process. It required viewing the tape over and over to determine the exact edit spots, then physically slicing the tape with a razor, removing the unwanted section and splicing the ends together. The editor, a technician, applied a "developing" fluid that made the sync pulses visible, then lined them up by peering through a microscope. The splice itself was made with silver-colored, self-adhesive, metallic tape. After all that, the assembled edit had to be carefully screened to be sure there were no jumps or glitches.

\* \* \*

**Paul Bogart:** Tape was brought in because General Sarnoff said, "Do it." At first, it was used instead of kinescopes for delayed broadcasts. It was live television on tape, with the same timing problems and with

mistakes and all. They would only allow you to edit from black to black
— after you faded to black, you could make a splice before fading in.

**Buzz Kulik:**  We tried to use tape as though it were live because
everyone was afraid that if we stopped the tape, television would start to
be put together like film, and nobody wanted that.

**George Schaefer:**  I have a two-inch tape, which I haven't tried to
transfer, of the second *Green Pastures* production. They taped it on the
West Coast for the delayed broadcast three hours later. Somebody managed to save a copy of it.

That was the first real use of tape, to take shows off the air live, and
not force the people out here to see them at ridiculous hours. I remember
a wonderful production on the *Producers' Showcase* of Robert Sher-
wood's *The Petrified Forest*. I was out here working, and I had to dash
home to see it at five-thirty because it went on the air in the east at
eight-thirty.

**John Frankenheimer:**  I did the first show all on tape that used cut
segments — that was *The Old Man and the Sea*. Just at the very beginning
there were some shots on film, and one shot of the tidal wave was film.
That's all.

It was taped scene by scene, over a three-day period at CBS. Putting
that tank up on the first floor, we practically had to shore up the whole
building with wooden supports. The scenes themselves were entities. We
shot them in one block, and did it until we got it right. The show was then
spliced together. I made the first splice ever done on tape. We had no
instruments to cut it; we cut the master with a single-edged razor blade,
and pieced it together. We'd look at it, and if the video rolled, we'd cut a
little bit more off the tape. And then I did *For Whom the Bell Tolls*, kind
of shot by shot, a lot of it on tape.

I hated tape. Hated it because it took away the immediacy. Also, we
never had a temperament problem on live television, because if anybody
wanted to argue, I'd just say, "Go ahead." My favorite remark was, "Look.
I've got all the time in the world to listen to all your horseshit. The point
is, it's on the air six-thirty on Thursday night. It's your face up there. Not
mine." It only happened once, let me tell you. But with tape, they always

knew that in the cool, cool, cool of the evening, if anything went wrong, they could do it again.

**Franklin Heller:** Until videotape came along, first black-and-white and then color, we only did live shows on *What's My Line?* There were kinescopes made, which were shipped out to Broken Elbow, Nebraska, and places like that, and to the West Coast for a while. Ultimately it was network all the way. Later, we'd do two shows in one night, the first on tape, the second, live. We would tape a total of six shows, once a month, for six months. We saved those six shows, and ran them in summer so we could have a vacation. We did that for only a few years — maybe four or five, but other than that all of the shows were live.

**Lamont Johnson:** In New York, I did an early tape for Worthington Miner — Tennessee Williams's one acts — with a perfectly splendid cast. It was like doing theatre but it was crude. We did large blocks, a whole act at a time. We didn't have the capability of the kind of editing that the highly sophisticated equipment makes possible now.

**Fielder Cook:** The *Playhouse 90*s, the *Hallmark* Bicentennial production of *The Rivalry* (about the Lincoln/Douglas debates), *Valley Forge* (up in Canada), and *Beacon Hill* (a gorgeous two-hour pilot) — I taped them all.

The tape that I liked the most, I would tape act by act. We fought to keep tape centered in that way. We would get as close as possible to that same adrenaline and excitement as a theatrical performance. Otherwise, it's a pain in the ass and not worth doing. If you're going to stop it, you can do much better on film, but it'll cost you more.

**Paul Bogart:** In 1960, after we had experimented a good deal, I did the first heavy show that ABC had ever done on tape, *The Citadel*, by A. J. Cronyn. Big production. We shot for several days in different studios at ABC and that's where I edited it, for the most part.

The editors at ABC were terrified of cutting the tape, of literally splicing it together, because they had very little experience at it, not nearly as much as CBS or NBC. We would cut it and put it together and look at it and then we would sneak up on each cut until we got it as close as we could. It took forever. But *The New York Times* said, "At last, tape editing has gotten so sophisticated that you can do anything with it." They didn't know what a labor it had been.

I think it was *Playhouse 90* that did a show in the late fifties in which Farley Granger played two parts. They pre-recorded half of his conversations and rolled them in against his live performance, so he had scenes with himself. The whole show was live except for those tape segments. Do you know what a risk they took and how brave they were? I would have loved doing that.

**George Schaefer:**  In live television you had the whole effects panel right in front of you and you could do anything you wanted to. But when you came to tape, you were suddenly very limited.

The first tape show I ever did was *Kiss Me, Kate*, the Cole Porter musical. We'd planned to do that live with a wonderful cast. There was Alfred Drake and Patricia Morrison, the original two stars, and people like Harvey Lembeck. But there was a threatened actors' strike, and rather than risk running into the strike period, it was decided to tape it.

This was when tape was really primitive. It would band and it was almost uneditable. You couldn't dissolve, and there was no way to do any effects. The machines, particularly when you were doing a ninety-minute or longer show, were less than accurate, the color would vary, and in the editing, the sound would pick up all sorts of funny noises. I was very unhappy with the sound quality. I really think *Kiss Me, Kate* would have been better as a live performance although it was still pretty good.

*The Tempest* was the first time that we used tape as tape, and from then on in, everything else was tape. That was in '60. With electronic editing, by the time we'd get done combing through and making edits, the originals would still be scarred, so I would pipe the sound on telephone lines from the studio — generally the NBC Brooklyn Studios — directly into the Reeves Sound Studios, where they would record it on 16mm mag track. Reeves was a very good studio. They would get the latest equipment and were always years ahead of the networks. Then we would take our two-inch tape and edit it electronically, get it down to length, make a 16mm, overnight, black-and-white, hot kinescope. Our sound editor would cut the original track to fit that, we would go ahead and mix it, very much the way you do when you make a film mix. The sound would be remarkably clean and good, and by running it through a mixing panel we were beginning to get quality that was comparable to the kind you get today on television.

When I did _Magnificent Yankee_ —which is an episodic play about Justice Holmes and his wife as they grow older through the years — I wanted the softness of the dissolves. At the end of a scene, we would do a slow dissolve through to the next set with one of the succession of different secretaries. The secretary would have the first line, then we would cut and stop, they'd make all their costume changes, we would pick up again and make the edit to the next scene on that cut. It was the first time that had been done on tape.

When I did _Victoria Regina_ we would have liked to have had that same effect but the script just didn't lend itself to it. What I did there was dissolve out of the scene to a big card that had the date on it, and start the next scene with that same card. But, we had to do a splice, so the letters would jump a little bit.

I think the most beautiful show we ever did, just visually, was a production of _Gideon_ that Warren Clymer designed, at the Burbank Studios. What would always give you away were the floors, because no matter what you did, you had this hard cement floor with all the camera marks on it, and the light would reflect on it. You could paint a rug or paint floorboards on it, but it didn't fool anybody. On _Gideon,_ we didn't show the floor. The entire set was built up about three feet off the floor. There wasn't a straight line in the whole thing. Everything was curved with this beautiful cyc around it. I had a path completely circling it, I had three Chapmans whirling around there, and I could get the camera below the ground level and be looking up.

_Gideon_ was tape, but shot in what they used to call "live on tape," which never meant completely live, but done in whole scenes. We'd record one master two-inch and a protection two-inch, and punch it up just as if we were live. You were dealing with low-band tape and the loss of one generation was very noticeable in terms of graining and banding. Today, with high-band tape, and particularly with one-inch tape, you can go two, three generations and it's not detectable. With electronic editing, it's like being in a whole other world.

**Marc Daniels:** In the early nineteen-sixties, I did do a tape project for the Westinghouse Broadcasting Company called _The Advocate_, which was a play that opened concurrently on Broadway. They played the television version as a Broadway premiere on five of their O-and-O [owned-and-operated] stations around the country. *The Advocate* was the SaccoVanzetti story, so that it didn't much have a movie possibility in any case. That was the first time I was able to use electronic editing.

**Ralph Nelson:**  Tape was coming along, and we who were in television welcomed it. We thought, Now we've got motion pictures backed off the map. But, when tape came into television, live was destroyed, because once the actors could do retakes, if they didn't feel the performance was going well, they would make a deliberate miscue so you'd have to start at the top and go through it again. So all that vitality and the adrenalin was gone. Then, when film came in, I decided if television was going to go to film, I would prefer to do on the motion picture screen rather than on the tube, so that's when I switched over.

**Delbert Mann:**  Some years ago, I came back to CBS to do a tape show — the first time I had been back in a long, long time. We did it in the old *Playhouse 90* studio and a lot of the crew were still around. They pushed like crazy to get back on camera, to be part of the crew, to be part of the team. It was really kind of a marvelous situation, from a decade gone by.

# Summing Up

**Paul Bogart:** I treasure those years because live was always a challenge and today there aren't the same risks, the same do-or-die that we had then. The shows were on once and nobody saw them again. When it worked, God it was thrilling. You'd sit there in the control room, it would get deathly quiet, and you'd watch these people making this marvelous event. If it wasn't any good at all, you got a bad notice occasionally, but, otherwise, who cared! It was all over with, down the toilet. The audience was not very demanding — they were just happy their sets were working and they got a picture.

It was a "Golden Age" because the top shows, like *Philco*, *Goodyear*, and *Studio One*, were in the hands of artists. I remember seeing *The Trip to Bountiful*, a play by Horton Foote, on *Philco*, with Lillian Gish and Eva Marie Saint. They played a long dialogue scene, sitting in a bus. The bus was the most rudimentary piece of scenery you ever saw. What you saw from the window was garbage — it wasn't even moving. Technically, it was a zero, but artistically, they were playing it so beautifully, and it was so superlatively well-written, that I was entranced by it.

I met the most wonderful people in my whole life in live television. The best actors, the best writers, the most willing people. Very few of them were bad people, and the bigger they were, the better person they were. I felt very fortunate to be there and to be having such a good time working.

**Allan Buckhantz:** After five years with *Matinee Theatre*, I got involved in a Broadway musical. After the New York show, I decided to take a vacation to Europe, and I stayed. CBS hired me to stay in Germany because they were helping to develop German television. I ran seminars training directors, stage managers and ADs. I was what they called a director-in-charge, and I supervised their *Playhouse 90*-type productions. It was one of the most productive times of my life.

In Berlin, I directed live TV again. Once a year they had a beautiful event they called a "British tattoo," where they flew in about five thousand musicians. I went to a rehearsal and said, "We should photograph it. Maybe we can sell it." We couldn't get a director quick enough, so they said, "What about you?"

I said, "You're crazy. It's twenty years since I've been in a control room." I walked into the truck, and it was as if I left it yesterday. Once you learn, I guess, you never forget.

It's odd that after twenty-five years, when I went back recently, I could not find a piece of equipment in that control room that wasn't there when I worked at NBC. They may have new monitors, but in principle ninety per cent of the control room hasn't changed.

**Fielder Cook:**  Nothing compares to live television. It was a whole media form of its own. It's not just that it was "Golden Years," it was an area of discovery and productivity, like the beginning of films, like the beginning of anything before it gets to be worth two zillion dollars.

Live television for me — and I would think for any director that did it — was the most exciting thing that ever happened. You had to be very young, ignorant enough and gifted enough to know that you could put it all in the pot and do impossible things and not worry. Going on the air, live, with ninety-five hundred things to have happen was a little crazy. You were rooted in fear because you had to be.

It is important to realize that a live television director had more power in the course of putting a play on the air and in preparing it and getting it done than any motion-picture director that I know of in history, except probably Chaplin, because Chaplin owned his own studio, wrote his own music, was his own actor, and did everything. Certainly I did, because I was the producer as well as the director, and I had complete control.

It was something none of us will ever have again because we'll never again be involved in that kind of revolutionary technical beginning. And it got one to dream of immortality.

**Marc Daniels:**  I was hired to direct *I Love Lucy* partly because I'd had the multiple camera experience. It was somewhat similar to live, except that the film cameras were much less flexible than the television cameras. You were stuck with the side cameras being the long lenses for close-ups and the center camera being the master camera, and you couldn't change a lens as quickly.

We began *I Love Lucy* using four cameras because they wanted to do the entire first half of the show without stopping. We had four Fearless dollies, four dolly grips, four camera assistants, two booms, two dolly grips for the booms, and a few cable men. You can imagine what that floor looked like.

The live period in general was very exciting, because it was all new, with everybody doing things for the first time. The shows themselves had a kind of tension that generally made for better performances. However, I think people's memories of this "Golden Age" are tricking them a little. With a few exceptions, if you saw the stuff today, you wouldn't think it was so terrific.

**John Frankenheimer:**   Live television was a collaborative medium between producers, directors, writers, and actors. We used to watch each other's work, we wanted to see what everybody else was doing. I suppose I admired Robert Mulligan more than any other television director. I loved the way he handled his cameras, and I loved the way he did his shows. I was also influenced by George Stevens, William Wyler, Fred Zinneman, Hitchcock, Orson Welles, Ingmar Bergman, Vittorio De Sica.

I was very young then. I didn't have to worry about having these long talks with actors and producers beforehand, then going out to sell it, getting the money to do it, and all that kind of nonsense. I did what I was good at, which is working with writers, actors, and cameras. I had tremendous adulation. I was very highly paid. I was able to do practically whatever I wanted to. I had my problems, obviously. Nothing was ever perfect, but I look back on it as really the best days of my career. TV was always a friend. I found it very flexible and very moveable and easy to work with. I liked it much better than directing films.

**Livia Granito:**   A director could work at all three networks, and I'd go wherever they had the best script to offer. After the period of working with Albert McCleery, I just kind of petered out. I had another child and became a mother and hausfrau. But, when he produced and directed another pilot at NBC, he asked me to join him as associate producer, but I actually sat in the booth and functioned as an AD.

**Walter Grauman:** Calling the shots of a live television show was very closely akin to flying, with all the equipment and all the monitors that you were watching constantly.

There was a lot of room for style — the angle, the cutting, the staging. I feel that directors evolved their own trademark styles, and that those who didn't did not succeed as directors. I've learned something from everybody I watched.

The live television style invaded the film world, and had a gigantic influence on the film medium. A lot of film directors came out of live television — Franklin Schaffner, Ralph Nelson, Delbert Mann, John Frankenheimer, Arthur Penn, Jack Smight, Sidney Lumet, George Roy Hill — all of the *Matinee* guys who are still working today. Those guys took over film, not vice versa.

**George Roy Hill:** There was always competition among directors, but it was a friendly competition. It was the greatest stroke of good fortune that we all started out in a business that was absolutely new. There was no bureaucracy, no vested interest, no wise old men to look over your work, because the wise old men, the established film directors, would have nothing to do with live television. We were all just kids, and we got training that was unexcelled.

Being involved in the writing of the script, working with actors — particularly actors of great stature — and doing it live, gave you a tremendous, across-the-board experience that I don't think can be duplicated in the present day.

I miss the excitement of those days. There's so much more riding on what you do now, just in terms of time. You have a year and a half to two years to take a project from beginning to end. The days when you did eight, ten shows a year was more physical strain but less emotional strain, because you had the chance to fluff it up one week and maybe make your comeback the next week.

Failure was the rule. You had to do so many shows that if you came up with a really good one out of three of four, you were ahead of the game. I can only remember four or five shows that I did during the whole time I was working on live television that I'm really proud of.

**Arthur Hiller:** By the time I started, it was near the end of the "Golden Age." *Playhouse 90* was coming out of Hollywood, and that was the top show then.

Live television was exciting because of the limitations. It all had to be done on a stage. On *Matinee Theatre*, we were even more limited because we only had a hundred twenty-eight dollars a week for sets. In a sense, though, that was good because your mind had to be constantly working.

No matter how prepared you were or no matter how organized, when that second hand hit the top, you had to pray, because there were eight hundred things that could go wrong — and often did.

When you finished a live television show, you really were off the ground. You were just flying! It would take you a couple of hours to get back down. When you finish a film, that's it.

If you asked the film directors that came out of live television, "What would you most like to direct if you had your choice?" I think most of us would say "live television."

The other night I was watching a rebroadcast of *Marty*, on KCET. I loved it. At one point my daughter said, "Are you crying, Dad?" I got a little tear from nostalgia. It was still just as good a show as when I saw it in the early nineteen-fifties, when I was still in radio in Canada.

**Lamont Johnson:** There was that early, fumbling, pioneer time in New York, late fifties, early sixties. Things were overwhelmingly theatre-oriented. There was a lot of cross-hatching in the techniques and the traditions. *Your Show of Shows* was a big borscht circuit show, with great echoes back to the Jewish art theatres of the Catskills. It grew to a whole new dimension through the genius of people like Sid Caesar and Imogene Coca and their producers, while the Woody Allens and Mel Brookses did their starveling apprenticeships.

And because it was a pioneer epoch, there was an enormous flavor of breaking new ground, but using old tools, depending on old talents and skills. It was a tremendous challenge to the initiative and the imagination and the creative juices. It is out of such challenges that remarkable new strengths develop. I think that young people today are hard pressed to have such challenges.

One was forced into invention — frequently by mediocrity — and that was one of the joys of pioneering. You had the sense that you were in on some kind of history, and that got the adrenalin zapping every time you had to get up at three in the morning to go to the studio to a four-thirty rehearsal. I wouldn't have missed it for anything in the world.

**Buzz Kulik:**   We watched each other and we learned. We all came from a different milieu. Fred Coe came from a little theatre down in South Carolina. Sidney Lumet's father was an actor. Yul Brynner was an excellent director. None of us had any preparation for this medium. None of us knew anything about cutting. It was on-the-job training, and because we didn't know so many things, I think we were a little less inhibited.

One of the things that was both good and bad at the same time was that we kept a stopwatch on everything. Time was our enemy, and very few casts ever stayed to their dress rehearsal timings. The excitement and energy of being on the air in front of thirty million people made them either speed up or slow down. As a director, you had very little control over that. They got into that kind of rhythm out of their own peculiar fears. That's the wonderful part of it, because sometimes, in the performances, you got an added zest.

Many of the things that happened can be thought of as funny in retrospect, but they weren't funny then, they were horrible. They occurred all the time, but we learned and became tough. There's nothing that could happen anymore that would throw any of us.

Some of these mistakes were things I wanted to kill myself over, yet my own wife wouldn't see them, and nobody else recognized them either. I came to realize that little errors are like a button not being buttoned. An audience accepts what you give them, because they don't know what you had in mind, and they assume that what they see is the totality.

The other thing I learned is that film directing is really the ultimate for the director. He can control every frame of the film, control the tempo, control the performances in so many ways. In the theatre, in live television, that wasn't the case, because even though we rehearsed as much, every cast had its own personality and its own rhythm and its own tempo.

**Ralph Nelson:**   When I joined CBS, the directorial staff was astonishing. Franklin Schaffner, Marty Ritt, Yul Brynner (when he had hair), before *The King and I*. Yul had to beg CBS to let him do it. He was supposed to return after the show, but by then, he'd forgotten it entirely.

John Frankenheimer and Robert Mulligan were among the associate directors. George Roy Hill and Buzz Kulik worked for J. Walter Thompson. Fred Coe brought Delbert Mann up from the south to be on the staff at NBC. Arthur Penn was a stage manager at NBC. All of us lucked into a time when a whole new industry was created, and we rode with the tide.

The majority of us went on to become top motion picture directors, because, just at the time, there was a big attrition of motion picture directors. The motion picture industry had never trained directors. Suddenly the motion picture companies became aware of the fact that here were young directors who were used to working with scripts, with actors, and with cameras. With film, they only had to deal with one camera at a time.

Now, our generation is passing on, and the new bunch are coming out of the film schools — the Spielbergs and the George Lucases and so forth.

**Arthur Penn:** My experience from 1951 through 1957 was very interesting. They were six remarkable years, where if you wanted to grow, the medium would give you just enormous numbers of opportunities. Everybody moved very swiftly if they could produce, but an awful lot of people couldn't take the tension.

Live TV was like flying a test plane. It was all full of difficulties of a technical nature. A lot of us ended up a little clutched because of that, but also rather proud of ourselves for being able to do it. But it was a tough baptism of fire, no question about that.

Fred Coe got an offer from Warner Bros. to produce a film and asked me to direct it. It was *The Left Handed Gun* with Paul Newman. Also, around that time I introduced Fred to a play called *Two for the Seesaw*, that was being written by a friend of mine. We made plans to produce that on Broadway. So in 1957 I said goodbye to television. We made the film, and we came to Broadway.

I didn't go back to television because it got less and less interesting — as you can see anytime you want to turn on the tube.

**John Peyser:** It was completely different from anything that you have today. The audience was a much more intelligent audience, a more schooled audience, a theatre-going audience. You had the upper strata of your social system watching television, because the mass market didn't exist. The business affairs people simply protected us and did for us what needed to be done, while the agencies merely supplied the commercials. Robert Montgomery, Tony Miner, Franklin Schaffner, Bob Stevens, and I — all these kind of people — controlled our own destiny.

**George Schaefer:**  I'm a great believer in Frank Capra's one man, one film theory. Even when they're bad, they're better than the committee-made projects. There was no way to make committee-made live television, and it had to be the director's way.

You really did it all, in the training ground that existed in live television. You worked with the authors, you cast, you rehearsed, you plotted every shot, you did all your editing. It was live, the music was put in at that moment, everything was under a director's control. Even when it was finished and off the air, you'd examine the shows and study the notices. You had an opportunity, in the course of a single year, to do six, seven very major productions. Some were better than others, and clearly the really great ones were somewhat far between, although I think our batting average was amazingly high on the *Hallmark* shows.

That was a wonderful piece of entertainment history that is gone and won't come back. Particularly, it provided an opportunity for directors to really direct. It's a training that the English directors are beginning to get, and it's not a coincidence, I think, that so many exciting directors of pictures are coming out of England these days.

**Martin Ritt:**  I went back to Broadway and acted in Clifford Odet's play *The Flowering Peach*. Also, I taught acting. Eventually, I did a film, *Edge of the City*, because Metro was in the proxy fight and didn't know what was going on. It was made for four hundred thousand dollars, and it turned out to be a good film. Metro didn't like the film, even after it opened to very good notices, which it did all over the world. But Fox decided to take a chance and hire me. That's how I came out here in 1956 or 1957. I never went back to the theatre, and I haven't done any TV since then.

I would say that there was a "Golden Age," and a lot of very gifted people came out of that time. That has happened before in the history of the world — a time when everything seems to blossom. But nothing has really come out of television in the last fifteen or twenty years.

**Franklin Schaffner:**  Once the coaxial cable came into existence, it introduced the possibility of reciprocity of broadcast from coast to coast. It was like growing up. Suddenly, the market expanded enormously.

I think it was inevitable that the combination of the Hollywood infusion, the expanding market, and finally the increasing cost of dramatic anthologies would change television. I use the word "cost" advisedly, because those dramatic anthologies had no syndication value. When we were recording on kinescope, what became valuable in terms of syndication was what was being done on film.

The live television experience was an invaluable training ground that directors no longer have — except perhaps in film schools. Our great advantage was having this kind of experience available *and* being able to make a living while we were learning our craft.

It's difficult to assess the quality of early television because the old kinescopes are so miserable to watch. They are so poorly recorded that you can't get a sense, in either visual or audio terms, of the excitement coming out of that tube. The early days are referred to as the "Golden Age" because people remember them as being great. Those of us who trained in it remember things as being "golden" because of the interchange we had, the education we received, the excitement we experienced, and the workload we carried.

**Delbert Mann:**  When I started directing films, I couldn't adjust for a long time to the tempo. Film work seemed terribly, terribly slow, a little bit done each day. Although the film of *Marty* was done in twenty shooting days, we had rehearsed for three weeks prior to that, as we had done on television shows. But even so, it still seemed terribly slow compared to the compactness of the time, compactness of the work, and the necessity to conform to the clock on a television show.

Television found its way, through a lot of trial and error and experimentation, into the kind of intimate, personal, small-story dramas that Paddy Chayefsky and Tad Mosel and JP Miller and Horton Foote and Reggie Rose epitomized. You didn't have the room or the capability to do action stuff, and because of the small black-and-white screen on which the viewer was seeing it at home, it proved to be the style of drama best suited to the medium.

I think it still is, and I find that the more the years go on, the more I like to work with that kind of material. I feel more comfortable as a director than with shows that have a lot of action to them, but at the same time, I enjoy a great deal doing something on film like *All Quiet on the Western Front*, which has a lot of action, but in front of it and as part of that action is a very intimate, personal story. The combination of the two is very satisfying.

From a network's point of view, the necessity of putting shows on film so they could be run a second and third time to amortize costs began to be seen. With the change of the production center of television from New York to California, it all added up to the very quick demise of live television. By the end of the decade, by 1959-60, live was really gone, and just never existed again. It lasted about ten years.

**Franklin Heller:** After *What's My Line?* went off the air in 1967, it came back a year or two later in the daytime on the network — five times a week, taped. They asked me to do it, and I said, "No, thanks, I was with the varsity. And I don't want to do dead television."

Aside from *Snap Judgment*, the game show with Ed McMahon that I directed, I never did any dead television. Once that show was over I said, "Oh, the hell with this, I don't want to do this anymore."

**Adrienne Luraschi:** When George Schaefer moved to L.A. and opened his office, I came with him. We started doing two-hour films for television, and I became assistant to George instead of AD. Gradually, I learned how film worked.

Television has brought a lot of good times, and I made a lot of friends. So often, though, you do a show and you may have been very close, but when the show's over, it's, "Bye, bye." Some of those people are still friends, which is nice. Even if you don't see them more than once or twice a year, you can pick up. I'm so thankful I got into television. It's been a wonderful life.

# Index

# About the Editor

After graduating from Dartmouth College in 1941, Ira Skutch spent a year working with producer Alex Cohen in the production of *Angel Street*, in which he also simultaneously made his debut and farewell Broadway appearance in the role of a non-speaking English Bobby. In the spring of 1942, he switched to radio as an NBC page. When World War II wound down, he transferred to the embryonic television department as a stage manager. By 1948, he was directing and producing four programs a week.

Starting out as a freelancer, he became commercial producer-director-writer for the *Philco Television Playhouse*. In 1954, Lennen & Newell, a Madison Avenue ad agency, hired him as a producer-director.

In 1957, he escaped the clutches of the ad world by joining Goodson-Todman Productions, where he served as producer-director and vice president until 1983, and logged over 10,000 episodes of such shows as *I've Got a Secret*, *Beat the Clock*, *Play Your Hunch*, *Match Game*, and *Password*.

He has since learned that there is life after game shows, co-producing A. R. Gurney's *The Middle Ages* at the Westwood Playhouse; writing a memoir, *I Remember Television*, published by Scarecrow Press; and editing other books for the DGA. These include Sheldon Leonard's *And The Show Goes On*, Joseph Youngerman's memoirs, *Five Directors from the Golden Years of Radio*, this volume, and Delbert Mann's *Looking Back*.